Reading *Clarissa*

Reading *Clarissa*

The Struggles of Interpretation

WILLIAM BEATTY WARNER

NEW HAVEN AND LONDON

YALE UNIVERSITY PRESS

1979

For Carolyn,
my wife and good physician

Published with assistance from
the Louis Stern Memorial Fund.

Designed by Sally Harris
and set in IBM Journal Roman type.
Printed in the United States of America by
Halliday Lithograph Corp., West Hanover, Mass.

Published in Great Britain, Europe, Africa, and
Asia (except Japan) by Yale University Press,
Ltd., London. Distributed in Australia and
New Zealand by Book & Film Services, Artarmon,
N.S.W., Australia; and in Japan by Harper & Row,
Publishers, Tokyo Office.

Library of Congress Cataloging in Publication Data

Warner, William Beatty.
　　Reading Clarissa.

　　Includes bibliographical references and index.
　　1. Richardson, Samuel, 1689–1761. Clarissa.
2. Richardson, Samuel, 1689–1761—Criticism and
interpretation—History. I. Title.
PR3664.C43W3　　823'.5　　79–1475
ISBN 0–300–02321–9

Contents

Preface

It is difficult to exaggerate the importance of the curious publication history of *Clarissa*. There is a sense in which the text can never be disentangled from the lineaments of that history. Most of us are used to bypassing the "Note on the Text" which marks the gateway to the standard edition we open to read. Only gradually does the serious student of *Clarissa* become aware of the strange circumstances that marked *Clarissa*'s entrance into the world—that Richardson circulated early handwritten copies of the novel so as to solicit comment and advice from his closest friends; that this practice led to heated debates about the novel, and extensive revision; that the novel was published in three long installments with five or six months separating each installment from the others; that this stimulated an unusual degree of reader independence which culminated in Richardson's celebrated debate with Lady Bradsheigh about the proper ending of the novel (tragedy or comedy, marriage or death); and that this debate, and others related to it, enter the novel and modify the text, with over two hundred pages of addenda Richardson places in the novel in the second and third editions; that Richardson's effort to reinterpret his text so as to control its reception lays down an authorized interpretation of the novel which is perfected by a group of eighteenth- and twentieth-century readers of the novel I have chosen to call "humanist"; that this interpretive alliance is so powerful that it has obscured its own operation and made it difficult to think the possibility of a radically different way of knowing *Clarissa*. This study reads *Clarissa* in relation to the history of its readings; it reads the readings of *Clarissa,* and explicates their history, so as to liberate *Clarissa* for another kind of reading.

The new reader of *Clarissa* may feel he can bypass this history of interpretation until he has read the novel. But he will find that history mediating his approach to the text the moment he seeks an edition to read. There is only one unabridged edition of *Clarissa* currently in print—the Everyman Edition, published by Dutton-Dent and edited by John Butt. It is based on the last edition published by Richardson (the third) and incorporates all the author's addenda to the text, except "the moral and instructive sentiments," collected from *Clarissa*. But there is one crucial difference between the third edition—the edition I have used for this study—and our modern one. Richardson placed inverted quotation marks in the margins of the third edition to mark those lines and passages he added to the text, while modern editions (including the Shakespeare Head edition) efface the distinction between new and old material. We shall see that this apparently innocent editorial procedure conceals two interpretive gestures: an embarrassment before the all-too-human struggles of interpretation that give birth to this text and a desire to hide the resulting striations of the text, so that it takes on the appearance of a finely woven, seamless fabric.

To fail to be aware of these apparently abstruse textual matters is to become an unwitting hostage of the interpretive history of this text. Matters only become worse if one chooses a less arduous way to know *Clarissa*—one of the three modern abridgments edited by George Sherburn, John Burrell, and Philip Stevick. In the reading which follows, I will try to show that the textual field of *Clarissa*, with its intricate history, is like a vast plain where Clarissa and Lovelace, and their respective allies, and the two ways of interpreting the world they embody, collide and contend. How one reads the text will depend, in the most crucial way, on how one experiences the struggle between Clarissa and Lovelace. Contemporary critics have in general been very hard on Lovelace. But no one has done more damage to Lovelace's reputation than George Sherburn and the other abridgers of this text, who deliver the editions that most modern students of *Clarissa* read. And this happens through their simple desire to shorten the story and keep it coherent. These abridgments enhance the plausibility of Clarissa as the simple victim, by removing Clarissa's language when it becomes contradictory, doctrinaire, or self-consciously artificial (as when she remarks on the art of narrative). And all this works to Clarissa's benefit, for she longs to appear to have the simple heart of a virtuous Christian. But when vast swaths of Lovelace's language are cut away from the book (and they will not be missed, for they often do not advance the chaste "plot" which fascinates the abridgers), then Lovelace loses all his mobility and variety. Instead of being open to many futures, Lovelace becomes what Clarissa sometimes accuses him of being: a rigid, implacable destroyer of her happiness. Now he is not a brilliant elaborator of fictions—he's simply insincere.

The difficulty of finding an edition of *Clarissa* to read can teach us something. Because of Richardson's eccentric practices in writing the novel, the text rises slowly out of the matrix sustained by the exchanges between the text and its readers. There is no neutral space where the text exists, or comes to rest. Even its most recent editors are protagonists in an interpretive struggle that has been going on for over two centuries. And when, in the study which follows, we are able to read *Clarissa* as part of the interpretive field it inhabits and engenders, we discover something significant: the struggles of interpretation between Clarissa and Lovelace "inside" the book are always already part of the struggles of interpretation that go forward "outside" the book.

However, this is a vantage point our study can only gradually achieve. So Part I of this study interprets the body of the novel and Part II recounts the incidents of reading that attempt to comprehend, interpret, deliver, and redeliver the text of *Clarissa*. Advantages accrue to attending to the text first of all. The strategies of encounter and struggle adopted by Clarissa and Lovelace anticipate the interpretive moves of all those who subsequently seek to control the meaning of this story. By reading the text before the interpretations of the text, we shall isolate an array of concepts, metaphors, and operations with which to interpret the interpreters. And by treating contemporary interpreters of *Clarissa* last of all, we shall be able to place them within the long and melodramatic history of interpretation they may imagine they stand outside.

This reading of *Clarissa* is informed and molested by theoretical questions addressed in the texts of Nietzsche, Derrida, Barthes, and others. But my reading is not an "application" of theory to literature—for the text of *Clarissa* opens the theoretical questions this study must pursue in order to read *Clarissa*. Our reading begins by demonstrating how Clarissa's two most characteristic activities—her mimetic narrative and her efforts at "self"-construction—are designed in and for Clarissa's struggle with her family and Lovelace (chapter 1). Lovelace responds with the arts of parody, the lie, the jest, and the stratagem—all ways to displace Clarissa out of her self-present virtue (chapter 2). Lovelace designs three melodramatic scenes to gain control of Clarissa's body; but Clarissa responds to the fire of Lovelace's art by using a Christian textual system which allows her to recuperate every loss, by making it part of the history of triumphant virtue (chapter 3). To pattern her past into a lasting monument to her virtue, Clarissa arranges to have a book edited that will tell her story. But, in order to make her past appear as an inevitable-looking cause-and-effect sequence that sweeps her toward death, Clarissa must repress and conceal the contingent moments of the past, the chancy moments in the genuine proposal scenes where the story of Clarissa and Lovelace suddenly opens out to comedy and love. And these moments persist in the text and continue to resist the impositions of Clarissa's (and Richardson's) tragic design (chapter 4).

It is at this juncture in our study that our reading is overtaken by a series of theoretical questions which were never really absent from the text, or our reading of the text. And these theoretical questions are engaged as they emerge in the debates which open around the text (Part II).

First, the question of authority and authorship. Richardson's particular compositional strategies, in writing this novel, put authority in play in and about *Clarissa.* For, to gain a hold on his reader, Richardson plays a game, by loosening his control over the text: he publishes the novel in three installments so as to keep his reader in suspense as to the story's outcome; he diminishes his overt role to that of an editor who collects and orders the letters of others; he lets characters take on a "life of their own" by writing their own narratives; and he tells an involving story of love to interest the reader he intends to instruct. Of course, Richardson only makes *Clarissa* into an inviting plaything so as to lure the reader into the coils of the fiction before sending the artifice (and its reader) on a swerve toward virtue. My study charts the discrepancy between this worthy and cunning design and the actual incidents of reading this text precipitates. It lays bare an affiliated divergence between the pure intentions that avowedly govern the text and the much more impure dispersal of meanings generated by the social network of unruly transactions that carries this text away and gives it a life in history. By tracing this history, we can investigate the inherent limits of an author's authority, watch how the very pressures calculated to consolidate this authority can disrupt it, and gradually shift our picture of the author—from that of the deity of a little kingdom of meaning (the book) to a sideshow illusionist (chapter 5).

Secondly, the active temporality of the text vs. the text as "unified whole." Because of the differing interests of the readers of this story, competing images of the text are evolved. Those like Joseph Spence, Aaron Hill, and others, who support Clarissa in the "fateful" design of her history, insist that the text is a "unified whole" whose "integrity" must be respected. Others, like Lady Bradsheigh, who wish to see the story end happily, assume the mobility of the action, and focus their readings around those chancy moments in the text, where Clarissa and Lovelace seem ready to forget their struggles and marry. For them the text is a function of the haphazard contingencies and discrete acts of will that are deposited by Richardson into the striated text he produces. When Richardson sees that many wayward readers threaten the moral goals of his fiction, he seeks to regulate the text with footnotes, a long index, and over two hundred pages of addenda. These additions help to conceal the disruptive, contingent moments of the text, by advancing an interpretation of the story of Clarissa and Lovelace, as the movement of "characters" of a fixed nature, through a series of actions that form a "plot," so as to deliver a certain "theme." This interpretation of the story represses the active temporality in the text, so as to make the novel's unfolding, and Clarissa's "history," appear to obey a natural (or divine) entelechy (chapter 6). This interpretation of *Clarissa* is perfected by humanist critics, who make Clarissa the heroine of a "rich" and "complex" inner life. Through the work of their reading, she becomes an exemplar of man's uniqueness and integrity (chapter 7).

Lastly, interpretation as judgment, assertion, desire. All the successive readers of this story—Clarissa, Lovelace, Spence, Lady Bradsheigh, Aaron Hill, Richardson, Diderot, modern humanist critics, myself—all these readers try to win a position of knowledge and judgment from which they can survey the story and describe things as they are. But if we attend to the language each of these readers uses to write their reading of the story, we invariably find that they fail to install themselves in a privileged position above the text. Instead, their interpretation is "in play" and part of the game, and the authority of each interpretation is thrown into question by the level of sheer assertion evident in their language, an assertiveness commanded by a desire from which none is exempt, and whose sources are finally unconscious (chapter 6 and the Tail-Piece).

But now let us approach Clarissa. For it all begins with the spare intensity of one simple situation—the vivid availability of a brilliant young English beauty named Clarissa. There is a constitutive instability about her very presence among an envious and inferior family, and before an inventive young rake named Lovelace. This situation invites adventure and activity: the plots to marry Clarissa and Solmes, Lovelace's complexly modulated desire, Anna's request for a narrative account, and finally every reader's interest and desire to know and interpret all the turns of this story. Clarissa stands like a figure in a Vermeer painting—bathed in the holy light that streams through the window on the left, but imprisoned in the mundane actuality of an ordinary room and prosaic activity. She is a descendant of the Christian saints but a daughter of modern experience. Like Vermeer's women, this middle position gives her form the sculpted energy of a profane icon, a beauty composed of earthly shape but heavenly color.

Acknowledgments

It is time to acknowledge my indebtedness. I am grateful to the Houghton Library at Harvard and the Berg Collection of the New York Public Library for allowing me access to their Richardson materials.

My study of *Clarissa* shows the way Richardson's acts of invention bear the impress of the responses and anticipated responses of his readers. And though I sometimes must subvert his will to power over his reader, my wife once reminded me how very Richardsonian my own acts of composition and revision appeared. Because of the fruitful but uneasy transactions between an author and his most taxing critics, I am indebted to a series of readers and potential readers who have been part of this text from its inception.

Laurence Holland—who let me get away with absolutely nothing, cheap. He gave this study as probing and generous and skeptical a reading as any writer could ever wish.

Ronald Paulson—for introducing me to *Clarissa*, for making me want to know how men and women of the eighteenth century might think, and for drawing me into the wake of his high standards.

Richard Klein—who, through his example and companionship, dared me to push every idea as far as it would go, and taught me to enjoy taking risks.

Sam Weber—who introduced me to Nietzsche, Derrida, and a bold new world of intellectual inquiry.

Frances Ferguson—for catching me when my argument went astray, for offering an abundance of sage advice, and for helping me to see the meaning of my harshness (and injustice) to Clarissa.

In addition, I wish to thank others who read this manuscript and graced it with their encouragement and advice: Carol Jacobs, Leo Braudy, Ellen Graham, Barbara Folsom, and Kevin Bowan.

In the late stages of revising this text I benefited from the unique intellectual atmosphere created by the students and faculty in the departments of English and Comparative Literature at the State University of New York at Buffalo.

PART I

TRAVERSING THE BODY OF *CLARISSA*

1: Clarissa and the Art of the Natural

The light of the body is the eye: if therefore thine eye be single, thy whole body shall be full of light.

Matthew 6:22

Truth is the kind of error without which a certain species of life could not live. The value for life *is ultimately decisive.*

Nietzsche, The Will to Power

Struggle is the pervasive and continuous reality of Richardson's novel *Clarissa*. Struggles between Clarissa and her family and Clarissa and Lovelace trigger the alibis and interpretations, the feints and representations that become the substance of the novel. Every word and sentence is a new move in this unremitting struggle, where prolixity and repetition become evidence that the energies of these struggles are undissipated. At no point in this novel can we get outside this struggle, above the turmoil and din, to a neutral place where we could take fine pictures and know things for what they are. This is most emphatically true of the editor's assemblage of the letters into a whole book. Midway through the novel's last installment we find Clarissa planning the editorship of the novel we are reading. This is her bid to turn all the contradictory movements of the text into a unified sign of her virtue and triumph.

Reading Richardson's novel is like entering a vast electromagnetic field. Even apparently neutral analytical instruments—like "plot" and "character"—have been magnetized, ingeniously slipped into place by one of the combatants, so an unwary critic will find them "lying around," pick them up, and employ them in his operations. When he's finished, he may discover himself playing a supporting role in an interpretive alliance directed by the text he intended to master. There may be no resisting the seductions of this text, but we can send in our minesweepers, and be suspicious of everything.

But where does struggle come from? In the first letter Anna Howe asks a version of this question. She has heard about the duel between James Harlowe and Lovelace and wants to have all the particulars from Clarissa. But Anna is already making statements we should distrust. She assures Clarissa that though the conflicts in her family

3

focus on her, they are not part of her and have no intrinsic relation-ship to her. She writes, "Everybody pities you. So steady, so uniform in your conduct; so desirous, as you always said, of sliding through life to the end of it unnoted. . . . *Rather useful than glaring*, your deserved motto; though now to your regret, pushed into blaze, as I may say; and yet blamed at home for the faults of others. How must such a virtue suffer on every hand!" (I,2).

Anna's comments open up Clarissa's basic attitudes toward the struggle she has become part of. The hardships of struggle are undeserved and are inflicted from without by the avarice and ambi-tion of others. Clarissa will be patient and obedient and only assert herself when she must. In her more reflective moments she wonders if these difficulties are not part of a providential design to punish pride or test virtue. Clarissa is especially fond of remembering the time before the family turmoil when the rhythms of her life were more justly tuned to her nature. She tells Solmes that when he first came into their family, she was "one of the happiest creatures in the world, beloved by the best and most indulgent of parents, and rejoic-ing in the kind favour of two affectionate uncles, and in the esteem of every one" (I,167). Anna completes this Edenic picture by saying of Clarissa's past, "thus happy in all about you, thus making happy all within your circle" (II,281).

But there is something wrong with this picture, especially when placed beside Bella's description of the same family circle. She tells her younger sister that she "half bewitched people" by her "insin-uating address. . . . How often . . . have I and my brother been talking upon a subject, and had everybody's attention till *you* came in with your bewitching *meek* pride, and *humble* significance; and then have we either been stopped by references to Miss Clary's opinion, for-sooth; or been forced to stop ourselves, or must have talked on unattended to by everybody" (I,216). It would be a mistake to try to adjudicate between Bella and Clarissa as to the tenor of past life at Harlowe Place. Neither is engaged in accurate description, for each sketch is invented for the ongoing struggle. Clarissa separates herself from the ugly exigencies of family strife by delimiting an innocent time before struggle, and putting herself there. Bella connects Clarissa with her present troubles by attacking her for what she insists Clarissa has always had—an ability to dominate others through a display of passive virtue.

This kind of opposition repeats itself throughout *Clarissa* and demonstrates something important. Characters habitually say and write things which have little meaning except as part of an attempt to gain comparative advantage in struggle. We cannot use this language to go behind struggle to find its origin or ground. We cannot find its cause in any character or group of characters and then chart its course and effects. Struggle is the matrix out of which the novel emerges, and all things are subdued to struggle. For this reason we shall find nothing in this novel that we can call neutral, objective, or true. Instead we shall uncover ingenious and elaborate pieces of artifice, inventions designed for warfare. And none is more powerful than Clarissa's—the idea of narrative, a narrative which is neutral, objective, and truthful.

The Weave of Narrative

The opening letter of the novel makes it clear that there are more reasons for Clarissa's narrative than satisfying the curiosity of a sympathetic friend. Anna explains that the duel has begun a debate among their mutual friends, Anna herself, and Anna's mother. The debate focuses upon whether Clarissa has been faultless and whether she must drop Lovelace. It is within this context that Anna makes her request for a narrative:

> I must desire you to enable me, on the authority of your own information, to do you occasional justice. . . . Write to me therefore, my dear, the whole of your story from the time that Mr. Lovelace was first introduced into your family; and particularly an account of all that passed between him and your sister; about which there are different reports; some people scrupling not to insinuate that the younger sister has stolen a lover from the elder. And pray write in so full a manner as may satisfy those who know not so much of your affairs as I do. If anything unhappy should fall out from the violence of such spirits as you have to deal with, your account of all things *previous* to it will be your best justification. [I,2]

The narrative Anna requests is to be a counterthrust against the "violent spirits" Clarissa must deal with to be sure she gains present "justice" and future "justification." To this end, Anna insists that

Clarissa provide a narrative which has a completeness that will satisfy
observers: "Write . . . the whole of your story . . . an account of all
that passed . . . in so full a manner as may satisfy." Here Anna
touches on something that will be important throughout *Clarissa*—
the motif of "the whole story." If we consider storytelling as the
recounting of facts, then it is difficult to imagine where, in the gradual accretion of interrelated details, a story might become "whole."
But we all know what Anna and Clarissa mean. A "whole story" is a
story that carries its own completed meaning, a story that is suffi-
ciently convincing in its method of narration as to obviate any need
for our interpretation, because it carries its own interpretation.

Anna invites Clarissa to weave enough facts into a seamless whole
to make her "justification" indisputable. But beyond the legalistic
context of justification, Anna's letter creates the framework for
Clarissa's participation in a fictional code: the debaters at Anna's
home are an audience; Clarissa and the "violent spirits" she must deal
with are the virtuous victim and dangerous antagonists of a sentimental fiction; and finally, Anna's fear that "anything unhappy"
should happen provides the suspense and possible catastrophe every
exciting fiction has. The mute presence of this fictional code behind
Clarissa's narrative can help affect Clarissa's justification. For if
Clarissa is able to complete the pattern of a sentimental fiction *while*
she gives a convincingly accurate account of her own trials, then her
auditors will be more sure than ever that they have heard the "whole
story." The idea of the "whole story," which grows into the idea of
the "whole book," is one of Clarissa's most effective feints. Were it
not for the story Lovelace tells, we could never take Clarissa's as
partial.

It turns out that Clarissa is quite willing to oblige Anna with the
account she requests. The way she accedes to Anna's request is
significant: "I will . . . be as brief as possible. I will recite facts only;
and leave you to judge of the truth of the report raised that the
younger sister has robbed the elder" (I,4). There is a note of confidence in her chosen strategy. It is not for her to descend into
tortuous efforts at self-justification. She will speak the facts and the
facts will speak for her. But beyond this, Clarissa's later critique of
Anna's description of Solmes shows she has moral zeal in her com-
mitment to an objective narrative: "you have such a talent at an ugly
likeness, and such a vivacity, that they sometimes carry you out of

verisimilitude. . . . [You] sit down resolved to write all that wit, rather than strict justice, could suggest upon the given occasion . . . should it not be our aim to judge of ourselves, and of everything that affects us, as we may reasonably imagine other people would judge of us and our actions?" (I,133).

Clarissa pairs this mimetic program with a deep distrust of any manner of expression which is consciously mannered and explicitly rhetorical. She sometimes even seems to regret that truth must find its expression in words. She criticizes Lovelace for his "elegant volubility." To Anna she writes, "He is too full of professions. He says too many fine things *of* me and *to* me. True respect, true value, I think lies not in words: words *cannot* express it: the silent awe, the humble, the doubting eye, and even the hesitating voice, better show it by much than, as our beloved Shakespeare says, *The rattling tongue/Of saucy and audacious eloquence.*" If Clarissa cannot convey her story by using this short lexicon of sentimental gestures, she will use words with a spareness and neutrality that will carry "facts" directly to the reader. This antirhetorical style will advance her rhetorical aims.

But, almost immediately, problems arise. Clarissa starts her narrative by describing Bella's "self-complacency" in receiving Mr. Lovelace's visits, and gives her long monologue before the mirror. Clarissa narrates Bella's final remarks in this way: "'she was always thought comely; and comeliness, let her tell me, having not so much to lose as Beauty had, would hold, when that would evaporate or fly off. Nay, for that matter' (and again she turned to the glass), 'her features were not irregular; her eyes not at all amiss.' And I remember they were more than usually brilliant at that time.—" At this point Clarissa seems to sense she has gone beyond the spare presentation of facts. In an aside to Anna she writes:

Excuse me, my dear, I never was so particular before; no, not to you. Nor would I now have written thus freely of a sister, but that she makes a merit to my brother of disowning that she . . . ever liked him, as I shall mention hereafter: and then you will always have me give you minute descriptions, nor suffer me to pass by *the air and manner in which things are spoken* that are to be taken notice of; rightly observing that air and manner often express more than the accompanying words. [I,5; my emphasis]

Clarissa, at first, only seems to be admitting to certain practical necessities. To present a clear picture of events, a measured amount of analytical pressure must be applied in narration. So Clarissa will not only give a printed version of Bella's words, but also her own account of the "air and manner" in which they are spoken. Then, to be a good storyteller, one must use earlier events, like Bella's infatuation with Lovelace, to elucidate later ones, such as her current denial of that infatuation. But embedded in Clarissa's aside are hints that other, less empirical factors are at work. The words and gestures of Bella, which Clarissa records, are not random events. They have a meaning and communicate their message to the most undiscriminating reader: Bella is jealous of Clarissa's beauty, and vain and self-deluded in finding something to admire in the mirror. Clarissa's narrative is shaped to communicate this meaning. But beyond this, once a battle begins, there can be no talk of neutral reportage. Clarissa almost had us thinking that it is an *accident* that the subject of this past-tense narrative has become her present adversary, when the whole narrative is *for* Bella: it's aimed at her, and would not exist if Clarissa were not engaged in a struggle with her.

A close analysis of Clarissa's narrative reveals the array of subtle instruments she has at her command. We can watch her using them in her account of Bella's difficulties with Lovelace. Bella is disturbed by Lovelace's reticence about proposing, "so," Clarissa narrates, "my sister found out a reason much to Mr. Lovelace's advantage for his not improving the opportunity that was given him. It was bashfulness, truly, in him. (Bashfulness in Mr. Lovelace, my dear!) Indeed, gay and lively as he is, he has not the *look* of an impudent man. But I fancy it is many, many years ago since he was bashful" (I,6). Here Clarissa contradicts Bella's characterization of Lovelace and enjoys a chuckle with Anna. But she has also quietly led the reader to some hard thoughts about her sister. If one can't explain Lovelace's hesitation through "a reason much to Mr. Lovelace's advantage," then perhaps a reason much to Bella's disadvantage—like her plainness—will do as well. None of this is said, but the thought comes quickly on reading Clarissa's narrative. To continue: Bella decides, since Lovelace is "bashful" and simply showing "reverence" for her, she will not play the flirt and make things difficult for him. Clarissa narrates: "In his third visit, Bella governed herself by this kind and considerate principle; so that, according to her own account of the matter, the man *might* have spoken out—but he was still *bashful*; he was not able to overcome this *unseasonable reverence*. So this visit went off as the former" (I,6). Clarissa is openly ironic in describing Bella's self-interested behavior as "kind and considerate." But her presentation of the results of the third meeting is more subtly undercutting. Clarissa combines two incompatible elements: an indirect narrative of Bella's disappointment (with a repetition of the words "might have," "bashful," and "unseasonable reverence") and a heavily ironic summary analysis of events ("but he was not able to overcome . . .").

The direct quotation of Bella's rationalizations might have won her sympathy. Instead, we get language that is at a middle distance—blending Bella's unlikely alibi with Clarissa's caustic irony so as to induce in us a smile at the elder sister's self-delusion. In the final part of her narrative Clarissa tells us Bella is irritated with Lovelace and decides to be quite "solemn and shy" on his next visit. She adds, "But my sister, it seems, had not considered the matter well. This was not the way, as it proved, to be taken for matters of *mere omission* with a man of Mr. Lovelace's penetration—nor with *any* man; since if love has not taken root deep enough to cause it to shoot out into declaration, if an opportunity be fairly given for it, there is little room to expect that the blighting winds of anger and resentment will bring it forward. Then my poor sister is not naturally good humoured. This is too well known a truth for me to endeavor to conceal it, especially from you. She must therefore, I doubt, have appeared to great disadvantage when she aimed to be worse-tempered than ordinary" (I,7).

Here Clarissa's narrative moves away from presentation into a blend of analysis and evaluation. For a variety of reasons the passage wins Clarissa an astonishing superiority over her sister. Its tone expresses a belittling condescension toward Bella. Clarissa's dominance of the situation is implicit in the great restraint used in phrasing her criticisms: Bella has "not considered the matter well. . . . This was not the way;" Bella is "not naturally good humoured." Naming Bella's fault—her bad temper—is something Clarissa is most reluctant to do, but it is "too well known a truth to endeavor to conceal it." In delivering her general sentence about love's declaration and shoots, winds and anger, Clarissa rises to the high metaphoric style. Finally,

Clarissa wins a laugh at Bella's expense, with a bit of gentle under-statement: "She must . . . have appeared to great disadvantage when she aimed to be worse tempered than ordinary."

Clarissa's narrative is not only designed to undercut the position of her adversaries. It allows Clarissa simultaneously to engage in an advantageous presentation of herself. We can follow this movement, and more completely apprehend the different modalities of Clarissa's narrative, by following her account of her brother's ambition. This account has three discrete segments, and each carries a covert message about Clarissa. Clarissa opens her account with some fanfare, telling Anna she has discovered an important new fact which casts new light on her brother's and sister's hostility to Lovelace. She had attributed this hostility to a "college-begun antipathy on his side" and to "slighted love on hers," but had still been unable to account for the suddenness with which their coolness toward Lovelace had flared into personal insults. Now it appears that their uncles, in a conversa-tion with Bella and James, had spoken of leaving all their wealth to Clarissa should she marry Lovelace. This was the hidden cause of their sudden insults to Lovelace and the duel which followed. Here Clarissa engages the reader in a drama of discovery, where we admire her adroitness in piecing together the evidence of Bella and James's con-spiracy. The account also displays her ability to sift and penetrate mysteries so as to insure her dominion over the material she presents.

Clarissa promises a narrative of this fateful conversation after she has "made a brief introductory observation or two" which, she writes Anna, "I hardly need to make to you who are so well acquainted with us all, did not the series or thread of the story require it" (I,53). There follows a two-paragraph account of the Harlowe's "darling view" of raising the family by concentrating all their wealth on James—a plan James embraces with undue fervor. In making this explanatory aside, Clarissa is quietly signaling another quality of herself as narrator. In unveiling a mystery, she had demonstrated her ability to see into the nature of things; now she shows her skill as a maker. She will construct a narrative that explains a whole chain of events by setting them in a linear cause-and-effect sequence. The full chain would be: a history of family ambition → James's avarice → James's jealousy of Clarissa's inheritance → conversation with the uncles → conspiracy with Bella → deliberate provocation of Lovelace → the duel → persecution of Clarissa and the Solmes project. Clarissa's "plotting" of the action into a cause-and-effect sequence designed to explain it is part of her interpretive control over the action. She will turn this skill to good use throughout the novel, and we shall look further at its efficacy later. (See, in chapter 4, "Building the Book" and in chapter 6, "Richardson's Defense of Clarissa.")

At this point in her narrative Clarissa is most intent on establishing the second term in her sequence, "James's avarice." She has just explained the background to that avarice, and now she clinches her point by telling the little story of James's anecdote about the chickens. This involves Clarissa in all the kinds of narrative counterthrusts found in her earlier account of Bella's difficulties. I have labeled them in the left margin. Clarissa's account also installs her as a lively teller of tales whose biting wit connotes her mastery over that which she narrates. Of James's ambition to inherit the family's wealth, Clarissa narrates:

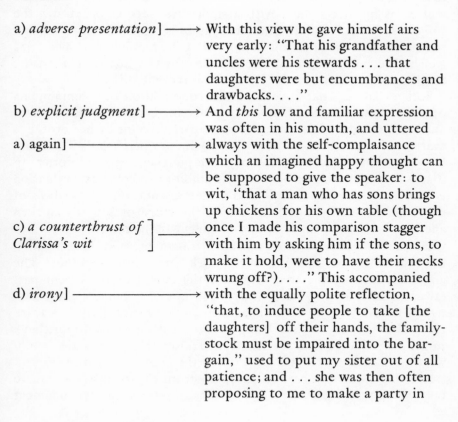

a) *adverse presentation*] ⟶ With this view he gave himself airs very early: "That his grandfather and uncles were his stewards . . . that daughters were but encumbrances and drawbacks. . . ."

b) *explicit judgment*] ⟶ And *this* low and familiar expression was often in his mouth, and uttered

a) again] ⟶ always with the self-complaisance which an imagined happy thought can be supposed to give the speaker: to wit, "that a man who has sons brings up chickens for his own table (though

c) *a counterthrust of Clarissa's wit* ⟶ once I made his comparison stagger with him by asking him if the sons, to make it hold, were to have their necks wrung off?). . . ." This accompanied

d) *irony*] ⟶ with the equally polite reflection, "that, to induce people to take [the daughters] off their hands, the family-stock must be impaired into the bargain," used to put my sister out of all patience; and . . . she was then often proposing to me to make a party in

e) *indirect slight*] ————→   our own favour against my brother's
rapacious views, as she used to call
them; while I was for considering the
liberties he took of this sort as the
effect of a temporary pleasantry,
f) *condescending generos-*   which in a young man not naturally
ity that encloses a "put- →   good-humoured, I was glad to see.
down."   [I,54]

The peculiar power of Clarissa's art comes from the way her quick fingers silently weave together three disparate threads of narrative: an apparently neutral act of presentation, a critical interpretation and analysis of what is presented, and a judgment or evaluation that brings to bear a rigorous paradigm of value. The first movement summons the subject into presence: here is Clarissa's summary of James's words, as he utters them with a smile. The second penetrates the subject so we learn its true nature: James is crude, ill-tempered, and self-satisfied in his apparent command of the family scene. The third weighs the merit of the subject: James's wit is not so acute as he thinks, and his contempt for his sisters is reprehensible.

Seeing Clarissa's narrative art as the coordination and commingling of these three activities helps us to probe the economy, the subtlety, and even the deceit of Clarissa's three-part account of her brother's avarice. The discovery of the cause of James's open hostility to Lovelace occasions an analysis and negative judgment of that motive. In Clarissa's description of her family's ambitions for James, evaluation is most explicit. But there is also some presentation and analysis of the logic of family plans. In telling the story of James's chicken anecdote, Clarissa's analysis and judgment of James are woven into what predominates in most narrative: direct presentation. Now all the elements of this sequence work splendidly together. The announcement of the true cause for the events of the recent past (avarice) leads to an abstract historical review of James's ambitions, which is followed by the climactic presentation of James as avaricious. Instead of Clarissa being content with a bare proposition—James is ambitious, even avaricious, and hopes to garner all the family wealth—Clarissa makes this proposition the preface to a little story.

But this story is a *very* powerful instrument, for it allows her to take her interpretive analysis of James's motives and her judgment of his ambition and weave them into a presentation of him. This makes interpretation and judgment look as sure, as real, as nonproblematic as any person or object summoned into presence by language. The triumph of Clarissa's narrative is to give James's avarice all the stability and finality Clarissa connects with "truth" and "nature." Note that Clarissa greatly enhances the rhetorical efficacy of this little story by having it represent not one occasion, but a host of occasions. We are told this anecdote was "often" in James's mouth, just as Bella was "often" for making a party with Clarissa against James. James cannot escape the verdict of this narrative, for it does not record one moment in his ambition, or one turn in his relationship to his sisters. It records James *as* ambition. Clarissa's narrative invites us to see judgment and interpretation under the aspect of nature as a part, a woven part, of James's very being. Thus we find Clarissa's art winning her a godlike authority—she grants James his nature.

It is not surprising that this narrative proves very effective in winning Clarissa her justification. When Clarissa elopes with Lovelace, Anna is shocked. But after she reads her friend's account of the matter, Clarissa is vindicated: "I have your narrative, my dear. You are the same noble creature you ever were. Above disguise, above art, above attempting to extenuate a failing" (II,1). For Clarissa, the special appeal of mimetic narrative comes from the logic of a truthful and virtuous passivity that is implied in it. After all, she has merely observed what lies before all men, and engaged in its repetition. If she has simply told the truth about a matter, how can she be held responsible for all that follows from that telling? But a problem arises for Clarissa when her narrative moves far beyond the kind of control we have found in passages examined above. Thus, in ending the letter which uncovers the conspiracy, she comments on James's plan to marry her to Solmes (James expects that Solmes will die before himself, thus bringing Solmes's wealth into the Harlowe family): "But by what a long-reaching selfishness is my brother governed! By what remote, exceedingly remote views! Views which it is in the power of the slightest accident, of a fever, for instance (the seeds of which are always vegetating, as I may say, and ready to burst forth, in his own impetuous temper), or of the provoked weapon of an adversary, to blow up and destroy!" (I,62). This display of aggressiveness toward James involves Clarissa in a dramatic lapse away from her program for a judicious and objective narrative.

But more importantly, Clarissa seems at times to be aware of the tension between her activity in writing and the passive virtue she strives for. Thus she writes, "But whither roves my pen? How dare a perverse girl take these liberties with relations so very respectable, and whom she highly respects? What an unhappy situation is that which obliges her, in her *own defense* as it were, to expose their failings?" (I,61) Here she deflects blame onto the "situation" which compels her to criticize. But on another occasion she seems to take responsibility for the rhetorical effect of her writing. She criticizes Anna for writing harsh things about her family: "when passion has subsided, and I come (upon reflection) to see by *your* severity what I have given occasion for, I cannot help condemning myself" (I,132). Clarissa may condemn herself, but since she cannot stop writing, a reader can only admire the ingenuity and versatility of her narrative creations. We can bypass Clarissa's scruples, however important they may be for her, and accept Anna's offhand manner of connecting storytelling with justification: "I fancy, my dear . . . there would hardly be a guilty person in the world, were each *suspected* or *accused* guilty person to tell his or her own story and be allowed any degree of credit" (I,186). Lovelace turns this piece of insight into practical advice: "It is much better, Jack, to tell your own story, when it *must* be known, than to have an adversary tell it for you" (III,408).

Clarissa's Investment, or the Mantle of Integrity

I have said that Clarissa is engaged in struggle and have shown how she creates a mimetic narrative to carry on that struggle. But though I have started the sketch of our heroine, the sketch is an impoverished one. For I have *not begun* to account for the immense interest she possesses for Lovelace, Richardson, and ourselves. I have not even found what she is fighting for. Luckily, Clarissa and Lovelace both have dreams which, taken together, tell us a great deal about our heroine. Clarissa's dream follows her decision to escape from Harlowe Place and accept Lovelace's protection. Lovelace's dream comes after the rape, when he is seeking reconciliation with Clarissa. That Clarissa's fondest fiction of transcendence occurs within the dream of her adversary is an irony I shall consider later. It is evidence that Lovelace has fallen on hard times. Clarissa dreams:

Methought my brother, my Uncle Anthony, and Mr. Solmes, had formed a plot to destoy Mr. Lovelace; who discovering it, and believing I had a hand in it, turned all his rage against me. I thought he made them all fly into foreign parts upon it; and afterwards seizing upon me, carried me into a churchyard; and there, notwithstanding all my prayers and tears, and protestations of innocence, stabbed me to the heart, and then tumbled me into a deep grave ready dug, among two or three half-dissolved carcasses; throwing in the dirt and earth upon me with his hands, and trampling it down with his feet. [1,433]

and Lovelace dreams:

Methought I had an interview with my beloved. I found her all goodness, condescension, and forgiveness. She suffered herself to be overcome in my favour by the joint intercessions of Lord M., Lady Sarah, Lady Betty, and my two Cousins Montague, who waited upon her in deep mourning; the ladies in long trains sweeping after them; Lord M. in a long black mantle trailing after *him*. They told her they came in these robes to express their sorrow for my sins against her, and to implore her to forgive me.

I myself, I thought, was upon my knees, with a sword in my hand, offering either to put it up in the scabbard, or to thrust it into my heart, as she should command. . . .

At that moment her Cousin Morden, I thought, all of a sudden, flashed in through a window with his drawn sword. Die, Lovelace! said he, this instant die, and be damned, if in earnest thou repairest not by marriage my cousin's wrongs! . . .

At this, charmed with her sweet mediation, I thought I would have clasped her in my arms: when immediately the most angelic form I had ever beheld, all clad in transparent white, descended in a cloud, which, opening, discovered a firmament above it crowded with golden cherubs and glittering seraphs, all addressing her with: Welcome, welcome, welcome! and, encircling my charmer, ascended with her to the region of seraphims; and instantly, the opened cloud closing, I lost sight of *her*, and of the *bright form* together, and found wrapped in my arms her azure robe (all stuck thick with stars of embossed silver), which I had caught hold of in hopes of detaining her; but was all that was left me of my beloved Clarissa. And then (horrid to relate!) the floor sinking under *me*, as the firmament had opened for *her*, I dropped into a hole more frightful than that of Elden; and, tumbling over and over down it, without view of a bottom, I awaked in a panic; and was as effectually disordered for half an hour, as if my dream had been a reality. [IV,135–36]

I am not at present concerned with the way these dreams fuse and displace the events of the novel. Without being "readable," in some psychoanalytic sense, these two dreams of the protagonists open a scene, the space of Clarissa's mind. They are two representations of Clarissa's death—the critical moment of her life and story. In both, death follows judgment, but judgment comes out of dramatically divergent power situations. In the first, Clarissa is alone with Lovelace and exposed to the full violence of his vengeance, in spite of "prayers and tears and protestations of innocence." In the second, Lovelace comes as a suitor, to ask forgiveness and be judged by Clarissa. She receives the respectful addresses of Lovelace's family, and her cousin appears, sword in hand, to protect her honor. From this position of strength, Clarissa is judged by God and ascends to Heaven. The bare fact of damnation or salvation is less important than the image of self that the dreams figure forth: there is the body violated, stained, and obscure, and the body whole, purified, and visible. These images are constantly present to Clarissa's mind and charge her life with their imperatives. Clarissa's dream enacts the first alternative. The body Lovelace stabs in the heart has been violated, the body he covers with dirt has been stained, and the body buried in "a deep grave ready dug" is obscured. This is what Clarissa dreads; it is what she must live through when she is raped. Her wish and choice is to have a whole body, a body purified and rising before all eyes in justification.

It is within the scene marked out by these stark alternatives that Clarissa works and struggles. The scene is that of judgment, where Clarissa, as both defendant and advocate, labors for a favorable verdict. This scene implies two contradictions present throughout the novel. Clarissa seems to champion an intensely personal Christian faith, where justification involves an isolated transaction between the self and God. But in fact, salvation, to be a victory, must be seen by others. Part of the horror of the churchyard is its darkness and isolation. Clarissa's victory gains glory from the attendant eyes of her cousin, Lovelace's family, and Lovelace himself, who must watch her ascend and be left grasping, with a galling sense of loss, the robe which is emblematic of her victory. There is another contradiction at work in these scenes of Clarissa's judgment. God's judgment of the self has no logical connection with God's judgment of others. But through an ineluctable logic peculiar to this novel of struggle, Clarissa's ascent into the firmament implies and necessitates Lovelace's descent into "a hole more frightful than that of Elden."

Since Clarissa's struggle is worked out in the courtroom—the place of judgment—it is not surprising that she is someone preoccupied with measuring, calculating comparative advantage, and judging herself and others. In winning an advantage over others, Clarissa's crucial move is the invention of a "self." This "self" is what makes Clarissa entirely unique, richer than the imaginings of those who know her, and quite beyond the range of their weak ideas. A short sketch of the form and activity of Clarissa's "self," implicit in her language, goes something like this: At the center of the self is the heart, the purest and most precious part of the self, which will not admit of the entrance of any foreign matter. The heart becomes the locus of virtue by being planted with principles that are the laws of God and man. If these principles are strictly adhered to, the self may become a paragon of virtue which shines in the eyes of men. But to do this the self must encourage the natural inclinations of the heart, those feelings of "pity" and compassion that link it with all men. All these activities require an immense and patient investment of time and energy, and a willingness to make headway slowly. Sometimes, quite unexpectedly, external adversity reveals something is *wrong* with the self. An examination of the heart leads to the discovery of a flaw or stain, which can only be removed through an arduous act of meditation. This act reintegrates the self and puts it back on course.

But to have given this sketch is deceptive—for it might set us thinking that this "self" is an actual thing in the world. This self is a fiction, not something simply false but rather an arbitrary construct like the hypothesis in an experiment which, by winning a provisional acceptance, can go out and do work in the world. This "self" is a fiction created in and for struggle, to ensure Clarissa a favorable verdict in her "case." It is there, in battle and in the courtroom, that we must watch how this "self" operates.

Clarissa's self comes into being with the simple but momentous gesture with which she marks the boundary between inside and outside. This allows her to empty the inside of that which is not pure, consistent, and identical to itself. She calls this purified interior "the heart." Clarissa's heart is like the small chapel at the center of a great fortress. No matter how violently the battle rages outside, she can win refreshment by returning to her heart and contemplating her own self-present virtue. Thus, after weeks of mutually acrimonious struggle with her family, Clarissa reflects, "O that my friends knew but my heart!—Would but think of it as they used to do" (I,411). A quick glance at her own heart usually wins Clarissa vindication from imputed wrong, for there she reads the text of her own innocence. Lovelace appreciates the strength of independence this gesture gives Clarissa. At one point he laments, "What can be done with a woman who is above flattery, and despises all praise but that which flows from the approbation of her own heart?" (II,31). Bella is familiar with Clarissa's appeal to her heart, but she is more skeptical as to its contents. In one tempestuous scene, Bella charges her sister: "Now Clary . . . would I give a thousand pounds to know all that is in thy little rancorous and reflecting heart, at this moment" (I,231).

Clarissa's appeal to the heart usually involves a double action—the vindication of her self accompanies a harsh judgment of others. When Captain Tomlinson wishes to speak with Clarissa about delicate matters, apart from the ladies at Mrs. Moore's, Clarissa declines to withdraw, saying:

> You may say all that you please to say before these gentlewomen. Mr. Lovelace may have secrets. I have none. . . . I should be glad that all the world knew my heart. Let my enemies sit in judgment upon my actions: fairly scanned, I fear not the result. Let them even ask me my most secret thoughts, and, whether they make for me or against me, I will reveal them. [III,109]

Captain Tomlinson gets the correct message, exclaiming: "Noble lady! who can say as you say?" Clarissa lays claim to special excellence by inviting a courtroom of enemies into her own heart. But this gesture also authorizes a judgment of Lovelace, who is unable to do the same thing. The use Clarissa makes of the idea of the heart and the concomitant opposition between interior and exterior, is most explicit in a systematic analysis Clarissa makes of Lovelace's pride:

> In other words, for persons to endeavor to gain respect by a haughty behavior is to give proof that they mistrust their own merit: to make confession that they *know* that their *actions* will not attract it.... Proud of what? Not of doing well: the only justifiable pride. Proud of *exterior* advantages! Must not one be led by such a *stopshort* pride, as I may call it, in him or her who has it, to mistrust the *interior*? . . . And this shows, that weighed in an equal balance, he would be found greatly wanting. [I,142]

Clarissa creates the heart by marking a boundary between outside and inside—and then the heart becomes the touchstone of her virtue. But here suddenly the same concept operates with more violence. The opposition of interior and exterior is brought to bear on Lovelace's demeanor and actions, so as to raise grave doubts about the quality of his heart. It is a short step from here to denying Lovelace any heart at all. Clarissa writes Anna: "I still am of opinion, that he wants a *heart*: and if he does, he wants everything. A wrong *head* may be convinced, may have a right turn given it: but who is able to give a heart, if a heart be wanting?" (I,202).

Clarissa's heart is not only a static locus of virtue; it is also a guide to action. For in her heart are sown principles which allow her to sift and judge her own conduct by the highest law. The strictest judgment of her own behavior allays concern over the actions of any future court. Her description of the way this inner tribunal works is significant. She finds that her reticence about Lovelace

> arises principally from what offers to my own heart; respecting, as I may say, its own rectitude, its own judgment of the *fit* and the *unfit*; as I would, without study, answer *for* myself *to* myself, in the *first* place; to *him*, and to the *world*, in the *second* only. Principles that *are* in my mind; that I *found* there; implanted, no doubt, by the first gracious Planter; which therefore *impel* me, as I may say, to act up to them, that thereby I may, to the best of my judgment, be enabled to comport myself worthily in both states (the single and the married), let others act as they will by *me*. [II,306]

The steady buildup of this long prose period, as it moves through its succession of antitheses, is expressive of Clarissa's confidence in the operation of these principles. They are like plants in the mind. They grow in Clarissa with the same sure, autonomous force that guides plants into accord with the rhythms of the natural world. Lovelace uses a similar metaphor in contemplating the singular way life and principle are linked in Clarissa: "Her LOVE OF VIRTUE seems to be [a] principle . . . so deeply rooted, that its fibres have struck into her heart, . . . and so blended and twisted themselves with the strings of life" (II,398). Acting on principle will not necessarily give Clarissa the pleasures of success, but it guarantees the more subtle pleasure of not having wilfully erred "against the light of [her] own judgment" (III, 153). This self-vindication is often paired with a confidence that her adversary in struggle must bear the burden of error. Thus Clarissa can write, "If we suffer by an act of duty, or even by an act of generosity, is it not pleasurable on reflection, that the fault is in others rather than in ourselves?" (I,92).

Clarissa's sober attachment to principle allows her to condemn Lovelace for "faulty principles" and his tendency to be, as she says, "so vain" and "so various" (II,95). But attachment to principle leads to more exotic activities than simple judgment; it engages Clarissa in the creation of the loftiest ideals of human conduct. Soon after Clarissa's departure from Harlowe Place, she and Lovelace are in the midst of a long and trying scene wherein Clarissa insists she has no regard for Lovelace, and he torments her by proposing marriage in such a way that she cannot accept. When Lovelace promises "generosity" as to marriage settlements, Clarissa decides to give things a more "diffuse turn," in order not to appear "too ready in [her] compliance." She channels her momentary frustration into an apostrophe to true generosity:

> You talk of *generosity*, Mr. Lovelace, said I; and you talk of *justice*; perhaps without having considered the force of the words, in the sense you use them on this occasion. Let me tell you what *generosity* is, in my sense of the word: TRUE GENEROSITY is not confined to pecuniary instances: it is *more* than politeness: it is *more* than good faith: it is *more* than honour: it is *more* than *justice*: since these are but duties, and what a worthy mind cannot dispense with. But TRUE GENEROSITY is greatness of soul.

It incites us to do more by a fellow-creature than can be strictly required of us. It obliges us to hasten to the relief of an object that wants relief; anticipating even such a one's hope or expectation. Generosity, sir, will not surely permit a worthy mind to doubt of its honourable and beneficent intentions: much less will it allow itself to shock, to offend, any one; and least of all, a person thrown by adversity, mishap, or accident, into its protection. (II,304)

The arc of the paragraph shows where Clarissa's ideal has its foundation. She begins by insisting that generosity is "more" than all that Lovelace imagines it to be. She gradually rises above his narrow conception to a climactic statement of what "it is" ("TRUE GENEROSITY is greatness of soul"). She closes by returning, not to what Lovelace thinks it is, but to what has been still more base, his actual behavior to Clarissa ("Generosity, sir, will not . . . shock or offend"). The exalted and airy heights of Clarissa's idealism rest on the lowlands of struggle. Her description of TRUE GENEROSITY becomes a yardstick of Lovelace's performance—and he is found woefully wanting. This idealism takes a more explicitly aggressive turn when she tells Belford to give up the "wicked friendship" with Lovelace because what they call friendship is "chaff and stubble," and that "nothing is worthy of that sacred name, THAT HAS NOT VIRTUE FOR ITS BASE" (IV,146).

The stability and identity of the "self" Clarissa creates is grounded on her inner nature; but that "self" gains its full validation by assuming its proper role among men. Clarissa's role is to be a paragon of virtue and an example to her sex. We can watch her assume that role in one subtle turn of her narrative. Clarissa is explaining to Anna the natural irritation of her whole family upon discovering that she has been left her grandfather's estate: "All thought themselves postponed, as to matter of right and power (who loves not power?); and my father himself could not bear that I should be made . . . independent" (I,54). The four-word parenthetical question seems innocent enough—everyone justifiably "loves" power. But it takes on new meaning when, in the next sentence, she dutifully gives up control over the estate to her father. The arrangement of the narrative has now given us an answer to what seemed a rhetorical question: Clarissa does not love power. *She* is unique in being above the power grabs of her family. In putting herself forward in this way, Clarissa seeks to realize the self as paragon and exemplar. This role takes on a rather grandiose turn by the way Clarissa phrases her loyalty to her parents. She tells her mother, "Were I to be queen of the universe, that dignity would not absolve me from my duty to you and my father. I would kneel for your blessings were it in the presence of millions" (I,79). "Queen of the universe" and "presence of millions" are suggestive phrases, for they connote the central position of passive dominance the paragon wins. Clarissa's apparent passivity helps to protect her dominance, by making her position seem "natural" and inevitable, rather than political (and thus saturated with effort, calculation, and consequence for others). Clarissa's position as a paragon of virtue and beauty is expressed throughout the novel by light imagery that makes her a source of light and a focus of attention. Although Clarissa has shaped her "self" as a paragon, it takes Anna to explain the implications and perils of this role. Early in the novel, Clarissa is surprised at the hostility Bella and James demonstrate toward her. But Anna explains the difficulty of being brother or sister to Clarissa: "Such a sun in a family, where there are none but faint twinklers, how could they bear it? . . . The distance between you and them is immense. Their eyes ache to look up at you. What shades does your full day of merit cast upon them?" (I,125).

But Clarissa's merit is no accident. It is the result of careful planning and systematic effort. When Lovelace retells their story as a transaction between a miser who protects the hoard of her virtue and the thief who steals it, the displacement of the main story line seems witty but only faintly apt. It suddenly becomes more appropriate when Anna gives her characterization of Clarissa. Anna describes the minute care with which Clarissa ordered the hours of the day. Here the analogy between time and money is explicit. If her friends wanted conversation after dinner, "she never scrupled to oblige; and would, on such occasions, *borrow*, as she called it, from other distributions." The remaining four hours around supper "she called *her fund*, upon which she used to draw to satisfy her other debits":

> Once a week she used to reckon with herself; when, if within the 144 hours, contained in the six days, she had made her account even, she noted it accordingly: if otherwise, she carried the debit

to the next week's account; as thus: *Debtor to the article of benevolent visits*, so many hours. (IV,507–09).

Clarissa's use of her time is like an investor's—she carefully apportions her reserves to different accounts so as to maximize her return. She defends the keeping of a strict account, for as she says, "It teaches me to be covetous of time; the only thing we can be *allowably* covetous of; since we live but once in this world; and when gone, are gone from it for ever" (IV,509). As is natural, she feels pride in getting a better return on her investment than others: "she calculated according to the practice of *too many*, she had actually lived more years at *sixteen* than *they* had at *twenty-six*" (IV,506). We are told that "Uncle Anthony, when he came to settle in England with his vast fortune obtained in the Indies," observed Clarissa's charity to the poor and remarked, "This girl by her charities will bring down a blessing upon us all" (IV,503). Uncle Anthony is the family miser, and this praise of his niece sounds like the admiration of one investor for another upon hearing of a successful venture.

It is easy to smile at the details of Clarissa's scheduling, but they are an important gauge of her ambition to plot a significant life story. Every hour she manipulates is an application of force, which sculpts her life and helps to structure her self. The range and magnitude of Clarissa's efforts are a mute testimony to the precariousness of her project. Below we shall explore the factors—such as temporality, laughter, or the unconscious—which constantly threaten to warp, fragment, or disperse Clarissa's construction. In spite of this, Clarissa hopes that self will become equivalent with virtue, that it will signify virtue to all who take her measure. It is in this context that the crisis precipitated by her struggles should be understood.

Clarissa's invention of the self—with a heart, its implanted principles, the role of the paragon, and its careful use of time—is her way of staking a claim on the future. This claim rests on a faith that if she can keep the self aligned with virtue, then her life will pursue a steady and prosperous course. But when family disfavor and her elopement alter the course of that life, Clarissa must confront an adversity which may conceal an explicit judgment against her. Clarissa's response is to engage in meditation. Meditation will test and examine the self, so as to bring it out of crisis. This is done by acting out a trial, in which

Clarissa is at once defendant, prosecutor, and judge. Systematic acts of meditation come at three points in the novel: when struggles at Harlowe Place reach their crisis (I,419ff.); when Lovelace manifests his first signs of dangerous violence (II,378); and immediately after the rape (III,205–13). What triggers meditation is the possibility that adversity may be a sign of God's negative judgment. This is the reason Clarissa feels so much horror at her father's curse: it is a little text which formulates his judgment, while linking Clarissa's disobedience to future ruin. In the key movements of the meditation, the past life is reviewed and interpreted, and this leads to the discovery of the heart's flaw: "I was the pride of all my friends, proud *myself* of *their* pride, and glorying in my standing" (I,419). "What a pride even in supposing I had not that pride! Which concealed itself from my unexamining heart under the specious veil of *humility*" (II,378). The ritual repetition of the word *pride* is a way of localizing sin previous to its excision. Sin is expelled by warring against the self. Clarissa writes, "I verily think, I more despise myself for my presumptuous self-security, as well as vanity, than ever I secretly vaunted myself on my good inclinations" (II,378–79). In spite of moments of backsliding (blaming others or wishing for death), the meditations do their work—they allow Clarissa to incorporate adversity into her life and purify the heart so as to realign the self with virtue. The goal of the meditation—a renewed equilibrium of self, life, and principles—is the unnamed moment of Clarissa's meditations. But there can be no doubt that this goal is reached, for Clarissa reenters the lists to engage her family and Lovelace in struggle. In meditation Clarissa protects the "self" she has created and demonstrates she has the spiritual magnitude to be a heroine of the inner life. This, of course, puts her far above the many mortals she meets who happen to be of simpler construction.

In anatomizing Clarissa's activities and creations we have encountered contradictions that we must resist attempting to overcome. Should we cut or untie these vexing knots, we would lose the design of her position, the peculiar way she eludes the logical. The word *reflect* is one knot of Clarissa's language that displays the contradictory quality of her position in the novel. Clarissa uses the words *reflect* and *reflection* incessantly. Each of the major meanings of the word *reflect* indicates one aspect of her position. *Reflect* may mean, first, "to bend back again"; secondly, to throw back light or images (by objects' being smooth and bright)"; thirdly, "to turn one's thought back *on* to fix the mind or attention *on* or upon a subject; to ponder, meditate on"; and finally, "to cast a slight or imputation, reproach or blame" (*OED*). As a paragon of virtue and beauty, Clarissa reflects light or images. This is a way of radiating light toward others, what Roland Barthes calls "action at a distance, the highest form of power."[1] The passivity of Clarissa's position as a paragon stands in sharp contrast to the arduous activity with which she turns her thoughts back on herself to engage in meditation. Neither the role of paragon, nor the activity of meditator, authorizes Clarissa's final form of reflection—the casting of a slight or imputation on others.

What do these activities have in common? All involve an application of force or an expenditure of energy, and this is to be expected in a heroine of struggle. But they also indicate what is implied by the first meaning of *reflect*—"to bend back, or to throw back again." Each involves a repetition, or a recuperation of what has been, so that it may become something *as* Clarissa. In being a paragon, Clarissa reflects the images of excellence native to her world. Her acts of personal scrutiny recuperate and reform her own past for use as part of a present identity. And in judging others, Clarissa names and condemns evil, so evil becomes a negative image of the self. In each case, a reflection or repetition by Clarissa of that which is other than self engenders the illusion of a stable self; a repetition of that which is fugitive and transient articulates a static image. Clarissa engages in reflection so as to "impose upon becoming the character of being." This, Nietzsche writes, "is the supreme will to power."[2]

Clarissa's investments of time and energy, the perfection of her virtue, are preparations for her reading by another. It is not surprising that she dedicates so much of her time to writing. Clarissa's narrative can justify acts which have a faulty appearance. In the eyes of her family Clarissa has scandalously eloped with a rake—but Clarissa is

1. Barthes is analyzing the power of a female character in Balzac's "Sarrasine." *S/Z*, trans. Richard Miller (New York: Hill & Wang, 1974), p. 36. Barthes seems to be indebted to Nietzsche's celebrated treatment of desire in *The Gay Science*, no. 60.

2. This sentence comes near the end of the section of *The Will to Power* which editors have described as "The Will to Power as Knowledge" (See Walter Kaufmann's translation [New York: Vintage, 1969], no. 617, p. 330). Nietzsche describes attempts to know and control the world in terms of an ontology (static conception of "being") as strategies to evade the indeterminate flux he here calls "becoming." Subsequent references to this book appear as *WP*.

sure of her innocence, though she may wither under their reproachful gaze. Thus Clarissa proclaims, with words that blend both defiance and fortitude: "Let me wrap myself about in the mantle of my own integrity, and take comfort in my unfaulty intention" (II,168). With these words Clarissa reasserts her singleness, her purity, her unity. Her will has not been faulty, the heart is not divided, and thus she can dress herself, invest herself, with a mantle of integrity.[3] But the gesture is a complex one—for it reiterates the marking of a boundary between inside and outside that creates the self. This is necessary because censorious eyes threaten the identity and meaning of that self. The gesture has a double action: it hides the self from other eyes, in the same gesture by which it dresses itself for those eyes. It draws back, in reliance upon itself, while it puts itself forward as doing so.

Here we come to what is so problematic about Clarissa. For though Clarissa dresses herself as innocent, we have seen how her behavior is everywhere linked to the struggle she wages with her adversaries. And this makes us ask: has she remained uncompromised by these struggles? or, is she hiding something unsavory beneath her garments? Can she be single (a whole purified body which *means* one thing) *while* she constructs that meaning? Can she engage in manipulation, assembling and composing while she is one single thing? The mimetic program she devises for her narrative is an attempt to hide her weaving fingers. The construction of a self is carried on so as to conceal the fact of construction: she *is* an assemblage and repetition of all her world's values. Her heart is sown with its principles; as a paragon she adopts a role that realizes its ideals. All this allows her art to take on the aspect of nature, allows its feverish activity of becoming to take on the character of being.

Clarissa's final signification of herself as virtue can only be ventured through her death. This is her last and most crucial act as an artist. And Lovelace's dream gives this act its most vivid expression. As she enters the cloud which opens for her, she can cast off the robe that is "all stuck thick with stars of embossed silver"—the emblem of her coming salvation. What is beneath that robe, whether it is "the whole body" "full of light" that Clarissa has worked toward, or the

---

3. After the rape, Clarissa will carry these tendencies to their logical culmination by choosing to die and constructing a book that repeats herself as paragon and a heroine of the inner life, and casts disparaging reflections on others. See below, chapter 4.

active and skilled artist I have detected there, whether the one or the other is the point at issue in my interpretive struggle. But whatever the answer, Clarissa could not have cast off the mantle of integrity, that costly garment of her investment, *while* she lived. For here the only single body, the only unified meaning we have, comes through the work of language and the signifying process: the repetition of signs, the weave of narrative, the turning and returning of pages. Thus we are left reading the folds of Clarissa's text, the only garment she has left us, and one that offers most uncertain evidences of her investment.

2: Lovelace and the Stages of Art

Oh, those Greeks! They knew how to live. What is required for that is to stop courageously at the surface, the fold, the skin, to adore appearance, to believe in forms, tones, words, in the whole Olympus of appearance. Those Greeks were superficial—out of profundity. And is not this precisely what we are again coming back to, we daredevils of the spirit . . . ? Are we not, precisely in this respect, Greeks? Adorers of forms, of tones, or words? And therefore—artists?

Nietzsche, The Gay Science, *Preface*

It is art that makes life, makes interest, makes importance. . . . I know of no substitute whatever for the force and beauty of its process.

Henry James to H. G. Wells

The Displacement of the Other

Clarissa has installed herself in something which looks like a metaphysical fortress. By weaving a narrative of her world and constructing a stable self, she can be and name "that which is." She wishes to denote, in the being of her very person, all the plenitude and inevitability of the real. In this way Clarissa appropriates immense authority to herself. Richardson's novel records Lovelace's attempt to subvert that authority. Lovelace enters with an ironic smile and a collection of weapons Clarissa has never seen before. Since Clarissa's position is rhetorical, that is, a thing constructed from language, Lovelace's counterforce to her comes from his own work with language—as artist, as parodist, and as contriver of fictions.

We can follow the Clarissa-Lovelace encounter by examining Lovelace's response to Clarissa's letter regarding his marriage settlements. Clarissa's letter reads like a legal brief. She assesses the degree of blame Lovelace must bear for proceedings, and ends by requesting Lovelace's detached judgment as to his charge that she has been diffident: "I appeal to your own heart, if it be possible for you to make my case your own for a moment, and to retrospect some parts of your behavior, words, and actions, whether I am not rather to be justified than censured" (II,396). Clarissa's appeal is characteristic. She invites Lovelace to engage in reflection and judgment—he is to look down into his own heart, and back over their past actions, so as to weigh her "case" fairly. In all of her language, Clarissa insists on the "real" "nature" and "value" of things. If Clarissa's reader or interpreter accepts these regulating categories, he finds himself in a kind of prison-house of reality, living under a fixed hierarchy of values, and tethered to a concomitant set of moral imperatives. But Lovelace subverts Clarissa's appeal. His first words, after citing the letter, are significant:

> The original of this charming paper, as Dorcas tells me, was torn almost in two. In one of her pets, I suppose! What business have the sex, whose principal glory is meekness, and patience, and resignation, to be in a passion, I trow? [II,396]

With these words, Lovelace refuses to mirror Clarissa's tone of sincerity and high seriousness. Instead, he takes her position, her language, and her style and marks a frame about them. He responds to her "charming paper" as art, as a move in a game, as a fine performance. By making Clarissa's letter the object of his own aesthetic interest, he frees it from its mooring in Clarissa's "nature," and opens a crucial space between Clarissa and himself. Now he can make Clarissa's letter the theme for his own set of variations. He does this by engaging in a displacement, inversion, and parody of Clarissa's position. The displacement has already begun in the passage quoted above: "What business have the sex, whose principal glory is meekness . . . to be in a passion, I trow?" Lovelace takes Clarissa's high-minded indignation and transposes it into the context of the rake's code. Now her response appears to be a gratuitous display of passion. His mastery is asserted by installing himself in the role of rake and connoisseur. Since women merely exist for the pleasure of men, he may prescribe the proper ingredients for their composition.

Lovelace's next move is to carry out an inversion of Clarissa's response by giving a picture of her opposite—the compliant wife. Clarissa's vigorous reply sets Lovelace to speculating on what kind of wife Clarissa might make. In the worldly-wise tone of the rake's manual, he maintains that it is "impudent" for a wife to be in a "passion,"

> for is it not rejecting at once all that expostulatory meekness, and gentle reasoning, mingled with sighs as gentle, and graced with bent knees, supplicating hands, and eyes uplifted up to your

imperial countenance, just running over, that should make a reconciliation speedy, and as lasting as speedy? [II,396]

In adding phrase to phrase in this long period, Lovelace indulges his love of display and baroque exuberance in composition. The reader's pleasure derives from the gross discrepancy between this picture of the compliant wife and Clarissa's vigorous independence.

Lovelace draws on the conventions of stage comedy to carry out his third and final displacement of Clarissa's letter. Now Clarissa's accusations are distilled into the type of the domineering wife:

> But for a wife to come up with a-kemboed arm, the other hand thrown out, perhaps with a pointing finger—Look ye here, sir! Take notice! If *you* are wrong, *I'll* be wrong! If *you* are in a passion, *I'll* be in a passion! Rebuff for rebuff, sir! If *you* fly, *I'll* tear! If *you* swear, *I'll* curse! And the same room, and the same bed, shall not hold us, sir! For, remember, I am married, sir! I am a wife, sir! You can't help yourself, sir! Your honor, as well as your peace, is in my keeping! And, if you like not this treatment, you may have worse, sir! [II,396–97]

The passage is a comic counterpart of all the vicious scraps the novel has given us. It also accurately reflects the clipped emphasis of parts of Clarissa's original letter. But here, there is a comic reduction of all Clarissa's lofty ideals into a blunt and masculine assertion of personal prerogative. This is not a truthful representation of Clarissa's defiance of Lovelace; it is a subversive and playful parody of it. But by winning our laughter and giving us pleasure, Lovelace helps to undo the matrix of truth and value through which Clarissa would have us see, know, and judge. All three displacements of Clarissa's letter help to attack the grounds of Clarissa's authority. But also, with every word written, Lovelace asserts his own very considerable powers of authorship.

Lovelace's ability to challenge other realities allows him to engage in the most pointed subversion of Clarissa's values. Clarissa's most acute anxieties come in fearing that a providential judgment is implicit in her misfortunes. She assumes a God-centered universe where human events are meaningfully linked to God's judgment of man. But when Clarissa chooses Sinclair's house for a London residence, Lovelace parodies the idea of providence and the verbal cadences peculiar to it:

Indeed, indeed, my goddess should not have chosen this London widow's. But I dare say if I *had* she would *not*. People who will be dealing in contradiction ought to pay for it. And to be punished by the consequences of our own choice—what a moral lies there! What a deal of good may I not be the occasion of from a little evil? [II,190]

The laughter Lovelace wins from his reader sends a fissure through the foundations of value Clarissa has labored so seriously and so patiently to build. Later, Clarissa and the editor seize on the idea of a great "deal of good" coming from the "evil" of Clarissa's fall, and weave it into the design of their book. But long before this, Lovelace has subjected that idea to parody. In a similar vein, Lovelace offers cogent parodies of Clarissa's desire to be an example and her concern for respecting the inviolability of the marriage vows (IV,40; II,250).

Displacement takes a wide variety of forms throughout the novel, but it always involves a twofold action: the disruptive shift of that which is in place, and its realignment or replacement by something slightly but significantly different. At times, Lovelace's plans for Clarissa only seem to lead to fruitless turmoil. In response, Lovelace evades the vexing character of the present and sketches future scenes of mutual bliss—either in or out of wedlock (II,251, 496). These images of the future recast their present struggle, but now in images that bear the impress of Lovelace's will. At other times Lovelace shields himself from Clarissa's seriousness by transposing their story into the form of a fable. Lovelace's mastery is expressed in the proud love-dance of the barnyard cock (II,67–68). Clarissa's frantic sorrow after an anticipated seduction is depicted in the transient protests of a newly caged bird (II,245–46).

But Lovelace's displacement of Clarissa and her values is most often won with a small and simple lie. When he brings Clarissa to St. Albans he brags to Belford that he has become a "master of Metamorphoses:"

To the mistress of the house I instantly changed her into a sister, brought off by surprise from a near relation . . . to prevent her marrying a confounded rake (I love always to go as near the truth as I can), whom her father and mother, her elder sister, and all her loving uncles, aunts, and cousins abhorred. [II,13]

This lie serves several practical functions, for it accounts for Clarissa's hostility and indisposition. But the way he tells his lie emphasizes its comic and parodic relationship to actuality. His aside about staying "near the truth" gives us a hint about his method. The slightest displacements of reality are the most powerful, for they win credence at the same time that they fundamentally transform. This is even more explicit when he weaves an alibi for Joseph Leman's false alarm at the garden gate at Harlowe Place. After Lovelace has told his story to Clarissa, he applauds himself for modulating falsehood in such a way as to create a convincing illusion of truth. He adds, "Yet how near the truth all of it! The only deviation, my asserting that the fellow made the noises by *mistake* and through *fright*, and not by previous *direction*" (II,54–55). There is an artistry and economy in Lovelace's use of the lie. But beyond this, the lie has a peculiar aptness for use in an assault on Clarissa. If Lovelace can get Clarissa to live within an acknowledged lie at Sinclair's—like the notion that she is his wife—he can disrupt the ground of her self-complacence: a conscious superiority born of the harmony between appearance and truth, social role and personal identity.

Emptying the Self and Beginning an Interplay

Displacement is an operation which denies Clarissa a secure being and ground of value. It takes the autonomous rounded body—with its "depth" and plenitude—and makes her a surface and mask that are turned toward the displacer, and at least partially subdued to his purposes. But with every displacement Lovelace must be willing to pay a levy by displacing himself: to make Clarissa a sister he must assume the role of brother, to make her the willing hen he must become the rooster, to adopt a succession of ironic and parodic voices he must forego any he could call his own. Of course, Lovelace is only too happy to do this. He empties the self, he makes it a surface, a mask, a series of folds, in the same moment that Clarissa is reduced to a surface and arrayed into a series of folds, so together they will constitute a manifold of struggle. Now the existence of each will become a function of the interplay, the play between Lovelace and Clarissa.

Lovelace gives us a glimpse of this process when he is meditating on what line he will take with Clarissa when he rejoins her at Hampstead, after her first escape from Sinclair's:

> But let me see, shall I be angry or pleased when I am admitted to my beloved's presence? Angry, to be sure. Has she not broken her word with me? . . . And is not breach of word a dreadful crime in good folks? I have ever been for forming my judgment of the nature of things and actions, not so much from what they are in themselves, as from the character of the actors. Thus it would be as odd a thing in such as we to *keep* our words with a woman, as it would be wicked in her to *break* hers to us. [III,34]

In this remarkable passage, two activities go forward together. Clarissa is not considered in the way we know her from her own letters—a frightened captive who has finally won a well-deserved escape. She is displaced and abstracted into one of the "good folks" who consider "breach of word" a "dreadful crime." By choosing to be angry, Lovelace makes himself a function of this aspect of her nature, this fold in her surface. Because Lovelace has consciously committed himself to the interplay of struggle, he looks outside to his opponent instead of inside to his own "heart"—where a Clarissa would try to find a fixed identity to repeat. He does not try to decide what the "nature of things and actions" is in itself, but considers how things and actions exist in relation to the "characters of the actors." Lovelace's aside about his method points to the radically fictional quality of his stance in the novel. He is forever adjusting his masks and roles according to the exigencies of the moment. At one point he worries that a fit of anger has "half forfeited" "the *gentle*, the *polite* part I had newly engaged to act" (II,99). More amusingly, he complains that Clarissa won't let him assume the role of devoted lover by vowing eternal fidelity: "And what can a lover say to his mistress if she will neither let him lie nor swear?" (II,15). This is why many recent critics of *Clarissa* emphasize Lovelace's position as actor and director in the novel.[1]

But Lovelace's choice of words, in his aside about method, takes us further than his particular role. "Characters of the actors" has a dual meaning. Its first meaning, as determined by his intention, is "the

---

1. See Margaret Doody, *A Natural Passion* (London: Oxford University Press, 1974), p. 104, and William J. Palmer, "Two Dramatists: Lovelace and Richardson in *Clarissa*," *Studies in the Novel* 5 (1973): 7–21.

natures of the agents"; its second meaning, as indicated by Lovelace's own behavior, is "the roles of the performers." Implied in Lovelace's displacement of Clarissa and his detached selection of a role is the radical claim that all persons engage in art by the way they do their "acts." Lovelace summarizes the relativity or groundlessness implicit in this position in his final antithesis: rakes keeping their word are as odd and wicked as Clarissa breaking hers. Lovelace's activity implies the absence of any ground upon which to posit a nature or identity for the self. But, paradoxically, his "act" (*his* actions and *his* performance), depends on there being a person like Clarissa, who predicates her "act" (*her* actions and *her* performance) on the presumed existence of something stable and determinate called nature. I shall look further into this paradox later.

Lovelace has set something going between himself and Clarissa that is more than the sum of the two combatants. It is an interplay, a manifold of struggle which sometimes takes on the aspect of a game. Soon after his first probings of Clarissa at St. Albans, Lovelace decides to test Clarissa's virtue as vigorously as he can. If she fails, he wins; if she holds, he loses and will marry her (II,41). Clarissa even acknowledges, at one point, that she is involved in a "desperate game" (II,82). But this "game" is more like a battle than the "play" Huizinga describes. For Clarissa has not volunteered to participate, and Lovelace has not agreed to respect any reasonable limits in testing Clarissa.[2] Nevertheless, the zest and suspense of the question "who will prevail?" does give this novel a lot of its interest. Lovelace concedes he is addicted to this excitement. He even invites Belford's criticisms of his behavior toward Clarissa: "I love opposition. As gold is tried by fire, and virtue by temptation, so is sterling wit by opposition" (II,185). Unlike Clarissa, who is not satisfied with activity that does not earn tangible and lasting returns, Lovelace realizes that the process of struggle is more dear to him than its goal. He admits to Belford that he has "ever had more pleasure in my contrivances than in the end of them" (II,147). In one moment, he tries

2. See Johan Huizinga, *Homo Ludens: A Study of the Play-Element in Culture* (Boston: Beacon Press, 1950), pp. 1–27. R. F. Brissenden suggests that Lovelace and Clarissa engage in a game of "Rapo," as described by Eric Berne in *Games People Play: The Psychology of Human Relationships* (New York: Grove Press, 1964). But Brissenden does not develop this idea. He is more interested in evidences of Clarissa's unconscious desire to be raped than in Lovelace's penchant for play.

to imagine how this transient adventure might become a permanent condition:

> What a delightful manner of life (oh, that I could persuade her to it!) would the life of honour be with such a woman! The fears, the inquietudes, the uneasy days, the restless nights; all arising from doubts of having disobliged me! Every absence dreaded to be an absence for ever! And then how amply rewarded, and rewarding, by the rapture-causing return! Such a passion as this keeps love in a continual fervour; makes it all alive. The happy pair, instead of sitting dozing and nodding at each other in opposite chimney-corners in a winter evening, and over a wintry love, always new to each other, and having always something to say. [II,187]

This passage offers a displaced version of an uncertain present into a future where Lovelace's mastery over Clarissa would be comprehensive and everlasting. But the passage is unusual, in committing Lovelace to a very idealistic vision of their relationship. The excitement of this vision comes from the immediacy, the presentness, and the drama Lovelace ascribes to their love. But there is an implied anxiety about the end of passion. The scene explicitly depicts the way love can be kept alive ("keeps love in a continual fervour").

Lovelace is correct in assuming that this magnitude of passion places Clarissa and Lovelace above ordinary mortals. But where does this vitality come from? It comes from the immediacy and presentness of the ongoing struggle, the suspenseful dramatic interplay that Lovelace and Clarissa know. That all of this must someday end, that time will close this game, is the somber reality which leads Lovelace to imagine—in an unusual flight of idealism—the possibility of distilling the energies of their transient struggle into a permanent "life of honour." During a moment of melancholy reflection, Lovelace seems to realize the temporal bind he is in. The very game he has constructed pushes him toward the goal that will finish his pleasure: "*Preparations* and *expectation* are in a manner everything . . . but the *fruition*, what is there in that? And yet that being the end, nature will not be satisfied without it" (I,172–73).

Lovelace offers something of a philosophy for what he and Clarissa are involved in. He writes Joseph, "I love to have you jest. All we say, all we do, all we wish for, is a jest. He that makes life itself not so is a

sad fellow, and has the worst of it" (II,149). Lovelace's first gesture
is to accept life as only a "jest" and so to acknowledge the ultimate
groundlessness of his situation and its inevitable passing. But then he
takes these severe limits, what we might call life's poverty, and
replenishes them, by making them part of his jest. What is trivial can
be fun; what is limiting liberates. Lovelace's double sense of the triv-
iality and value of the jest helps to explain his horror at Clarissa's
solemn determination to die after the rape: "A *jest*, I call all that has
passed between her and me; a mere jest to die for—for has not her
triumph over me, from first to last, been infinitely greater than her
sufferings from me?" (IV,261)

Lovelace is not acknowledging, in this complaint, the way he has
made use of Clarissean seriousness. For each one of his displacements
is a jest which releases its energy of laughter at the moment it comes
into a lively tension with Clarissa's austere sincerity. A parody of the
idea of providence borrows much of its power from the force of
Clarissa's serious adherence to that idea. What is fun and liberating
in the jest comes from its interplay with what is serious and "real."
Thus the jest is always a form of battle that conceals a certain dependence. Baudelaire explains, in his famous essay "L'Essence du rire,"
that one who laughs seeks to subvert the other, especially an authority, so as momentarily to assert his own superiority;[3] but he does
this with the secret knowledge of his own weakness. For Baudelaire
supposes that only since the terrible losses of the Fall has man known
poverty and sorrow and needed to assert superiority over another
with laughter.

Clarissa must appear to most readers as one of the genuinely
superior heroines in fiction—and all the art of the jest is needed to
disturb her self-present virtue. But to accomplish this mission, Lovelace must wear the fool's cap and be the lowly jester. Belford often
insists that Clarissa's virginity is simply not worth all this trouble. But
Lovelace argues for the value of his game and jest, while acknowledging its humble limits, in words that propel him back into the manifold
of struggle:

> To be serious, Belford, I must acknowledge that all our pursuits,
> from childhood to manhood, are only trifles of different sorts and

---

3. "L'Essence du rire," *Oeuvres Complets*, ed. Claude Pichois (Paris: Gallimard, 1961),
pp. 975–93.

sizes, proportioned to our years and views; but then is not a fine woman the noblest trifle that ever was or could be obtained by man? And to what purpose do we say *obtained*, if it be not in the way we wish for? If a man is rather to be her prize, than she *his*?

Lovelace is the inventor of the particular game that comes to mediate all the action in *Clarissa*, and he consciously commits himself to the terms and consequences of this mutual struggle. This explains something which at first seems most surprising: it is Lovelace, not Clarissa, who gives us the novel's most convincing versions of human attachment. In saying farewell to Belford, Lovelace passes over their recent differences and shows a respectful regard for Belford's plan to reform his ways. Lovelace artfully modulates his expression of affection so as to respect a masculine code that eschews any effusive display of feeling. As Belford narrates:

> Taking me aside, and clasping his arms about me, "Adieu, dear Belford! said he. May you proceed in the course you have entered upon!—Whatever airs I give myself, this charming creature has fast hold of me *here* (clapping his hand upon his heart); and I must either appear what you see me, or be what I so lately was. O the divine creature!" lifting up his eyes. . . . "*You*, Jack, may marry, continued he; and I have a wife in my eye for you. Only thou'rt such an awkward mortal" (he saw me affected, and thought to make me smile); "but we don't make ourselves, except it be worse by our dress. Thou art in mourning now, as well as I: but if ever thy ridiculous turn lead thee again to be beau-brocade, I will *bedizen* thee, as the girls say, on my return, to my own fancy, and according to thy own *natural appearance*— thou shalt doctor my soul, and I will doctor thy body: thou shalt see what a clever fellow I will make of thee. . . . And now, thou sorrowful monkey, what aileth thee?" (I do love him, my lord.) "Adieu!—and once more adieu!—embracing me. And when thou thinkest thou has made thyself an interest *out yonder* (looking up), then put in a word for thy Lovelace." [IV,486–87]

Lovelace's feeling of attachment, to both Clarissa and Belford, seems more genuine for being largely concealed. It has been resolved into the artful raillery of this goodbye: the willed gaiety, the mild insults, the promises of future play, and finally a muted confession that he is

in a bad way and could use Belford's support ("then put in a word
for thy Lovelace").

There is another moment in the novel when Lovelace seems to
move even further toward an unselfconscious expression of his need
for another. After Clarissa's first escape from Sinclair's, he wanders
through the spaces they have shared, numb with loss:

> I have been traversing her room, meditating, or taking up every-
> thing she but touched or used: the glass she dressed at, I was
> ready to break, for not giving me the personal image it was wont
> to reflect of *her*, whose idea is for ever present with me. I call
> for her, now in the tenderest, now in the most reproachful terms,
> as if within hearing: wanting *her*, I want my own soul, at least
> everything dear to it. What a void in my heart! what a chilliness
> in my blood, as if its circulation were arrested! From her room to
> my own; in the dining-room, and in and out of every place where
> I have seen the beloved of my heart, do I hurry; in none can I
> tarry; her lovely image in every one, in some lively attitude, rush-
> ing cruelly upon me, in differently remembered conversations.
>   [II,524]

The repetitions of "I," "my," and "her," and the circular motion of
the syntax, give this passage a brooding and incantatory quality, as it
turns around the one thing present in Lovelace's mind—the image of
the absent Clarissa. This stunning expression of loss may be a lineal
descendant of the extravagant displays of emotion that were common
in heroic drama. But here, an absence of allusion, the way metaphors
are woven into the narrative, the familiarity of the domestic context,
and the subtle manner in which love and anger are blended, all give
the passage a firmness and immediacy that connote an absence of
self-conscious artistry. It is not that Lovelace has ceased being artful.
Rather, it is that here, as in his final farewell to Belford, Lovelace's
art can coexist with a surprising degree of directness, honesty, and
attachment. And this does not actually conflict with all we have come
to know of Lovelace. Lovelace's displacement of self and other, and
his invention of a game, combine to engender a pervasive theatricality
that becomes a gift for the other so as to give himself reality. His way
of operating engenders something shared and mutual.

By contrast, Clarissa seems irreducibly self-centered, and her friendship with Anna Howe chill and uninteresting. For Clarissa habitually talks about her friendship with Anna in terms of a mediating concept of virtue. She makes it the object of her discourse and the occasion for instruction. These speeches assume what she explicitly asserts in dying—her radical autonomy, an existence quite apart from all human ties. By contrast, Lovelace's life is a function of Clarissa as antagonist in struggle, and of Belford as recipient of his narratives. Each gives him the possibility of playing, performing, and feeling alive. That he is a function of the manifold of struggle and the interplay between self and other means that he is an uncertain and changing quantity, but also that he acknowledges, with every story and gesture, that he needs the other person and will feel the most acute sense of loss on their departure.

The Perils of the Practice of Art

Lovelace tricks Clarissa out of Harlowe Place and defers any drastic step, like rape or marriage, that might simplify their relationship. This brings them opposite one another, alert and distrustful. Then Lovelace uses a series of displacements to shift himself and Clarissa out of any fixed identity into the motion of surfaces and gestures which mark their interplay. But what goes on in the space between Lovelace and Clarissa? With these preliminary steps, Lovelace has drawn a boundary within which he can practice his arts: the art of the stratagem, the art of representing himself to Clarissa, and the narrative art with which he reports his adventures to Belford. Lovelace's stratagems, like the Tomlinson ruse and his sudden "illness," are designed to control the terms of Clarissa's situation, limit and define her options, and test her responses. A continuous Lovelacean performance is paired with these stratagems. It stages the shifting representations that Clarissa must reckon with: an ardent Lovelace, a dangerous Lovelace, a reformed Lovelace, etc. Finally, Lovelace creates his own text, a text that allows him to display the self-conscious pleasure he receives from the exercise of power through art. At times, Lovelace experiences an almost orgasmic joy at the success of his contrivances (I,515; III,20). He also entertains the most grandiose expectations for the text he writes for Belford. It will not only secure his own position in "rakish annals," but it will also test

Clarissa in such a way that the "whole sex" will be "concerned" (II,250, 40).

In contemplating the grandeur of his own artistic conception, Lovelace rises to a style that seems a conscious echo of the Milton of *Paradise Lost*: if Clarissa's virtue should hold,

> well will she merit the sacrifice I shall make her of my liberty; and from all her sex honours next to divine, for giving a proof, 'that there was once a woman whose virtue no trials, no stratagems, no temptations, even from the man she hated not, could over-power.' [II,42]

All Lovelace's arts are arts of imitation. His stratagems must seem to be actual events, his performances must seem to be natural behavior, and he works to give his narrative the immediacy of direct presentation. This leads Lovelace to propound a mimetic aesthetic which is a parodic version of Clarissa's mimetic program. He is vexed with Belford for calling his stratagems "trite, stale, and poor": "In thy opinion, I suffer for that simplicity in my contrivances, which is their principal excellence. No machinery make I necessary. No unnatural flights aim I at. All pure nature, taking advantage of nature, as nature tends; and so simple my devices, that when they are known, thou, even *thou*, imaginest thou couldest have thought of the same" (II,491). His final taunt emphasizes the difficulty of giving one's art the simplicity of nature.

He gives a further hint of his method in discussing the letter that describes the London lodgings from which Clarissa is to choose. Of Sinclair, Lovelace writes, "And her features being broad and full-blown, I will suppose her to be of Highland extraction . . . I never forget the minutiae in my contrivances. In all matters that admit of doubt, the minutiae, closely attended to and provided for, are of more service than a thousand oaths, vows, and protestations made to supply the neglect of them" (II,115). Lovelace knows that a generous scattering of details will create the impression that reality has been faithfully recorded. Clarissa habitually apologizes for the art necessary in presenting her story to Anna. In contrast, Lovelace revels in the artifice of his "narrative of narratives": "I will continue it as I have opportunity; and that so dexterously, that if I break off twenty times, thou shalt not discern where I piece my thread" (III,34).

One page before the announcement of the rape, Lovelace breaks off his narrative to give an aside about his technique. These words actively reassert, at a moment when the reader has been most powerfully projected into unfolding events, the art which lies behind every presentation of nature: "Thou'lt observe, Belford, that though this was written afterwards, yet (as in other places) I write it as it was spoken and happened, as if I had retired to put down every sentence as spoken. I know thou likest this lively *present-tense* manner, as it is one of my particulars." Taken together, these remarks commit Lovelace to a mimetic aesthetic. But in contrast to Clarissa and her mimetic program, Lovelace is a confessed illusionist. To be effective, his art, like Clarissa's, must seem not to be art. Here realism is not a moral obligation, or an apparently detached repetition of the actual— as it has been for Clarissa; it is a trick, a piece of Lovelacean magic.

There are unexpected perils for Lovelace in committing himself, as completely as he does, to the practice of art. Since sign systems and language are part of the public domain, each of his arts can be turned against him by his adversaries. This is the significance of the allegorical letter Clarissa writes about returning to her "father's" house (IV,157). When he discovers it is a ruse, Lovelace is shocked to find he does not have a monopoly on the use of the stratagem. He had lulled himself into thinking he had an artist's control over all the sign systems of his fiction, that all that lay before him was an intelligible text of his own devising. We can follow the peculiar power-bind that develops from Lovelace's practice of art by looking at what happens when he becomes the love-poet who "creates" Clarissa.

In seeking to explain his youthful disappointment at being spurned by a "quality-jilt," Lovelace describes his early ambitions in art and love. If the passage is read closely, it discloses ambiguities not at first apparent, which go a long way toward elucidating the tensions in Lovelace's position throughout the novel:

> it was . . . a vehement aspiration after a novelty, I think—those confounded poets, with their serenely-celestial descriptions, did as much with me as the lady: they fired my imagination, and set me upon a desire to become a goddess-maker. I must needs try my new-fledged pinions in sonnet, elegy, and madrigal. I must have a Cynthia, a Stella, a Sacharissa, as well as the best of them: darts, and flames, and the devil knows what, must I give to my

Cupid. I must create beauty, and place it where nobody else
could find it: and many a time have I been at a loss for a *subject*,
when my new-created goddess has been kinder than it was proper
for my plaintive sonnet that she should be. [I,145–46]

Through most of the passage there is a willed confusion of what one
might call the boundary between art and life. It is clear that "confounded poets" are having great influence on the young Lovelace, but
is the "novelty" he aspires to as a "goddess-maker" a real lady or a
lady in art? The next two sentences seem to settle the matter. Lovelace is to have his "Cynthia" or "Stella" by writing "sonnet, elegy,
and madrigal." But what then of the "quality jilt"? The next sentence
answers this question by overcoming the art/life opposition. Lovelace
aims at a radical fusion of the lady in art and the lady in life. He
wishes to "create beauty," like a poet, but he will place it in a real
lady, like a lover. In order to protect his "creation," he will put her
beyond the reach of other men, like the ethereal beauty of art. But a
problem besets his task. Often his "subject" slips out of the position
created for her by a plaintive sonnet, and Lovelace loses his "goddess." Lovelace's peculiar way of living through art, of loving Clarissa
as the canvas for his art, helps us to apprehend their situation. Lovelace is correct in claiming that he is "no sensual man," for sexual
possession would end the practice of art (II,147). Lovelace relishes
all the different moments of their struggle, for each gives him a new
view of his model and a new canvas to work on. Of course, Clarissa is
a particularly apt "subject" for him. No fear that she will be "kinder"
than is "proper" for his art.

   What kind of portrait does he paint? What kind of Clarissa does he
create? We can get at the answer to this question through a bit of
indirection. Throughout the novel, Belford's responses are an accurate
gauge of the farthest tendencies of the arts Clarissa and Lovelace
practice. Just as late in the novel Belford becomes Clarissa's epigone,
early in the novel he is a naïve or gullible "reader" of the Clarissa
whom Lovelace "creates" in his narrative letters. Lovelace invites
Belford and their brother rakes to a dinner party at Sinclair's. Clarissa
is imprisoned, surrounded by evil, and in danger of violation; in other
words, she is an image of virtue in distress. The fact that she does not
know the full measure of her danger is all the more poignant. This is
a situation constructed by Lovelace. With an artist's detachment, he

writes to Belford, "I want thee . . . to see and admire her while she is serene and full of hope: before her apprehensions are realized, if realized they are to be . . . before her beamy eyes have lost their lustre . . . and before the plough of disappointment has thrown up furrows of distress upon every lovely feature" (II,214). After the dinner party, Belford writes to Lovelace appealing to him to spare Clarissa any more trials. His way of describing her allows us to trace the tendency of Lovelace's art. He stands in awe of her understanding and declares her a "perfect beauty." He continues:

> I have done nothing but talk of this lady ever since I saw her. There is something *so awful*, and yet *so sweet*, in her aspect, that were I to have the virtues and the graces all drawn in one piece, they should be taken, every one of them, from different airs and attitudes in her. She was born to adorn the age she was given to, and would be an ornament to the first dignity. What piercing, yet gentle eye; every glance, I thought, mingled with love and fear of you! What a sweet smile darting through the cloud that overspread her fair face; demonstrating that she had more apprehensions and grief at her heart than she cared to express. . . . I am ready to regret such an angel of a woman should even marry. She is in my eye all mind; and were she to meet with a man all mind likewise, why should the charming qualities she is mistress of be endangered? Why should such an angel be plunged so low as into the vulgar offices of domestic life? Were she mine, I should hardly wish to see her a mother, unless there were a kind of moral certainty that minds like hers could be propagated.
> [II,243–44]

How can such a description of another human being happen? Perhaps we'll understand if we look at the elements of Belford's description. He begins by testifying to his obsession with Clarissa, an obsession that impels him to "talk." Since he cannot designate her nature, he will tentatively probe her mystery. Thus he writes, "there is something . . ." and what follows is a paradox, a series of oxymorons: Clarissa's aspect is "awful" yet "sweet," her eye "piercing" yet "gentle," and her smile mingles "love" with "fear." The abundance of these excellences and the hyperbole of Belford's praise signals an excess or surplus of energy in the object. It is this energy

which allows her to do a most astonishing thing—she reconciles contraries into one image.

Where does this power come from? Belford's language makes art
the matrix which engenders Clarissa's transcendent position. Belford
insists that Clarissa be the model with which to have "the virtues and
graces all drawn in one piece." She should "adorn" her age and be an
"ornament" to the first dignity. Belford is not interested in the
circular interdependence of art and life; it is the apartness, the self-
completeness, and the perfection of art which lead to his final claim,
that of Clarissa's radical superiority. Clarissa is "all mind," an "angel
of a woman" who should not be touched—she should not even
marry.

Now, although Belford writes on Clarissa's behalf, one can't escape
the sense that he is indulging *himself*. He has described the perfectly
desirable woman, and then denied her to all men. There is a very
rarified pleasure in this, an aesthetic rather than a sensual pleasure. It
is an extension of the "game" Lovelace has begun, a "game" that
modulates delay, self-denial, and desire. Several passages on art in
Nietzsche's *The Will to Power* illustrate what Belford and Lovelace
are doing with Clarissa. They have contrived one of those "states in
which," Nietzsche writes, "we transfuse a transfiguration and fullness
into things and poetize about them until they reflect back our fullness
and joy in life."

There are two successive moments in the realization of the art
object: the first, when the art object is filled with the artist's energy
and life, and the second, when the art object "reflects" this life and
energy back. There is the same double movement when Nietzsche
compares art with "states of animal vigor:" "It is on the one hand an
excess and overflow of blooming physicality into the world of images
and desires; on the other, an excitation of the animal functions
through the images and desires of intensified life" (*WP*,802). When
the object is perfectly realized, it is said to have beauty. This is the
highest reach of the artist's power, that which gives him the most
pleasure:

"Beauty" is for the artist something outside all order of rank,
because in beauty opposites are tamed; the highest sign of power,
namely power over opposites; moreover without tension:—that

violence is no longer needed; that everything follows, obeys, so easily and so pleasantly—that is what delights the artist's will to power. [*WP*,803]

Belford's "rendering" of Clarissa shows the danger of Lovelace's activity. Belford endows Clarissa—the art object—with so much energy, beauty, and spirituality (with so much of his own power) that he becomes impotent. Even if she belonged to him, he would not want her to be a mother unless "minds like hers could be propagated." For Belford, the art object has appropriated so much authority to itself, that the only justifiable activity is its duplication. Of course, Clarissa turns this thought, the idea of her duplication, into a moral program, when she installs herself as an exemplar to the sex in the novel she arranges to have edited. Lovelace's danger comes from the two contradictory ways he is involved in the "perfection" of Clarissa. Lovelace invents the scenes within which Clarissa shines, and he magnifies her roles with his own opposition. But he also sits back and savors the beauty of her performance. The greater the Clarissa he creates, the greater his pleasure in creation and the grander the images of life she will reflect. But precisely at this moment—the moment of his maximum pleasure and passivity—Lovelace can be mastered by his own creation. This happens on several occasions in the second installment. Lovelace finds himself strangely assimilated to Clarissa's will, abandons all his schemes, and proposes to her with complete genuineness.

Two scenes display all the modalities of this process. The first scene is at St. Albans, after the discovery of James Harlowe's plan to kidnap Clarissa forces her into greater reliance on Lovelace. She even harbors an unacknowledged love for her antagonist. Lovelace begins the scene determined to tease Clarissa for "her past indifference" by proposing at the same time that he reminds her "of her injunction" not to talk of marriage. But Clarissa's response is captivating:

I never beheld so sweet a confusion. What a glory to the pencil, could it do justice to it, and to the mingled impatience which visibly informed every feature of the most meaning and most beautiful face in the world! She hemmed twice or thrice; her look, now so charmingly silly, then so sweetly significant; till at last the lovely teaser, teased by my hesitating expectation of her answer, out of all power of articulate speech, burst into tears. . . .

Then she spoke, but with vexation; I am—I am—*very* unhappy—
tears trickling down her crimson cheeks, and her sweet face, as
my arms still encircled the finest waist in the world, sinking upon
my shoulder; the dear creature so absent that she knew not the
honour she permitted me. . . . Then recovering herself and her
usual reserves, and struggling to free herself from my clasping
arms; How now, sir! said she, with a cheek more indignantly
glowing and eyes of a fiercer lustre. I gave way to her angry
struggle; but, absolutely overcome by so charming a display of
innocent confusion, I caught hold of her hand as she was flying
from me, and kneeling at her feet, O my angel, said I (quite
destitute of reserve, and hardly knowing the tenor of my own
speech; and had a parson been there, I had certainly been a gone
man), receive the vows of your faithful Lovelace. Make him
yours, and only yours, for ever. This will answer every end.
[II,141]

The second scene makes explicit what is only implied in the first—
at the moment when Clarissa becomes the object of Lovelace's art, he
perceives her as transcendent, himself as abject and powerless. Here
the whole sequence takes only three short paragraphs. The scene
follows the copying of Anna's letter, Lovelace's violent anger, and
Clarissa's troubled and reproachful meditation on herself (II,370–79).
A turbulent debate about the justice of Miss Howe's criticisms of
Lovelace culminates, thus, as Lovelace narrates:

I cast myself at her feet. Begone, Mr. Lovelace, said she, with a
rejecting motion, her fan in her hand; for your own sake leave
me! My soul is above thee, man! with both her hands pushing me
from her. Urge me not to tell thee, how sincerely I think my soul
above thee! Thou hast, in mine, a proud, a too proud heart to
contend with! Leave me, and leave me for ever! Thou hast a
proud heart to contend with!

  Her air, her manner, her voice, were bewitchingly noble, though
her words were so severe.

  Let me worship an angel, said I, no woman. Forgive me dearest
creature! Creature if you be, forgive me! Forgive my inadvertancies! Forgive my inequalities! Pity my infirmities! Who is
equal to my Clarissa? . . . And till she had actually withdrawn . . .
all the motions of my heart were as pure as her own. [II,382–83]

After the first scene, Lovelace wonders at Clarissa's sudden power over him. He asks, "Was the devil in me! I no more intended all this ecstatic nonsense than I thought the same moment of flying in the air! All power is with this charming creature . . . this sweet creature is able to make a man forego every purpose of his heart that is not favourable to her" (II,142).

How can we make sense of this "ecstatic nonsense" for Lovelace? Each scene begins with Lovelace in full control, testing or teasing his victim. For different reasons, Clarissa feels acute distress, a distress which suddenly becomes fascinating to Lovelace. In the crucial, unnamed moment of this sequence, Lovelace suspends his own will, marks a frame about Clarissa, and engages in a detached regard of her. Now he can name and sketch her excellences in a verbal portrait.

What kind of portrait does Lovelace sketch? As with Belford, Lovelace finds that Clarissa can reconcile contraries. In the first scene Clarissa's pride and independence come into collision with her love for Lovelace and her need for him. This inner conflict is the dramatic backdrop for the "sweet confusion" Lovelace relishes. This "confusion" is primarily "shame" before Lovelace's gaze and "perplexity" about what to do. But it also implies a mixing "in which the distinction of the elements is lost by fusion or blending" (see *OED*). This fusion of the distinct is explicit in "the mingled impatience" which informs "the most meaning and most beautiful face in the world." Clarissa's beauty is blended with something quite different—a "meaning" aspect, a face that "conveys or expresses meaning or thought"; it is "expressive, significant" (see *OED*). Lovelace's attention is arrested by a face that holds opposites in one unified image. He finds her "now so charmingly silly, then so sweetly significant." Her moods also juxtapose opposites. First she is "so absent" to herself she lets her head rest on his shoulder; then she resents his freedoms with a cheek "indignantly glowing and eyes of fiercer lustre."

The second scene Lovelace narrates also makes Clarissa an object that is fascinating in the way it reconciles contraries. Her reproach to him is haughty and majestic: "My soul is above thee, man!" But her way of warning Lovelace off contains a serious self-reproach. In her meditation, just before this scene, Clarissa has castigated herself for having too much pride. Now she says, "thou hast, in mine, a proud, a too proud heart to contend with!" Her heart is "too proud" to submit to Lovelace, but also "too proud" to lead the kind of Christian

life she strives to lead. It is the double-edged quality of this reproach
—anger at Lovelace and distress with herself—that allows Clarissa to
become an aesthetic object for Lovelace (and the reader). Again Lovelace expresses this fact with an oxymoron: "her air, her manner, her
voice, were bewitchingly noble, though her words were so severe."

In isolating Clarissa as a self-complete object, and naming the
splendid elements she holds in tension, Lovelace feels her overabun-
dance, her excess of energy. This is expressed with exclamations and
hyperbole: "I never beheld . . . What a glory to the pencil" (II,141);
"the most meaning and beautiful face in the world. . . . Who is equal
to my Clarissa?" (II,383) As Clarissa's image appropriates all power to
itself, Lovelace feels himself to be abject and worthless. He kneels,
now not from design but to express her superiority. He pleads,
"Forgive my inadvertancies! Forgive my inequalities! Pity my infirmities!" (II,383). Now Clarissa is seen as pure spirit. Lovelace writes,
"O my angel, said I . . . an angel, said I, no woman" (II,141, 383).
Lovelace's final failure is expressed as an inability to compass
Clarissa's exalted new reality with his language. After the "fire scene"
he writes, "*Imagination* cannot form; much less can the pencil paint;
nor can the soul of painting, *poetry*, describe an angel so exquisitely,
so elegantly lovely!" (II,499).

Now we are ready to see that Lovelace's portraiture engages the
same process as his other arts—parody, the lie, the stratagem, and the
performance. Here too Lovelace empties the self in the same motion
with which he displaces Clarissa into a surface. Here too the willed
simplification of the two adversaries prepares for an intricate play
between them. In framing Clarissa and making her a portrait, Lovelace abstracts aspects of her into one reduced but intensified image.
But he is so generous in his adornment of the surface, he gives it such
complex tones and enigmatic shadings, that it threatens to overcome
him. The myth of Pygmalion, as told by Ovid, is the aptest traditional
description of the situation. One's own creation expresses so much
beauty, holds so much energy in tension, that miraculously it comes
alive. Now it can master (i.e. seduce) its creator.[4]

---

4. We shall see (in chapter 6, "The Reader as Pygmalion") that Richardson and his most
important correspondent, Lady Bradsheigh, make the story of Pygmalion an apt one for
interpreting their relationship to the object they adore—the text of *Clarissa*.

Toward the Rape: Venturing a Mastery of Meaning

In a novel full of piety and fun, the rape is an astonishing event. It ranks with Clarissa's death as one of the great deeds in the novel. It has the power, in the minds of the characters, to become the end of all that happened before it and the beginning of all that will come after. Why must Lovelace rape Clarissa? We should not discount the simplest motive—a violent and reflexive striking out so as to level Clarissa. She has taken a very high line with Lovelace in declaring, "My soul is above thee, man!" Lovelace responds by writing, "there is no bearing the consciousness of the infinite inferiority she charged me with" (III,154). But Lovelace feels justified by other factors. Clarissa has violated his "game" by escaping to Hampstead (II,256). Also, rape is the most cogent response to Clarissa's fictional projection of her self as a whole unified body "full of light." He can subvert this fiction by introducing a small part of himself *into* Clarissa. Thus the rape, like all Lovelace's displacements, will seek to induce the slight difference that will make all the difference. Lovelace playfully speculates upon the effect of this displacement, should she reject him after the rape. The fallen Clarissa becomes a parody of the upright virgin we know:

> And thus may her *old* nurse and she; an *old* coachman; and a pair of *old* coach-horses; and two or three *old* maid-servants, and perhaps a *very old* footman or two (for everything will be old and penitential about her), live very comfortably together; reading *old* sermons, and *old* prayer books . . . and giving *old* lessons, and *old* warnings, upon new subjects, as well as *old* ones, to the young ladies of her neighbourhood; and so pass on to a good *old* age, doing a great deal of good both by precept and example in her generation. [III,177]

But the rape is more than the logical next step in the conflict between Clarissa and Lovelace. Lovelace calculates that it will initiate a new phase in their history. All through the novel, Clarissa's chief projection of her self, and Lovelace's displacements of her, have been representations and counter-representations—attempts by each to win a decisive battle in a war of meaning. By raping Clarissa, Lovelace expects to end her counterthrusts by fixing her meaning. She will simply be a "fallen" woman, his woman, and significantly, silent—

one who will "tell no tales" (III,190). All of this depends on what the rape is supposed to be: the moment when Clarissa will be decisively marked, and the moment when Lovelace will "know" her.

Marking and knowing are the two stages of Lovelace's definitive interpretation of Clarissa—his determination of her meaning. In proceeding, Lovelace is confident that her rape will mark her. It will be the stain that becomes a publically accepted sign that designates her nature. After her second escape, Mowbray writes, "she has gone away with thy marks, I understand. A foolish little devil! Where will she mend herself? For nobody will look upon her" (III,307). But notice. The decisive significance of this "mark" is predicated upon, built upon, Clarissa's own fictional constructs: the marking of the self's inside/outside boundary, the idea of her purity, the notion that her hymen is her crucial anatomical structure. The force of Lovelace's act is dependent upon the authority of Clarissa's fictions. This is its hidden flaw, and something Clarissa can work with. She *also* knows how to interpret, and how to reinterpret. For while the rape violates Clarissa, it merely validates the fictional design of her innocence, allowing her to re-mark her self as pure, in a powerful new way, after the rape.

The rape is also to be a moment of knowing—the moment when Clarissa will be undressed, seen, penetrated, and known. These are activities which engage every reader, like Lovelace, who wishes to win authority for his interpretation. He "lays bare" the text, "sees" its significance, "penetrates" to its real meaning, and thus "knows" it. Lovelace's interpretation of Clarissa is dependent on the prestige, or the mystique, of these sexual metaphors for "knowing." In raping Clarissa, Lovelace attempts to undermine the power of her wholeness, to break her into parts, to show she's made of the same stuff every-one else is, and therefore can be read by the text of the rake's creed: "once subdued, always subdued." All this will subject Clarissa to Lovelace's interpretation of her, and so the rape becomes Lovelace's venture to master, once and for all, Clarissa's meaning. But Lovelace should beware. For even the commonest slut knows how to weave new veils to cover the body with a seeming freshness. And Clarissa is *not* common.

Pulling off the rape is no simple matter. It requires all the resources of Lovelace's art. After Clarissa's flight to Hampstead, he must engage in constant performance—not only for Clarissa but for all the ladies at

Mrs. Moore's. He is quicker and more elaborate in the stratagems he executes: the bridegroom disguise, an impromptu impersonation of Clarissa, the prompting of "Lady Betty" and "Cousin Charlotte," and the drug which drastically curtails Clarissa's powers as an artist of the sentimental. Lovelace's narrative to Belford becomes more stagey and, as he moves toward the rape, his displacements of Clarissa increase in range and intensity. For, in spite of all his assumed confidence, Lovelace confesses to doubts about what he's doing and an "enervating pity" which would "unsteel" his heart (III,191). In fact, he needs to keep displacing, distancing, and undoing Clarissa *in order* to steady his own heart for the rape. Thus he subverts Clarissa's claims of piety with a comic description of her virtuous life with Mrs. Norton (see above, p. 49). He overcomes the pleas of "Love," in an imaginary debate, by insisting that Clarissa is the avowed "rebel" to real love, for she would modify its claims through an appeal to "merit" and "prudence" (III,156–57). Finally, in the last letter before the rape, Lovelace cleverly evades the social laws which ordain that sexual relations only exist as part of marriage. He presents their marriage license, marked by a succession of witty interpolations, and coupled with his scheme for annual marriages. In his charming demonstration—and Lovelace *is* charming—he contrives to show how his plan would bring connubial bliss, personal health, and social peace (III,179–84).

All of these displacements are part of a defensive strategy. They displace Clarissa's situation out of its conventional social matrix and subdue it to Lovelace's own art. This procedure receives its sharpest test with the unexpected appearance of "conscience." Lovelace has been engaging in various casuistical arguments for the rape. He explicitly parodies Clarissa's appeal to her conscience: "I can justify myself to *myself*; and that as the fair invincible would say, is all in all" (III,144, parodying II,306). But then, quite suddenly, an "imposter" named "conscience" steals Lovelace's pen and considers matters in an entirely different way. First it decides to "reflect" on "the manifold perfections" of Clarissa "before it be too late." It considers possible consequences of the rape and offers well-reasoned advice: "she perhaps will refuse and abhor thee. . . . Thou canst not live without her. Thou wouldst rather marry her than lose her absolutely" (III,146). In considering alternatives, this "conscience" discovers Lovelace's lack of freedom. He can't go back on his plans, and is compelled by the expectations of his own agents. He declares, "I am a machine at last and no free agent." Finally this "conscience" offers Lovelace something of a temptation to the Clarissean ideal of a consistent self that knows the joys of a harmony between self, life, and value:

> What a happiness must that man know, who moves regularly to some laudable end, and has nothing to reproach himself with in his progress to it! When, by honest means, he attains this end, how great and unmixed must be his enjoyments! What a happy man, in this particular case, had I been, had it been given me to *be* only what I wished to *appear* to be! [III,146]

Now, "conscience" is a completely Clarissean idea. Conscience broods about past and future, considers options prudently, conceptualizes its own freedom, and strives for an internal consistency of self. It has been the absence of anything one might call a conscience which makes Lovelace what he is—one who displaces, empties the self, and engages in many varieties of art. To do this, he must attend to the present and near future, ignore the ultimate consequences of his actions, bracket the very idea of freedom, and look away from anything called the self. The sudden appearance of a conscience in Lovelace displaces the displacer. It resolves all the intricacies of his "game" into contradictory nonsense. That is why the scene unfolds like a temptation, and Lovelace must kill this ghost or demon "conscience." "She" is an emanation of Clarissa and would eliminate Lovelace and his whole mode of being. As he says over her corpse: "Lie there! Welter on! Had I not given thee thy death's wound, thou wouldst have robbed me of all my joys. Thou couldst not have mended me, 'tis plain. Thou couldst only have thrown me into despair" (III,147).

Lovelace's murder of "conscience" dramatizes the fundamental violence of the Clarissa-Lovelace encounter. Lovelace's displacements of Clarissa always implied the rape, and, for all their subtlety and wit, are as violent as Clarissa's desire to subdue him to her system of values by "reforming" him. This scene also shows us Lovelace moving toward the rape with an inexorable necessity. As he does so, we seem to catch him assuming a tone of regret with regard to his anticipated action. He begins by subverting his remorse at the same time that he gives expression to it: "there is a mixture of gravity in me. This, as I grow older, may increase; and when my active capacity begins to abate, I may sit down with the preacher, and resolve all my past life into vanity and vexation of spirit." Then he gives a less playful turn to the moment by displacing the novel's action into a metaphoric journey. Lovelace presents his relationship with Clarissa, in this metaphor of the journey, in such a way as to incorporate the two forces working on him: his genuine regret for continuing with his plot and the absolute necessity of his doing so. He writes:

This is certain, that I shall never find a woman so well suited to my taste as Miss Clarissa Harlowe. I only wish that I may have such a lady as her to comfort and adorn my setting sun. I have often thought it very unhappy for us both, that so excellent a creature sprang up a little too late for my *setting-out*, and a little too early in my *progress*, before I can think of *returning*. And yet, as I have picked up the sweet traveller in my way, I cannot help wishing that she would bear me company in the *rest* of my journey, although she were to step out of her own path to oblige me. And then, perhaps, we could put up in the *evening* at the same *inn*; and be very happy in each other's conversation; recounting the difficulties and dangers we had passed in our way to it. [III,178]

The passage begins with Lovelace adopting the rake's complaisant egotism, the stance of a connoisseur making a choice: she is "so well suited to my taste." But Lovelace quickly softens his tone to "I only wish," and then to the still more muted expressions of will, "before I can think" and "I cannot help wishing." The third sentence establishes the tone of detached regret and resignation that characterizes Lovelace's use of the analogy ("I have often thought it very unhappy"). What emerges, almost despite Lovelace's intention, is the fact of his absolute need for Clarissa. It would seem that all that's in question is the terms of their relationship, the way they will get together. But all the struggle and conflict of that great question have modulated into a wish for a graceful reconciliation. Her rape or seduction has simply become a "step out of her path to oblige me." The rake's exercise of will is modified into a mild proferring of a wish. Clarissa goes from "a woman" to "such a lady as her" to "the sweet traveller." The deeper meaning of the passage is concealed in its ostensible statement. Lovelace offers this as a kind of prospect, but its tone of loss and the conditional of the last sentence—"And then, perhaps we could"—show that Lovelace is really figuring forth what might have been if their intractable positions had been a little different. The absolute reconciliation of the end—"recounting the difficulties and dangers we had passed"—is in dramatic tension with the deception and violence Lovelace finds himself projected toward.

Here, in writing about Lovelace, in interpreting and analyzing him, I have constructed a subject for him, I have sketched a psychology. But Lovelace does not stoop to meditation, though we can do a meditation with his language. The moment we do we must remember that we've modulated into a Clarissean mode: we have centered his self, we have turned his condition into a proposition. Lovelace always escapes this gesture, and leaves us doubting our proposition—perhaps now he's mocking all our sentiment and seriousness. For Lovelace escapes into language, displacing himself and his situation not into a form or a space but onto the next page of his letter, or the next moment of the game. Thus no motive is stabilized to explain an action, no clear cause can be found for his effects.

Lovelace is always taking us to the limits of analysis, always getting us to question our own need to explain. In his display of himself in writing, he resembles writing as it is figured forth by Derrida in "La Double Séance." Derrida is explicating Mallarmé's conjunction of writing with the dance. The ballet dancer does a pirouette on one toe. But the stability of that held moment of a turn on one point is in part illusion. For as the foot turns it is slightly displaced in preparation for the next figure of the dance. In the same way, the pen on the page turns through one word, one phrase, one idea on its way to another; it tries to hold in the pirouettes of language one meaning and one gesture *while* it is moving toward another. In *Clarissa*, only Lovelace can detach himself from his experience through his use of the jest and the game. His writing is a succession of fugitive and provisional gestures which detach him from his experience as much as they articulate it—they detach *while* they articulate. His life becomes a kind of dance around Clarissa, with every pirouette a graph of their interplay, and he, his writing, and his displacements become a chain of pirouettes which, to quote Derrida, "are linked one to another, forming one another, and moving like silhouettes, stamped as dark shadows on a white ground, profiles without face, ever presenting themselves as a series of skewed sketches, turning around a circular shaft, this invisible axis of writing, displacing itself without end."[5]

5. *La Dissémination* (Paris: Editions Seuil, 1972), p. 272. Translation mine.

3: The Battle for the Body

For Clarissa at the garden gate:

> They looking back, all th' eastern side beheld
> Of Paradise, so late their happy seat,
> Wav'd over by that flaming brand, the Gate
> With dreadful faces throng'd and fiery arms.
> Some natural tears they dropped, but wiped them soon;
> The world was all before them, where to choose
> Their place of rest, and Providence their guide:
> They hand in hand with wandering steps and slow
> Through Eden took their solitary way.
> —Paradise Lost XII, 632–41

For Clarissa in the "pen-knife" scene:

> And I saw a great white throne, and
> him that sat on it, from whose face the
> earth and heaven fled away; and there
> was found no place for them.
> And I saw the dead, small and great,
> stand before God; and the books were
> opened: and another book was opened
> which is the book of life: and the dead
> were judged out of those things which
> were written in the books, according to
> their works.
> And the sea gave up the dead which
> were in it; and death and hell delivered
> up the dead which were in them: and
> they were judged every man according to
> their works.
> And death and hell were cast into
> the lake of fire. This is the second death.
> And whosoever was not found written in
> the book of life was cast into the lake of
> fire.   Revelation 20:11–15

For Lovelace and his fire:

> Fire is thus a privileged phenomenon which can explain anything. If all
> that changes slowly is explained by life, all that changes quickly is
> explained by fire. Fire is the ultra-living element. It is intimate and it is
> universal. It lives in our heart. It lives in the sky. It rises from the depths of
> the substance and offers itself with the warmth of love. Or it can go back
> down into the substance and hide there, latent and pent-up, like hate and

vengeance. Among all phenomena, it is really the only one to which there can be so definitely attributed the opposing values of good and evil. It shines in Paradise. It burns in Hell. It is gentleness and torture. It is cookery and it is apocalypse. It is a pleasure for the good child sitting prudently by the earth; yet it punishes any disobedience when the child wishes to play too close to the flames. It is well-being and it is respect. It is a tutelary and a terrible divinity, both good and bad. It can contradict itself; thus it is one of the principles of universal explanation. . . .

. . . The Feminine heat attacks things from without. The masculine heat attacks things from within at the very heart of the essential being. Such is the profound meaning of the alchemist's reverie. . . . This inner, masculine fire . . . is the fire which can "open bodies." An anonymous (alchemist) writes . . . 'Art, in imitation of Nature, opens a body by means of fire, but uses a much stronger fire than the Fire that is produced by the fire of confined flames.'

—Gaston Bachelard, The Psychoanalysis of Fire, pp. 7, 53

In the first two chapters of this book we have looked at the two epicenters of Richardson's text, seeing things first from Clarissa's angle, then Lovelace's. But the separateness of these angles is an interpretive fiction—parts of *our* act of mimesis and *our* act of displacement as they comprise aspects of a larger activity called interpretation. We must begin to think of these two centers of the text together; for Clarissa's mimetic narrative and Lovelace's parodic displacements, her construction of a self and his way of opening one out into play, are invented for the same struggle and go forward simultaneously.

All this activity is directed toward one goal—the control of Clarissa's body. In this battle, the moment of Clarissa's physical violation has a crucial place. We have seen the way it becomes the final move in Lovelace's game-plan to subjugate Clarissa. In addition, Clarissa's nightmare burial in the churchyard prefigures the rape, and her last papers keep returning the reader to the rape scene. But when we look to the letters, we find two lacunae at the points where the rape should be described. Lovelace sends Belford his short code message: "the affair is over," and Clarissa censors her account to Anna: "Let me cut short the rest . . . then such scenes followed—O my dear, such dreadful scenes!" (III,196; III,371) The very absence of a representation of the rape invites the reader to feel the imaginative power—the horror and the fascination—the rape has for Lovelace and Clarissa.

But since the rape is an inaccessible center of Richardson's novel, where does the battle for the body unfold? We must look to the three melodramatic scenes that come at points where control of Clarissa's body becomes an urgent question: the abduction scene at the garden gate (I,476–87; I,511–13), the fire scene (II,501–07), and the pen-knife scene (III,287–92). Each scene is the occasion for the arts Lovelace and Clarissa practice. Lovelace's use of the stratagem is integral to his contriving these scenes; he uses Leman's false alarm, the fire at Sinclair's, and Dorcas's offer to help Clarissa. Each scene engages him in a performance: Lovelace as ardent deliverer, Lovelace as lover overcome with passion, Lovelace as indignant prosecutor. In all these ways Lovelace works to overcome Clarissa's self-control. Clarissa responds by using her practiced allegiance to truth-telling and the idea of a self to reassert her adherence to a personal ideal of virtue.

While Lovelace's affiliations with the dramatic are explicit through-out the novel, Clarissa's talents in this direction are obscured by her apparent yearning for a tranquil life of virtue. But the *way* she does battle with her family engages her in an active development of the dramatic potential of the situation. In discussing marriage to Solmes with her aunt, Clarissa composes a pathetic scene: "And what will any of my relations be answerable for, if they force my hand into his, and hold it there till the service be read; I perhaps insensible, and in fits all the time!" Clarissa's aunt is bemused by the way Clarissa has read herself into a fictional scene: "What a romantic picture of a forced marriage have you drawn, niece!" (I,404).

Clarissa's efforts to contrive scenes of poignant drama are most apparent when they fail. During one of Solmes's proposals, Clarissa refuses her brother's advice, and her father thunders his disapproval from the next room. Clarissa runs to the locked door and seeks to stage an impromptu scene:

> O my papa!—my dear papa, said I, falling to my knees at the door —admit your child to your presence! Let me but plead my cause at your feet! . . . I will not stir from my knees, continued I without admission. At this door I beg it! O let it be the door of mercy! [I,390]

Suddenly, the locked door Clarissa is leaning against is opened and she falls "flat on [her] face into the other parlour." She stands up, only to find all but the maid gone. The pathos of this moment comes from her family's stern refusal to give Clarissa the audience she needs. Lovelace takes a very different line in discussing Clarissa's aptitude as an artist of the sentimental:

> Then this lady is a mistress of our passions: no one ever had to so much perfection the art of moving. This all her family know, and have equally feared and revered her for it. This I know too; and doubt not more and more to experience. How charmingly must this divine creature warble forth (if a proper occasion be given) her melodious elegaics! Infinite beauties are there in a weeping eye. [II,252]

Lovelace will not avoid exposure to Clarissa's "art of moving" as her family does. He plans to give Clarissa the "proper occasion" for the practice of her arts, so as to bring out their charm and beauty. In addition, he will engage, test, and compete with Clarissa, for he relishes the sport and theater of it all. In spite of the vast differences between Lovelace and Clarissa, each has dramatic inclinations, and Lovelace decides to use his dramatic art to solicit Clarissa's.

The scenes Lovelace contrives create a single space in which these antagonists compete to win a prevailing, a mutually accepted, signification. They are like two children at a blackboard, wrestling for the possession of a single piece of chalk with which to write their own word or image. Of course, the drama of these scenes is enhanced by the implicit presence of other eyes: for Clarissa, her friends and family; for Lovelace, his rakish compatriots and the women "below." But each goes much further than the expectations imposed by these other eyes. Thus, after the scene where Clarissa says, "My soul is above thee, man!", Lovelace reflects, "How poor indeed was I then, even in my own heart! So *visible* a superiority, to so proud a spirit as mine!" (II,400). Both Clarissa and Lovelace believe in the innate power of the visually manifest—that which has been written and displayed for the eye to see. This motivates strenuous efforts at representation. For Clarissa this means making what is present to her self present to all. She will so represent herself that her hidden nature (i.e. her virtue) will become a generally accepted display. Lovelace attempts representations that will subvert Clarissa's equanimity and give him control over her person. To enter a space of rival signification is to be threatened with being a passive receiver of meanings, an audience and nothing more. Power, at this moment, consists in being the active encoder of significations, the controller of language, and the director of the unfolding scene.

The Play of Rival Significations

Outside the garden gate at Harlowe Place, Lovelace wins almost complete control over the tone and direction of his encounter with Clarissa. He does this by giving a particular meaning to the scene. He makes it the moment of an apocalyptic convergence of all the forces arrayed around Clarissa. Clarissa has habitually complained of being embattled on every side, so she is especially susceptible to this idea. Lovelace begins by insisting on the dangerous and critical nature of the moment: "And here we shall be discovered in a moment. Speed away, my charmer—this is the moment of your deliverance" (I,476). These words serve to define their roles for the scene Lovelace is constructing: Lovelace is the deliverer, Clarissa the delivered. To give emphasis to this point in the long colloquy that follows, Lovelace recalls all that Clarissa has suffered and insists that Wednesday will bring her forced marriage to Solmes. When Clarissa holds firm, he threatens to enter the garden gate with her and personally confront the family: "I will face them all: but not as a revenger, if they provoke me not too much" (I,480).

Lovelace's arguments, and his barely veiled threat, serve to put his violent resistance to the Harlowe family before Clarissa. Now all is prepared for a fictive crisis. He hears a sound, whispers, "*They are at the door my beloved creature*," and Joseph's voice responds to the cue and materializes the combatants: "*Are you there? Come up this moment!—this moment! Here they are—here they are both together! Your pistol this moment!—your gun!*" At this point Lovelace uses a grandiloquent gesture and an urgent verbal appeal to complete his illusion. He draws his sword, claps it "naked under his arm," saying, "Fly, fly, my charmer; this moment is all you have for it. . . . Your brother!—your uncles!—or this Solmes! They will instantly burst the door. Fly, my dearest life . . . if you would not see two or three murders committed at your feet, fly, fly, I beseech you." Unknown to Clarissa, her account of this moment tells us the signification Lovelace's artifice has been designed to realize:

Now behind me, now before me, now on this side, now on that, turned I my affrighted face in the same moment; expecting a furious brother here, armed servants there, an enraged sister screaming, and a father armed with terror in his countenance more dreadful than even the drawn sword which I saw, or those I apprehended. I ran as fast as he; yet knew not that I ran; my fears adding wings to my feet, as the same time that they took all power of thinking from me. [I,484]

Clarissa imagines she is standing at the center of a scene of hyperbolic violence. The scene reenacts her story. She is the defiant and undutiful daughter with a resolute lover, sword "drawn," pulling on one side, and her family threatening on the other—a "furious brother," "armed servants," and a father with "terror in his countenance." The scene skillfully crystallizes her deepest anxiety: the physical violation and dismemberment of her unified body. It is suggestive that "all power of thinking" is taken from Clarissa. The scene Lovelace has contrived carries its signification so immediately that it impels Clarissa to move according to its rhythms. In remembering her flight, Lovelace is bemused by the "charming contradiction" of her "flying from friends she was resolved not to abandon to the man she was determined not to go off with" (I,513). He sets down his pen to laugh. That Clarissa and Lovelace were fleeing swiftly from nobody, that all her panic at the gate and all the energy of her description are directed at a convincing illusion, a compelling but mendacious signification— all this is Lovelace's joke. This justifies his laughter and verifies the power of his art.

In the fire scene at Mrs. Sinclair's, Clarissa becomes a coequal participant in the melodrama of signification. The scene opens with Clarissa presented, by Lovelace's narrative, as an assemblage of beautiful parts composing a glowing erotic image: "her bared shoulders and arms, so inimitably fair and lovely: her spread hands crossed over her charming neck; yet not half concealing . . ." (II,502). Lovelace immediately tries to translate the occasion into a night of passion: "I mentioned the morrow as the happiest day of my life." Clarissa counters by insisting on the primacy of the present instant: "Tell me not of tomorrow. If indeed you mean me honourably, *now*, this very instant NOW! you must show it, and be gone!" (II,503). If Clarissa is to escape Lovelace's assault, she must do what he accomplished before the garden gate. She must convince him of the extraordinary quality of this particular moment, and then try to give that moment a meaning which will direct him away from his accustomed mode of action.

Clarissa responds in a range of contradictory ways: she reproaches him with the utmost vehemence, threatens self-violence, reproaches him in stern indignation, condemns herself as forever shamed, and appeals to him as "my *dear* Lovelace" and "*blessed* Lovelace." Lovelace does what we have seen him do before. He comes under the spell of an object that he himself in part creates—a Clarissa that reconciles contraries of sensuality and virtue, feminine beauty and masculine strength. He writes, "Oh, what additional charms . . . did her struggles give to every feature, every limb, of a person so sweetly elegant and lovely!" This leads to a crucial hesitation and a very familiar description of Clarissa: "I sat suspended for a moment. By my soul, thought I, thou art, upon full proof, an angel and no woman!" It is at this moment that Clarissa intercedes to give her version of the unfolding scene: this is no night of erotic passion, but an instance of virtue in distress!

> See, Mr. Lovelace!—Good God! that I should live to see this hour, and to bear this treatment!—See at your feet a poor creature, imploring your pity, who, for your sake, is abandoned of all the world! Let not my father's curse thus dreadfully operate! Be not *you* the inflicter, who have been the *cause* of it: but spare me, I beseech you, spare me! For how have I deserved this treatment from you? For *your own sake*, if not for *my sake*, and as you would that God Almighty, in your last hour, should have mercy upon *you*, spare me! [II,504]

With the repetition of the word *see*, Clarissa insists that Lovelace turn from his own passion and regard her as an object with a particular meaning. She is the innocent and helpless heroine of sentimental drama caught up in a whirlwind of turbulent forces: curses, judgment, good, and evil. He must choose to be the villain who undoes her, or the hero who can save her. Lovelace's "heart" is "penetrated" by the power of Clarissa's words. He tells her, "I will submit to my beloved conqueress, whose power never was at so great a height with me as now" (II,504).

How has Clarissa prevailed over Lovelace? Clarissa emulates

Lovelace's procedure in abducting her from Harlowe Place. She uses a series of devices to push the scene into an absolute clarity of meaning: repetition of catch phrases, comprehensive bodily gestures, a relentless overstatement, stage business and props. The symbols displayed through these scenes, and the pen-knife scene, dramatize the possibility of the body's exposure, entrance, and violation (gates, doors, sword, fire, key, scissors, pen-knife). But it is important to note the subtle interweaving of agency that drives this scene toward its conclusion. Lovelace constructs the initial situation (Clarissa exposed and helpless), Clarissa offers the counterpoint of her innocence, Lovelace experiences her as an art object, then Clarissa offers the climactic verbal formulation of the scene and is spared.

Lovelace designs the last of the "big" melodramatic scenes, the pen-knife scene, to overcome Clarissa's continued resistance after the rape. He hopes to place Clarissa in the position of a guilty defendant being tried for bribery. This takes careful planning. He gets Dorcas to feign sympathy for Clarissa, Dorcas receives a bribe from Clarissa, and Lovelace "finds" the letter that contains the bribe. Mrs. Sinclair's feigned indignation hints at the renewed physical assault Lovelace has planned: "I hope you will find a way to hear this cause in her presence. I value not my doors on such an occasion as this." We have noted that the scene of judgment has a special centrality in the organization of Clarissa's mental life. It is not likely that she would miss her trial, even one constructed by her adversary. Clarissa uses her not inconsiderable resources to counterattack.

Lovelace's description of her entrance into the "courtroom" emphasizes an eruption into presence of a Clarissa who has intensified her self's very "nature." He writes, "and then *hear* her step toward us, and instantly *see* her enter among us, confiding in her own innocence; and with a majesty in her person and manner, that is natural to her; but which then shone out in all its glory!" The language here makes plain the signification which Clarissa's entrance has accomplished: outraged innocence. Lovelace's use of light imagery —"shone out in all its glory"—emphasizes an excess or surplus of Clarissa's "nature." A long silence indicates her control and their awe before this overwhelming embodiment of innocence. Lovelace writes, "Such the glorious power of innocence exerted at that awful moment" (III,287).

Clarissa's first step is to discredit Lovelace's construct—his "trial":

"O thou contemptible and abandoned Lovelace, thinkest thou that I see not through this poor villainous plot of thine, and of these thy wicked accomplices?" Clarissa refuses to be a passive reader of the scene he has composed. She systematically discredits all the components of Lovelace's artifice and simultaneously asserts her own role of judge and truth-teller in a trial, not of herself, but of Lovelace and his agents. Mrs. Sinclair is "my detestation" who "shouldst once more have provided for me intoxicating potions"; the "vile women" are openly told that she is not married, thus undermining the pretext upon which Lovelace was living with her ("and, to your utter ruin, [I] will find friends to pursue you"); Dorcas is praised ironically for her role in Lovelace's "farce": "Thy shameful, thy poor part, thou hast as well acted as the low farce could give thee to act!" Then Clarissa, like a judge in her own courtroom, dismisses Dorcas: "No inquiry after this will be made, whose the first advances, thine or mine." Here Clarissa proves to be as clever as Lovelace in revising the meaning of a preexistent situation. She uses the trial scene Lovelace has constructed, but shifts herself from defendant to judge.

Dorcas's flight leads to Lovelace's attempt to regain control of the scene. He advances toward her "with a fierce aspect, most cursed vexed." Now Clarissa brings out the crucial device of her own performance—the pen-knife with which she threatens suicide. She signals her absolute earnestness of purpose with her stern words ("The LAW only shall be my refuge!") and the disposition of her body:

> she held forth a penknife in her hand, the point to her bosom, grasping resolutely the whole handle, so that there was no offering to take it from her. . . . She withdrew to the door, and set her back against it, holding the pointed knife to her heaving bosom.

With this vivid bodily gesture, Clarissa parodies her own physical violation in order to avoid rape. Clarissa's performance wins complete mastery over the meaning of the moment. The women weep as though at a sentimental tragedy, while Lovelace gives verbal form to the signification Clarissa has won:

> The mother twanged her damned nose; and Sally and Polly pulled out their handkerchiefs, and turned from us. They never in their lives, they told me afterwards, beheld such a scene.

Innocence so triumphant, villainy so debased, they must mean! [III,290]

In the fire scene Clarissa enjoins Lovelace to accept her sense of the moment through a long and delicate interchange. But here Clarissa completely overpowers Lovelace and wins a unified signification that is so compelling it takes on public authority—it overwhelms all in the room and he can extract no promises. It is entirely appropriate that Lovelace loses his power of speech. He writes, "[Clarissa] heard my broken voice—my voice was utterly broken."

Lovelace's dominant emotion after the scene centers on the mastery of Clarissa's art and the impotence of his own. He is fascinated with the authority she has won. Of her exit he says, "Then, taking one of the lights, she turned from us; and away she went, unmolested. Not a soul was *able* to molest her." He revolves the components of her carefully orchestrated performance; and his awe, at the power of her act, in both senses of the word, is compared to the frothy impotence of his own once vaunted stratagems (III,292).

The Sources of Melodrama: Pyrotechnics and the Book of Life

There is a pleasing clarity about these melodramatic struggles to control Clarissa's "person." At least for a passing moment the stakes are primitively simple, and a bypass of the mind and its complications seems to have been managed, so all energy can be focused into the histrionics of signification. But questions remain. And these questions can take us a long way toward apprehending the grounds of Clarissa's triumph. Clarissa repeatedly asserts the central importance of these scenes by subjecting them to retrospective interpretation. They help to indicate the logic behind the course of the struggle between Clarissa and Lovelace. So first, why does Lovelace design this particular mode of encounter? And second, why does Clarissa gain power and authority as we proceed from scene to scene?

Lovelace organizes these scenes in order to exploit his talents as a master of pyrotechnics, so each can become an occasion for the display of his verbal agility and wit. But the purpose of these linguistic skills also aligns him with pyrotechnics in its etymological sense, as the art of using fire. By likening Lovelace to fire, we can intuitively apprehend the coherence of a character who at first seems hopelessly

contradictory or paradoxical. Lovelace's displacements, his performance, and his portraiture, are like fire as Heraclitus and the whole
alchemical tradition described it: they are "agent[s] of transmutation." At the garden gate Lovelace works to transmute Clarissa from
being her father's daughter to being his lover; at Sinclair's, he labors
to transform her from being her own person to being his woman.
When Lovelace tries to find a way to describe the passion which
impels these transformations, he links himself with fire. In his very
first letter (I,147) he finds, "the passion in [his] stormy soul"
expressed in the last three of these six lines from Dryden:

> Love various minds does variously inspire;
> He stirs in gentle natures gentle fire:
> Like that of incense on the altar laid.
>
> But raging flames tempestuous souls invade:
> A fire, which ev'ry windy passion blows;
> With Pride it mounts, and with Revenge it glows.

Lovelace continues this letter by explaining the means by which he
manipulates James Harlowe, "cooling or inflaming his violent passions
as may best suit my purposes" (I,147). Lovelace completes the
analogy with fire by worrying about the diffidence of "this charming
frost piece," Clarissa (I,148).

   Through the course of the novel fire becomes a privileged image for
giving definition to Lovelace. He is linked with fire by his wrath, his
sexuality, and the changeable and uncontrollable quality of his passions. In explaining to Clarissa his attempted theft of Anna's letter,
he asks if it is not natural to "burn with desire to be admitted into so
sweet a correspondence" (II,272). But while Lovelace's calculated
violation of social norms aligns him with the destructive side of fire,
fire also gives expression to something about him which is relent-
lessly alive. His multifarious projects commit him to the ever-active
and the ever-new. In his idealized picture of the "life of honour" with
Clarissa, Lovelace makes use of an anthithesis between heat and cold.
He wonders how he might keep "love in a continual fervour"
("fervour" from the Latin *feruoem*, "to heat"). He abhors time and
convention, which drive lovers into "opposite chimney corners" to
doze "in a wintry evening and over a wintry love" (II,187; see also
above, pp. 58ff.). A great deal of Lovelace's attractiveness comes

from one's sense that he embodies a principle of boundless energy and life, what Gaston Bachelard attributes to fire by calling it the "ultra-living element."[1] It is appropriate that Lovelace "ignite" the action; his activity drives the story into new and interesting places.

It is Lovelace's affinity with fire and its qualities which both invites and frustrates a moral judgment of him. We are invited to judgment because, as Bachelard points out, fire is the only phenomenon "to which there can be so definitely attributed the opposing values of good and evil." But if we try to judge Lovelace for his transgressions we are balked by his firelike way of fusing virtues and vices in one elemental projection of energy. The persistence with which he is an agent of change makes it impossible to call him "innocent." But the apparent necessity for his working in the contradictory ways he does makes it difficult to hold Lovelace responsible for all that happens because of him.

Lovelace makes a most literal use of fire to drive Clarissa from her room at Mrs. Sinclair's. But beyond this, he designs all these melodramatic scenes to expose Clarissa to the transmuting power of his fire. He, like the alchemist Bachelard quotes, hopes to use his art to "open a body by means of fire." He does not wish to destroy Clarissa, though she accuses him of this. He wishes to take her from the enclosure of a father's house and violate the personal enclosure called "virginity." He hopes to undo the body's integrity, its system of self-enclosed meanings, and open it to new meanings—his own meanings. And to do this he knows that all the fire of his person will be necessary. But how can this "fire" transmute? Fire is the ever-changing element. It never has the fixed boundaries of an object. It is an unstable surface which makes what it meets unstable. It has the power to melt and burn, disfigure and transfigure all that comes too near. And, what is still more startling, it can make the "other" part of its own relentless progress . . . it can feed on the other. This is the fascinating power of fire. But—and here is the danger for Lovelace—when it ignites what it meets, Lovelace's fire releases new and unimagined energies that lay dormant in Clarissa.

In the scene at the garden gate, Clarissa receives a most vivid instance of the transmuting power of fire. There, her self is momentarily opened into a swirl of alien meanings that allow Lovelace to seduce her away

1. *The Psychoanalysis of Fire*, trans. Alan C. M. Ross (Boston: Beacon Press, 1964), p. 7.

from her father's garden. Clarissa's response gives us a clue to the counterforce she employs to meet Lovelace. During her first long argument
with him, Clarissa places the garden scene within a peculiar complex of
meanings. She says, "But here, sir, like the first pair (I, at least, driven
out of my paradise), are we recriminating" (I,502). With this sentence
she accepts Eve's guilt, gets Lovelace to double as Adam and Satan,
and equates her father's house with Paradise. For the reader with any
memory of recent affairs at Harlowe Place, the last equation must
seem rather dubious. But this act of interpretation, however forced
or inaccurate, has the utmost importance for subsequent events.

   To apprehend the meaning and force of this act of interpretation
and sharpen our images of Lovelace and Clarissa, it will be valuable to
consider Nietzsche's comparison of the Prometheus story and the
myth of the Fall. Nietzsche finds the Prometheus story to have the
"same characteristic significance for the Aryan character which the
myth of the fall has for the Semitic character." The Aryans attached
immense value to fire, assumed the gods would never simply give so
precious an element away, and concluded that it must have been
stolen. This transgression is glorified by the story of Prometheus's
theft and his subsequent suffering. Nietzsche comments, "What
distinguishes the Aryan notion is the sublime view of *active sin* as the
characteristically Promethean virtue. . . . This is an idea which, by the
dignity it confers on sacrilege, contrasts strangely with the Semitic
myth of the fall in which curiosity, mendacious deception, susceptibility to seduction, lust—in short, a series of pre-eminently feminine
affects was considered the origin of evil."[2]

   Nietzsche's comparison helps us to understand the divergent ways
our combatants work against their adversary. Lovelace comes to
Clarissa to exercise a Promethean enterprise in committing sacrilege;
he shows a certain zest in planning his theft. When accused of evil,
he is defiant, or minimizes his own fault. Clarissa's "sin" is a
"curiosity" about Lovelace, a "mendacious deception" about their
correspondence, and a "susceptibility to seduction" in meeting Lovelace at the garden gate. The Prometheus story tells of transgression
against an unfair ruler (Zeus), assumes the give and take of struggle,
and does not posit any higher metaphysical law standing above the

   2. See *The Birth of Tragedy* in *Basic Writings of Nietzsche*, trans. and ed. Walter Kaufmann (New York: Modern Library, 1968), p. 71.

antagonists. But the myth of the Fall is about a transgression against the law of a good and all-powerful God. This engages man in a guilt-ridden calculation of error and a bewildering attempt to atone for an acknowledged sin. What is necessary, above all, is the keeping of an accurate history of man's sin, and the ways God gives to man to overcome the terrible burden of the Fall. The name of that history is the Bible. It gives Clarissa an interpretive system within which she can work to win out over Lovelace and the "sin" that this system defines him to be.

An acknowledged Christian sinner, like Clarissa, may seem to be at a serious disadvantage in meeting the exuberant transgressions of a Lovelace. But Clarissa has access to an interpretive system predicated on God's final judgment of man. It is partially described in the passage from *Revelation* found on the title page of this chapter. There, God's judgment of man at the end of time is described as a relationship between two kinds of books. All men are judged "by their works" as they are "written in the books" that record men's lives. God's reading, interpretation, and judgment of a man's life is not represented as taking place. It simply exists. It is inscribed in the contents of another book, "the book of life." Here interpretation appears nonproblematic. It is embodied in the writing of a name in a book, the book of life, which in turn depends on the meaning of another book, the book every man "writes" by the way he lives, by his "works." This helps to explain the central necessity of Clarissa's life. She must live her life—in other words, write her book—so it is shaped into a meaningful pattern that guarantees her inscription in the book of life.

How can she do this? Through an ingenious use of the Bible. The Bible records the history of man's relationship to God, the story of Christ's life, and the many texts of Old Testament law and New Testament teaching. Taken together, they function as a collection of fictional paradigms and moral dicta which allow man to compose his own life and book according to a divinely ordained typology. God's "Word" informs man so that he may be in conformation with the book of life. When Clarissa aligns her father's garden with paradise, she solicits a whole series of meanings which open on her eventual triumph. One of these is the *felix culpa*, by which man's fall is a necessary preliminary to his greater glory in a final Christian redemption. The idea is frequently repeated late in the novel, but it is

implied in Anna's words early on. She writes Clarissa that there is
"a kind of fate in your error . . . for the sake of a better example to
be collected from your sufferings . . . for, my dear, ADVERSITY *is
your* SHINING-TIME" (II,282).

The meeting at the garden gate receives its final interpretive turn
when Clarissa puts "April X" on her coffin as the date of her death;
for this, as she explains to Belford, "was the fatal day of her leaving
her father's house" (IV,257). At first, this may seem to make her
culpability all the more emphatic. But the words selected for her
coffin from Psalm 116 establish the correct interpretive context:
"Thou hast delivered my soul from death; mine eyes from tears; and
my feet from falling." Clarissa's design of her coffin invokes a familiar
Christian paradigm: Man must die to this world before being reborn
in Christ. The many assurances of salvation she receives in dying
allow her to reinterpret her departure from Harlowe Place as the
"death" to this world which is the first important event in her long
spiritual journey toward God—a journey we are to believe she has
nearly completed.

The Fall has a privileged position within the interpretive system
that Clarissa operates in the novel. The Fall inaugurates man's life in
sin, the necessity of the coexistence in man of good and evil. The
Fall also points toward a final moment of judgment—when the little
which remains will be taken from man, or all losses will be made good
in a paradise regained. This temporal situation—life between fall and
judgment—necessitates a continuous struggle to shape the unfolding
life so its meaning will be prepared for judgment. Thus, the fall of
man out of God's grace is also a fall into all the problematics of self-
representation. Events in *Clarissa* dramatize man's movement from
fall to judgment. Clarissa may begin her narrative in order to justify
her behavior in the eyes of her friends; but Clarissa's "fall" opens up
the interpretive system Clarissa deploys for the rest of the novel and
gives new urgency to her compositional efforts. Her father's curse,
however unfair, is a preliminary judgment by an earthly father which
invites her eternal damnation by a heavenly one. The curse shows
that Lovelace has succeeded in opening up Clarissa's life to the
possibilities of evil, and raising the first serious doubts about her
future judgment. The sense of adventure thereby gained, links their
lives with the story of the Fall in yet another way. That Lovelace's
challenges will continue, that Clarissa's response will be vivid, that

they will be held accountable for what each makes of the encounter—this is the sense in which, on leaving Harlowe Place, they, like Milton's Adam and Eve, find "the world lay all before them."

Now we are in a position to understand how Clarissa overcomes the transmuting power of Lovelace's fire. She does so by working within an interpretive system that coordinates three books: the "book of life" as a goal; the "book" of her "works" as the substance of her personal history; and the Bible as a set of fictions that mediate between the second and the first. Within this system Clarissa's essential self—the one that will come up for judgment—is defined by the succession of actions and events that compose her personal history. This system gives Clarissa ways to deal with compromising events like her escape with Lovelace. However many extenuating circumstances surround Clarissa's departure from Harlowe Place, neither Clarissa nor her inventor ever authorizes us to separate her from that moment. It is not a gratuitous or accidental event, nor is it simply imposed by force. It might easily have been arranged for Lovelace to kidnap Clarissa on her being sent to her Uncle Anthony's for a forced marriage.

But the meeting at the garden gate "belongs" to Clarissa, it has a necessary relationship to her "case," and it is one of those "works" in her personal history that will someday come up for judgment. As such, this somewhat alien and potentially corrupting event must be incorporated into Clarissa's life. How is this done? We have seen that she interprets the event or action as a type of the fall from God's grace. This has two important consequences. First, she makes the event her own action, she takes responsibility for it, by accepting it as a sinful moment in her own history. Second, and more subtly, since it is only one moment of her life, she keeps its final meaning open. For judgment of the self will be based on the whole course and meaning of her history, and the final import of Clarissa's departure from Harlowe Place is still in question. It is worth noting the almost magical quality of this interpretive system. For when Clarissa incorporates an action into her history, even an acknowledged error, a "loss" can be turned to advantage and a fall can become the beginning of a spiritual ascent.

The Christian interpretive system gives Clarissa the idea of the self as a continuously unfolding history. During the first melodramatic scene, this self and history are particularly impoverished. Clarissa is

simply a very virtuous young daughter who is determined to resist the
efforts of her family and lover to direct the course of her life. But by
the time of the fire scene, Clarissa has lived more. She has suffered
the misunderstanding of her motives that comes from her departure
with Lovelace, she labors under a father's curse, and she has struggled
against Lovelace's treacherous advances. All this personal history is
incorporated into the image of her self she presents to Lovelace at
the crucial moment of the fire-scene:

> See at your feet a poor creature, imploring your pity, who, for
> your sake, is abandoned of all the world! Let not my father's
> curse thus dreadfully operate! Be not *you* the inflicter, who have
> been the *cause* of it. . . . For *your own sake*, if not for *my sake*,
> and as you would that God Almighty, in your last hour, should
> have mercy upon *you*, spare me! [II,504]

Clarissa's words carefully coordinate an interpretation of their recent
history, so as to magnify the ethical content of Lovelace's choice. She
holds Lovelace responsible for both her isolation and the hardship of
the curse. This gives the rape—the dire possibility of the present—
a particularly abhorrent meaning. In raping Clarissa, Lovelace would
fulfill a curse initially inflicted because of him. This compounds the
perversity of such an action. But beyond this, her present appeal to
Lovelace is an earlier type of his future appeal to God at the last
judgment.

Now, it is not so much the content of this interpretation of the
rape which "penetrates" Lovelace. He frequently demonstrates his
immunity from the most pathetic moral argumentation. It is the force
of Clarissa's presentation of her self that overcomes Lovelace's will to
act. Where does this force come from? It comes from the high stakes
of Christian judgment (salvation or damnation); the internal consistency of a life-sequence everywhere related to this judgment; and
the temporal reach of Clarissa's representation of this one moment—
she organizes their personal histories and future prospects around the
present instant. Stated most concisely, Clarissa makes use of the
immense authority and privilege which the Judeo-Christian tradition
accords to the interpretive system we call "history."

The rape is the genuine catastrophe of Clarissa's personal history.
But it gives Clarissa this advantage. Lovelace can no longer deceive
her, for his final intentions have been exposed. Since his future has no

legitimate connection with hers, he cannot emit a single signification that has any consequences for her. For Clarissa, the rape has unalterably fixed Lovelace's meaning—he simply *is* evil. His artifices can now be reinterpreted to be a succession of the darkest contrivances, designed expressly to destroy her. This new interpretive control of their mutual situation is evident in Clarissa's entrance in the penknife scene. She discredits Lovelace's stratagems—the drug, their "marriage," the letter to Dorcas—as items in the history of his treachery to her. They simply augment Clarissa's signification of her self as outraged innocence.

Clarissa's version of her self is not just one among many. For Clarissa can now organize their shared past around her own identity and make use of Lovelace, Sinclair, and the others as subordinate figures in her own baleful history. The confidence Clarissa has in the coherence of that history is implicit in the assurance with which she can see, name, and act. Gone is the anxious indecision of the garden gate. When she threatens her own life, it is not a futile, histrionic gesture as in the fire scene, but a shrewd and carefully calculated part of a plan. Her appeal to God, at the moment Lovelace advances toward her, places their total situation within the matrix of Christian providence, and makes God the only legitimate audience of this performance. She counts on God's mercy should suicide be necessary, she thanks God for a "present" deliverance, and an appeal to God's final judgment is explicit throughout. Thus, all that Clarissa does is for God's "immediate eye." The power of this signification rests on her ability to make this moment a carefully calculated incident in her unfolding history. All those present become bystanders in this process —they offer no countervailing representations. They are simply "placed" in the history Clarissa "writes" as she acts this scene and emits a singularly convincing image of herself as virtue.

The third and last melodramatic scene is important in putting out the fire of Lovelace's art. A transfer of power to Clarissa is expressed through his meditations after the scene: "Then, taking one of the lights, she turned from us; and away she went, unmolested. Not a soul was *able* to molest her" (III,291). If Clarissa's rape is prefigured in Lovelace's use of fire in the fire scene, her final triumph is implicit in the mastery of this exit. In Bachelard's last chapter to *The Psychoanalysis of Fire*, he discusses the tendency of fire to become purified into its idealized form: light. Light then becomes the "symbol" and "agent of purity."[3] And this is analogous to the transformation Clarissa succeeds in making. Lovelace's challenge to Clarissa ignites her substance, it opens her body into more luminous modes of being. The melodramatic struggles to control Clarissa's body, with their wanton expenditures of energy, often resemble nothing so much as two flames contending.

But Clarissa's interpretive system gives her a peculiar and unexpected advantage. With the passage of time, Clarissa draws all the light of Lovelace's fire, all its heat and destructive potential, into one refined, stable, idealized image of the self. And this image is made of light—the light regularly associated with Clarissa's position as a paragon, the light of her beatific transmutation after death, her transcription into the book of life. How is this done? Clarissa turns the contending flames into one, unwavering, steady light through the superior force of her signification, and this can be done because the self is enhanced, the self is magnified by a history which incorporates her adversity, repeats and renames *his* outrages, so as to stabilize *her* meaning. And it is the work of this "history," this repetition of Lovelace and Clarissa *as* evil and good, which turns Lovelace's fire into Clarissa's light, makes his evil, and the adversity it brings, the occasion for her brilliance—a time for her to shine.

---

3. Bachelard, pp. 106–07.

4: Building a Book into an Empire of Meaning

I could a tale unfold whose lightest word
Would harrow up thy soul.
        Hamlet, *act 1, scene 5 (The Ghost)*

It seems probable that if we were never bewildered there would never be a story
to tell about us.

                    Henry James, The Princess Cassamassima, *Preface*

The Choice of Death

Clarissa and Lovelace bear no children, but their union is not unfruitful. For Lovelace's violence against Clarissa plants the seed for a more insidious will to power over others: Clarissa's idea for a book that will tell her story. In the tenth paper written during her derangement, we see the first trace of this idea: "I could a Tale unfold —/Would harrow up thy soul!" (III,209) Clarissa's use of the ghost's words in *Hamlet* is apt, for her "tale" will be told in the tragic mode and it will enact a revenge. The book involves a quantum leap in the art of self-representation, for it attempts to fix the meaning of Clarissa's life and story for all time. Before the rape, Clarissa acts and reacts within a fluid situation where meaning never seems to come to rest. Her narrative of her brother's avarice becomes suspect when we see how it serves her. Her solemn institution of a "self" seems to invite the irreverence of Lovelace's parodic displacements. Even the triumph of the pen-knife scene cannot silence Lovelace for long. Thus, in the early phases of Clarissa's struggle, meaning is always only half of a transaction: it never "holds" for much longer than the moment of its elaboration; and it seems unchaste—forever marred by the struggle that provoked it.

After the rape Clarissa goes from being an agile tactician of self-representation to being a master-builder. By building a book, and putting her friends and adversaries *in* her book, she tries to assume a Godlike authority and dominion over them. She will be the center and subject that reigns over a multiplicity of objects. She will invent the terms of their presence and reconcile them with the animating *telos* that directs the unfolding of her book and story. The pen-knife scene gives us an early glimpse of how Clarissa appropriates others for her own meaning and purpose. A book will try to make this transient victory a permanent condition. Once they are placed within the confines of this book, all that Lovelace, James, Bella, and the rest can think or do simply predicates their subject, Clarissa.

To the unalert reader it may appear that Clarissa has a book edited to tell her story *because* she is going to die. In fact, precisely the opposite is true. Clarissa dies so that she may produce the book that will guarantee her triumph. Death is the crucial initial act in the generation of this book. It serves her in many ways. It seems to tie the ends of life into a neat circle, something complete and secure and apparently immune from the gross fluctuations of futurity. If Clarissa dies in the right way, with the right blend of pathos and reproach, summoning the higher forces of Fate and Nature and God, then she will be able to solicit the tragic code that gives life a mysterious meaning through death. The heroine will be exalted and the witnesses of the tragedy will begin an invidious meditation on the causes of Clarissa's fall. The book ends by pointing an accusing finger toward everyone but Clarissa: Lovelace, James, Bella, and others.

Death also imposes a substitution upon Clarissa's friends and adversaries. Instead of dealing with her, they must accept this book, where both Clarissa and they have passed, in reduced form, into the arabesques of language. Through this reduction Clarissa evades the undignified chatter and ambiguous crosscurrents of mutual transaction. By dying to life, Clarissa can be born again in a book. Now Clarissa will incarnate an entirely fresh clarity of meaning. And should anyone question her story, Clarissa tells Anna that her own death will be a "voucher" for the "veracity" of her book (III,381). But, in enumerating the subtler uses of death, we must not forget its crude and sensational appeal. No book ever got better prepublication publicity: death always insures interest—it's the bright spot of blood that arrests the attention of us all. Finally, if the book has done its job, it, like all good craftsmanship, will efface Clarissa's artistry—the decision to die and her use of the code of tragedy. Because of the book, Clarissa's death will begin to seem natural, appropriate, and inevitable—yes, even "fateful."

The Axis of Comedy (and a Temptation to Life)

Clarissa's compositional efforts do not go uncontested. Lovelace, Anna, James, Bella, and others have participated in the same scenes, they have their own ideas and desires, and wish to end this story (which contains their lives and stories as well as Clarissa's) very differently. Instead of death as the end of Clarissa's story, they would turn all the conflicts surrounding Clarissa's courtship into the moments of dissonance and adventure previous to the general reconciliation and happy union of Lovelace and Clarissa. The question at issue—life or death—is the key source of tension in the novel following the rape. Behind this question lies a larger issue: who will end this story so as to give it its predominant meaning? This struggle extends beyond the boundaries of the novel, becomes the principal issue of Richardson's correspondence, and leads him (by forming an authorial alliance with the goals and procedures of his heroine) to modify the body of the text so as to bolster the authority of Clarissa's ending. I shall narrate the formation and career of these compositional alliances below in chapter 6.

Clarissa is neither a comedy, nor a tragedy, nor a clearly definable hybrid. Instead it is a text whose comic design and tragic design converge and contend, because each gives expression to the wills and compositional strategies of Clarissa, Lovelace, Anna, Belford, and the rest. In his discussion of drama, Lovelace asserts his general preference for comedy in this way: "there was enough in the world to make our hearts sad without carrying grief into our diversions, and making the distress of others our own." Acknowledging Clarissa's preference for tragedy, he makes a playful and telling remark: "for the devil's in it, if a confided-in rake does not give a girl enough of tragedy in his comedy" (II,340).

Lovelace's use of the possessive—the comedy is "his"—reflects his confident control over events. The remark comes in a scene staged for Clarissa to overhear so she will give credence to a series of Lovelace's latest contrivances (going to the theater, the Fretchville scheme, the dinner party). He can make their story his comedy because he has more power than Clarissa. The tragic resonances of her suffering will be placed within "his comedy," the one he is now composing and at another time entitles, "Quarrelsome Lovers." What he does not suspect is the way Clarissa will later be able to invert these relationships, and subordinate "his comedy" to her tragedy. Then the witty schemes and manipulations of appearance so congenial to comic design will be transposed into the dark deeds that precipitate the catastrophe of Clarissa's tragedy. Lovelace's remark indicates the way the predominance of comedy or tragedy is fundamentally arbitrary and depends upon the force of the interpretive pressures that Clarissa and Lovelace bring to bear on a situation open to both.

Shakespearean drama shows how a comedy or a tragedy can emerge from a single situation. Plays as different as *King Lear* and *As You Like It* both commence with court intrigue, sibling rivalries, banishments, and the removal to a natural world where a realignment of the social order can begin. But what would one say if these two plays were one play? What if *King Lear* incorporated half the fun and romance of *As You Like It*, and then ended in disaster? Only if someone is given complete control of an interpretive field by fiat—as when a believer posits the existence of God as a guarantor of meanings—only then can a stable relationship between comedy and tragedy be asserted. Thus Frye tells us that: "Christianity sees tragedy as an episode in the divine comedy, the larger scheme of redemption and resurrection."[1]

By contrast, the conjunction of tragedy and comedy in *Clarissa* is violent and inharmonious. For tragedy and comedy are still, by Frye's typology, "contrasting" pairs that are more different from each other than either is different from romance and irony. We must not forget the simple side of a reader's experience, where comedy and tragedy are still as different as love and hate, joy and sorrow, life and death. The copresence of comedy and tragedy in *Clarissa* is early evidence that this text is not a unified organic body dominated by a single mythic design. Instead, this text is much more like a geological formation, with layers of sharply differentiated strata that tell us of the successive acts of interpretation, each with its own peculiar set of haphazard intensities, that give this text its ambiguous shape. This invites us to look at the contradictory tendencies of this text: first, all that pushes this story toward comedy, and then the pressures, originating in Clarissa, to compose a book to disseminate her tragedy.

The first readers of *Clarissa* can hardly be blamed if they thought they were reading a comedy that would end in marriage. When the story opens, a beautiful young lady is being courted by a handsome young man over the strenuous objections of her family. An awkward and jealous elder sister, an ambitious younger brother, and an ugly suitor named Solmes all contribute to the heroine's distress. A duel

1. Northrop Frye, *Anatomy of Criticism* (Princeton: Princeton University Press, 1957), p. 215.

has just been fought which attests to the bravery and magnanimity of the hero. Lovelace and Clarissa dwarf those around them, and though the heroine's sentiments about the hero are delicately veiled, her jealousy on hearing of Rosebud, and the electricity given off by their brief encounter at the wood-house, invite the reader to complete a very romantic tableau.

But the first installment goes beyond giving us a romantic situation reminiscent of new comedy. When Solmes comes courting, Clarissa describes his entrance with a good deal of humor:

> The man stalked in. His usual walk is by pauses, as if (from the same vacuity of thought which made Dryden's clown whistle) he was telling his steps: and first paid his clumsy respects to my mother; then to my sister; next to me, as if I were already his wife, and therefore to be last in his notice; and sitting down by me, told us in general what weather it was. Very cold he made it, but I was warm enough. [I,105]

The mechanical manner of Solmes's entrance, Clarissa's reflection on her suitor's intelligence, the play on "cold" and "warm," and the joke about a wife's unimportance all link this passage to the humor of stage comedy. Clarissa further develops the farcical potential in this scene, and sets everyone aflutter, by continuing her appeal to be spared Solmes's attentions because of "an invincible dislike" of the man. Later, when Clarissa is dying, and all grows somber and meaningful, the reader must strain to recall light moments like this one—moments that are "comic" in every sense of the word.

The second installment tells of Clarissa's and Lovelace's life together, previous to her first escape, and develops another aspect of comedy: the battle of the sexes. Here, the man and the woman are attracted to one another, but each is anxious to protect his or her personal independence. This sets up the kind of game we see between Beatrice and Benedict in *Much Ado About Nothing* or Mirabell and Millamont in *The Way of the World*. If the man plays his part with the right grace and audacity, and the woman hers with a just blend of wit and resistance, then we get moments of delightful banter that exaggerate the prerogatives of each sex so as to make their final mutual capitulation all the more delicious. In witnessing the course of these battles, part of the reader's fun comes from seeing how each character modifies the other. We get pleasure from watching how

Lovelace unbends Clarissa's maidenly modesty and forces her to feel her first pangs of love. In a complementary vein, Clarissa guides Lovelace into his first tears of compassion for another. In a battle between lovers, perverse actions will often obscure much more gentle feelings. At one point Lovelace reflects upon this. He wonders: "Strange, I should thus delight in teasing a woman I so dearly love" (II,342).

It is the comic strain in *Clarissa* that makes us expect the contradictory and accept the inconsistent. Many times Lovelace expresses his intention of reforming in some comfortably distant future. In doing so, he elides the gap between will and action, the whole space in which ethics holds sway (I,453). But Lovelace's shortcomings are not held against him by the readers of comedy. Spurred on by their own desire for a happy reconciliation, they generously make up the difference between the Lovelace they know, and the man who would be worthy of Clarissa.

Finally, in a comedy, all the obstacles to the union of the hero and heroine are overcome in deference to the prerogatives of a community of observers. This helps to explain what happens when Lovelace tells Moore, Rawlins, Bevis, and Captain Tomlinson the "whole story" of his troublesome "married" life with Clarissa. Lovelace shyly confesses his inability to consummate their "marriage," everyone smiles or conceals a smile, and the captain delicately expresses his hope "that all matters would be happily accommodated in a day or two" (III,86). The widow Bevis chimes in that "it would be a very happy conclusion of a very knotty affair . . . and I see not why we may not make this very night a merry one" (III,87).

Several elements contribute to make this moment quintessentially comic: the playful allusions to sex, the collective solution of a love problem, and the promise of a festive celebration. Lovelace contemplates the zeal of these new allies and then entertains a thought that might be the key assumption of all comedy: "And indeed the women and I, and my beloved too, all mean the same thing: we only differ about the manner of coming at the proposed end" (III,87).

That this whole scene is orchestrated by Lovelace as part of his plot to regain physical control of Clarissa and pursue his revenge is one of the ironies of the text. For at Hampstead, both the comic and tragic strains of the text are simultaneously moving to a climax. Even after the rape, the possibility of a comic resolution is never entirely relinquished. Thus Anna writes insisting that Clarissa must marry Lovelace: "The Alliance is splendid and honorable. Very few will know anything of his brutal baseness to you. All must end, in a little while, in a general reconciliation" (III,416). Lovelace even imagines a romantic reunion catalyzed by his own illness, with Clarissa "flying to my comfort; her duty and her choice to pray for me, and to bid me live for her sake!" (IV,116).

Up to now we have been following the opposed pressures for a tragic or comic resolution of the action. But there is one moment in the text where comic design actually almost prevails over tragic design. This is the first, and most important, of the three genuine proposal scenes. We must approach this scene with a good deal of circumspection, because the narratives with which Clarissa and Lovelace provide the reader function as much to conceal and repress what is happening in this scene as to report it. If we reduce the two accounts to a common factual thread, we come up with this:

The encounter begins like many others—with each sparring for advantage. Lovelace reproaches Clarissa for putting trust in a family that has shown they don't deserve it rather than in himself, who has shown he does. Clarissa girds for battle, telling Anna, "[I] resolved not to desert myself." Then Lovelace unexpectedly makes his proposal, but in a harsh and discouraging manner. Clarissa finds herself suddenly weakened and in a position of unaccustomed vacillation. She feels anger at Lovelace's cunning way of blending love and reproach, but she recalls Anna's politic advice to seize the first opportunity to marry. She feels Lovelace's eyes upon her, taking in her whole person. She does not know that Lovelace is composing a portrait of her which he finds inexpressively beautiful. She bursts into tears, turns to go, and he throws his arms about her waist. He promises not to take unfair advantage of her difficult situation with her relatives, but holds back from repeating the proposal. Clarissa chafes under the embarrassing silence that seems to ask that she take the initiative. She feels "fresh tears" and declares she is "very unhappy." Lovelace becomes more mild in manner, but still keeps some reserve as he savors the freedom she's given him in allowing him to hold her close. Then there's a sudden turn in Clarissa's disposition. She "recollects" what a "tame fool" she must look

like, gathers herself together, and turns to fling from him. Overcome by the brilliance of her anger, he suddenly relinquishes all
manipulative control, seizes her hand, and gives a "clear" and
"explicit" proposal of marriage. But the moment of Clarissa's
opening towards him is gone. She adopts a pose calculated to gall
him: all the chafing vacillation he has witnessed is not a sign of
budding affection or dependence, it is merely her distress with
her family's cruelty. This validates Lovelace's worst suspicions
and he explodes in wrath.

The accounts Clarissa and Lovelace offer of this encounter partly
conceal the great impact this scene has on the protagonists. Clarissa
is agitated at the emergence of a stark alternative to the incessant
struggles that have mediated all the transactions of her story. This
proposal, however flawed and compromising, confronts her with a
completely new possibility—a life where her stiff separateness would
cease to be necessary. The proposal is an offering and a temptation
to be something radically different from the self-enclosed entity that
is an adjunct of struggle. With this question, what we might call an
"axis of comedy," with all its ability to organize the disparate threads
of her life, enters the scene, crosses her story, and threatens to transform her life. In addition, Clarissa is disturbed by the feelings she
harbors for Lovelace—enough love to welcome a simple acceptance
of him, a resolution of all their conflicts in an acknowledged
mutuality of feeling.
    But this path is frightening; it demands a radical change in her
public manner and her private conceptualization of herself. It is
alarming that Lovelace has this power. With a few words he can
penetrate her whole situation with all the terms of comic design—of
a man's proposal, of a woman's acceptance, of Eros, and of a simple
"yes" that would change everything. It is on the brink of that
possibility, the sudden presence and tyranny of that "yes," that
Clarissa chafes, frets, and hesitates. It is completely appropriate that
at this moment Lovelace, who has been relatively isolated from this
predicament, finds himself enchanted by Clarissa's unaccustomed
vulnerability; and, sensing her openness to him, he begins to move
toward reconciliation and acknowledged love.
    That Lovelace reaches Clarissa, with a genuine proposal and a new
and fervid opening toward her, just moments after she has pivoted

away, that their timing is off, that they are out of "synch" (coming so near but never touching), is the bit of contingency upon which the whole comedy of Clarissa and Lovelace turns toward tragedy. But there is no "fateful" necessity here. In spite of all the causes for Lovelace's initial reticence and Clarissa's sudden withdrawal, the opening that each has suddenly seen is real. We can think of it as an axis on which the story of Clarissa and Lovelace could have unfolded (as tragedy) and been refolded (as comedy). But once each has felt the force of this alternative, once they have been shaken by its brushing so near, their main efforts are directed at repressing its presence and denying the potentiality that has opened before them.

A close comparative analysis of Clarissa's and Lovelace's narratives of this scene will allow us to follow the formal means each employs to repress the potentiality of comic design. Clarissa defends herself against the coercive pressure of this presence by organizing her narrative around an explicit argument: Lovelace's manipulative and provoking way of proposing, and the embarrassing initiatives he would impose on her, leave her no choice but to put him off with a "saving art." Thus Clarissa follows the quotation of Lovelace's opening proposal with the rhetorical question, "What a *recriminating*, what a *reproachful way*, my dear, was this of putting a question of this nature?" Clarissa's narrative is punctuated with apology: she justifies her reticence logically (thus, it is not love that paralyzes her, it is weighing Anna's advice against Lovelace's harshness); she reproaches his way of wooing: "He knows not . . . respectful love"; she confesses to being vexed and chafed by the discrepancy between his self-possession and her weakness; and finally she repeatedly insists that he refuses to press his proposal—thus their failure to get together is *his* fault.

In his account to Belford, Lovelace's narrative pose neatly complements Clarissa's: he claims a manipulative control over events that is punctuated by a lapse in which he proposes earnestly only to be rejected. Lovelace asserts his control by mocking himself with a light-hearted analogy: "And now, Belford, what wilt thou say, if, like the fly buzzing about the bright taper, I had like to have singed the silken wings of my liberty?" This gay manner eases the transition to the narrative of his lapse toward love and comedy. After the narrative of his second proposal—which is highly charged and urgent—Lovelace steps back and asks, "Was the devil in me! I no more intended all this ecstatic nonsense. . . . It is I, not she, at this rate, that must fail in the arduous trial." And after this long aside, which reestablishes the whole situation of struggle that has dominated the novel ("the contention," Lovelace calls it, "that her vigilance has set on foot, *which* shall overcome the *other*"), Lovelace brushes his genuine proposal aside with these words:

> Well, but what was the result of this involuntary impulse on my part? Wouldst thou not think I was taken at my offer?—an offer so solemnly made, and on one knee too? No such thing! The pretty trifler let me off as easily as I could have wished.
> [II,142]

In order to hold the other at a distance, each adopts a rigid pose: Lovelace claims to be engaging in a callous manipulation, even after he loses control; and Clarissa, after turning away from Lovelace, claims that her vacillation and emotion come from worry about her family, though they are obviously a function of Lovelace's proposal. Now, ironically, each accepts a radically simplified pose as an adequate account of the *other*'s motives, and is thereby led to an essential error about the other. Clarissa feels Lovelace's genuine proposal was "half extorted" from him and more the result of "compassion" than "love"; thus she fails to perceive the very genuine passion he feels for her. Lovelace feels that Clarissa's willingness to listen to a proposal comes from "fear of her brother" and "not her love of me," so that "marriage" with him would become a "second class refuge." Thus he fails to take full account of the signs of love and openness implicit in her hesitation, her letting him encircle her waist, her fit of anxiety and flight, and the very intensity of her alibis.

Why do our protagonists—who have on so many occasions demonstrated themselves to be astute psychologists—experience these lapses in evaluating each other? These lapses help Lovelace and Clarissa swerve away from the opening toward comedy and spare them the burden and anxiety of seriously entertaining an alternative to the whole mode of struggle both have adopted. This also explains the many minute ways in which Clarissa and Lovelace sculpt their narratives so as to end up with widely divergent versions of the same scene. Each is faithful to a common factual sequence, but their narratives of the proposal scenes give radically different impressions.

Clarissa quotes the first, manipulative and insincere proposal (which Lovelace only alludes to), while she only refers to Lovelace's "clear" and "explicit" proposal, which Lovelace quotes in full. Clarissa omits mention of Lovelace's vacillation between anger and sympathy between the two proposals, while Lovelace omits the "half sentences" and half-hearted apology for proposing which he utters during the long, embarrassing silence while he gazes at Clarissa. Clarissa insists that he refused to take the available chances to propose again, while in direct contradiction, Lovelace says that he "reurged" the question.

Perhaps the most striking contrast between the two accounts comes with regard to Lovelace's promise, after her first hesitations, not to take advantage of her family difficulties. In Clarissa's account, his words come after her awkward vacillation between anger and love, and they only prolong Clarissa's trial. They seem artfully designed by Lovelace to make her suffer while he parades his own good intentions. In Lovelace's narrative, he has just finished his hushed rapture over Clarissa's "most meaning and . . . beautiful face," so that when "fresh tears" come to her, he puts his arms around her and his speech has a very different force. The language is very different, and though —like much in the novel—it can be read in two ways, it is much less taunting than Clarissa's version, and implies that Lovelace is extending genuine sympathy to Clarissa.

If one arranges Clarissa's and Lovelace's narratives of this scene opposite one another, one finds that they approach and withdraw from each other so that they never touch a midpoint of acknowledged love at the same moment. Throughout the proposal scene, and their narratives of that scene, Clarissa and Lovelace do a frenetic dance which keeps them always separated by the smallest distance. This suggests something about their relationship. There is a bar or slash-mark between Clarissa and Lovelace which helps to keep them apart, but paradoxically this bar is composed of love, reconciliation, and an orientation toward the other. Right in the midst of struggle is the possibility of union which is the "other" of struggle. Through most of their story this bar is invisible to the combatants, but it makes all the oppositions activated by their struggle appear (real).

In the proposal scene, this bar or axis of union makes a transverse movement through the plane of struggle as the "axis of comedy," becomes visible to the combatants, and is repressed and concealed by their narratives. The reader only becomes aware of this "axis of comedy" in a negative fashion. The very parallelism of the hero and heroine as they mirror each other in their approaches and withdrawals, in their succession of poses and arguments and errors, this reciprocity of movement, invites the reader to link the two lovers— to collapse a distance *so* actively sustained; to countermand negatives so inadequately recounted; and to join two lovers apparently only separated by the unlucky timing of their moments of obstinacy. Lovelace himself whimsically invokes this idea at the end of his narrative: "A confounded thing! The man to be so bashful; the woman to want so much courting!—How shall two such come together, no kind mediatress in the way?" (II,143)

The "axis of comedy" is not an anatomical element of *Clarissa*. It, like the tragic currents in the novel, is more like a potential, activated along the bar separating and linking Lovelace and Clarissa by one event (the proposal). This event is a bit of contingency which involves Clarissa and Lovelace in a moment of genuine play, where "play" might be defined as a random movement of elements that frustrates every attempt at prediction or retrospective explanation, because it is a moment when things really can "go either way." Now, within the particular terms of this scene, these alternatives can be schematized as tragedy and comedy, so comedy becomes the new stage, the arduous new level onto which Clarissa and Lovelace could move so as to transvalue all the previous terms of their relationship. Their repression of this possibility can be understood in terms of the Nietzschean notion of "self-overcoming."[2] At certain moments the self can, through a movement of violence to the old self, gain access to an entirely new life, just as a new fire can be built on the ashes of an old fire which it transcends absolutely. Thus, to give an example entirely apt for Clarissa, a virgin of eighteen looks with horror upon the loss of that which seems to define her whole life (virginity) but which will, at twenty-eight, exist merely as a threshold she moved through on the way to a new organization of her self (as woman). But when this potentially transvaluing moment occurs (where comedy could enclose tragedy), it is repressed by the narratives so as to make it seem nonreal, not an actual possibility. Instead, we get a book which takes Clarissa's life and story and replaces what is contingent

2. See *Thus Spake Zarathustra* (New York: Viking Press, 1954, 1966), ed. and trans. Walter Kaufmann, pt. 2, sec. 12, "On Self-Overcoming," pp. 113–16.

and arbitrary with an account governed by the logic peculiar to tragedy—life as an inexorable movement toward death, where alternate paths are only acknowledged to make death seem more poignant.

The Will to Power of the Subject

What does Clarissa choose to do instead of turning toward Lovelace? If I were to characterize all of Clarissa's activities—her invention of a "self," her narrative of her story, her use of the meditation, her casting of herself as the heroine of melodrama, and finally her construction of a book—if I were to describe this progression with one analytical proposition, I would say that Clarissa *engages in a more and more comprehensive will to power of the subject over the world.* Clarissa's magnification of herself as a subject begins with a kind of primitive vanity: she has a keen sense of her own superiority, likes the way she looks, and likes to look at herself. This helps to explain a prodigious development of the subject in this young girl. The subject comes into existence in the moment the self imagines itself as separate from everything else by sending itself signals on how it looks to the eyes of others. One of Richardson's most intelligent correspondents, Sara Chapone, doesn't care for this side of Clarissa. She explains her preference for Anna Howe by discussing the virtue of "simplicity," which she finds in Anna but finds lacking in Clarissa.

> Simplicity is that Rectitude of Mind which suppresses all useless Reflections upon itself and the Actions which spring from it. It differs from Sincerity, but is more excellent. Many persons are sincere, who are not simple: they are ever at the Glass to study and adjust themselves: they are in continual Fear of being taken for what they are not: whereas the simple Person forgets that *Self* of which the other is so jealous: And provided the Action be right, makes no further Reflection upon it. [*Letters,* 210]

Richardson did not like these remarks about his heroine, but we may concede, with him, that Clarissa's self-consciousness develops in large part from the crisis she finds herself caught up in. Thus Richardson tells one correspondent that he "makes" the genial, talented, and spirited heroine of *Sir Charles Grandison*, Harriet Byron, "what I would have supposed Clarissa to be, had she not met with such persecutions at home, and with such a tormentor as Lovelace" (*Letters*, 179). Clarissa's struggles and suffering impose a certain independence on this young girl, and lead to a rich development of the inner life. Thus, with every turn in her adventure Clarissa's subject grows in strength and stature.

But if this subject "is" any-"thing," it is radically evanescent. It begins as the agent of an activity (consciousness of any other) and is more vividly present in the reciprocal gesture by which the subject catches itself being aware of the other (i.e. experiences self-consciousness). As the subject becomes an active presence, it confirms and is confirmed by an intuition of its superiority. This is why the idea of the subject, once it takes hold, is so vastly seductive. This intuition of superiority is born of the subject's apparent (and perhaps illusory) autonomy, and the way consciousness always seems to float *above* in being aware of something *below*. ("Subject" is derived from the Latin word *subiectum*, "to put under" or "to cast under.") But since these activities are as quick as thought, they need to be stabilized—given a comforting duration—by some palpable form and action.

In the first chapter of this book we considered two early instruments used in Clarissa's struggle: narrative and the invention of the "self." Both help to exalt and embody the subject. When Clarissa narrates, her subject hovers over the world, makes it an array of inferior objects, a set of knowable entities, which the subject grasps, arranges in a coherent pattern, and presents to the reader. Thus, in Clarissa's narrative of her brother's and sister's plot against her, James's avarice becomes an obedient subject which pays fealty to Clarissa. Two likely responses to reading Clarissa's narrative—how well Clarissa understands James's avarice! Clarissa would never stoop to such activities!—confirm the subject's awareness and moral superiority, the two hidden correlatives of the subject's narrative. The objects of the subject's narrative never seem to win an independent existence. They are the subject's possessions: James is "Clarissa's brother" and Bella, "Clarissa's sister." They are the subject's subjects—her topics, and ones ruled by her artifice.

There is one potential danger in Clarissa's use of narrative. Since the subject's dominion over her objects (or subjects) is a function of her position as narrator, her dominance depends upon incessant narrative. With the end of every letter, the subject is threatened with lapsing back into impotence. But Clarissa meets this danger through the second activity discussed in the first chapter: the elaboration of the "self." All the elements of Clarissa's "self" are ways of embodying the subject, of giving it a quasi-physical permanence: the boundary between her self and the world, the existence of the heart with its implanted virtues, her role as a paragon, and the careful sculpting of her personal history so as to develop the "self." Now we have seen that Clarissa defines her "self" as superior to others: she demands more of her life, she has more exalted goals and loftier ideals. This superiority of character gives an objective appearance to the superiority the subject gains by making others its object. In fact, the whole notion of a "self" gives Clarissa as subject the sure, steady presence of a body. The "self" is the body of the subject.

But notice that something curious has happened. By giving a narrative, Clarissa assumes the position of subject in her world; but by elaborating a "self" she makes herself the object of her own analysis and representation. She becomes the most important object to her own subject. This neatly enhances Clarissa's authority by doubling her presence before the reader. It is not the last time we shall find her occupying *both* positions in an apparent opposition.

We may probe further into the problematics of Clarissa's representation of her self and story by linking her activity with the etymological history of the word *subject*. This is important for us, because we shall come to see her construction of a book as the way in which she attempts to control and occupy simultaneously several disparate positions described by the word *subject*. In its earliest use a "subject" was a person who was under the dominion of another; a vassal, or retainer; a dependent or inferior. *Subject* is subsequently used to describe a whole series of passive objects or entities (people or things) which receive the force, attention, judgment, or discourse of some higher, more powerful force. This second general meaning of *subject* is very close to its apparent opposite, *object*. In this sense a "subject" may be a topic to be discussed, the participant in an experiment, or a corpse to be dissected. From these two early meanings of the word, there evolves the active verbal sense of making subject, subordinating, or subjugating a person or thing to some stronger force or process. This more noble and active use, "to subject," and the grammatical notion of the subject as the "part of a sentence concerning which something is predicated," prepares for the

much more belated philosophical usage we have utilized to designate
the agent of compositional activity. The *OED* describes this meaning
of *subject* with these words:

> 9. *Modern Philosophy*. More fully conscious or thinking subject:
> The mind, as the 'subject' in which ideas inhere; that to which all
> mental representations or operations are attributed; the thinking
> or cognizing agent; the self or ego.
>
> The tendency in modern philosophy after Descartes to make
> the mind's consciousness of itself the starting point of enquiry led
> to the use of *subjectum* for the mind or ego considered as the
> subject of all knowledge, and since Kant this has become the
> general philosophical use of the word (with its derivatives *sub-
> jective*, etc.).

With this philosophical usage, the word *subject* is applied to something powerful, important, and comprehensive. As the faculty of
understanding that sits at the center of experience, it is that to which
"all mental representations are attributed"; it is "the subject of all
knowledge."

Now what strikes *this* reader of *Clarissa* is the way in which Clarissa
habitually fluctuates between appearing as a passive victim "subject"
to the arbitrary forces around her, and as an active agent who
"subjects" others to analytical scrutiny and literary representation. In
fact, Clarissa's acts of representation (from a single letter to the whole
book) often recapitulate a movement through the etymological circuit
we have just described. Clarissa presents herself as immersed in a
situation which is crisis-ridden, open-ended, and out of control. But
the *means* she uses to represent her life and situation shift her from
appearing as a "subject" who is "subject" to another, to appearing as
a "subject" who "subjects" her self, others, and her own past to
ultimate control. Thus Clarissa's narrative letters work to give the
"subject" (as a center of consciousness) dominion over several more
passive and compliant "subjects": the self, others, and the transactions between the self and others in time.

We can see how this happens in Clarissa's presentation of the
"proposal scene." In our analysis we tried to locate a chancy and
unpredictable "present" behind the two narratives offered by the
protagonists. This "present" engenders all the anxiety of a ninth-
inning rally, because it can go "either way" and is not under the

control of any presiding subject. But Clarissa's narrative works to overcome the risky presentness of this scene. For however much Clarissa, Lovelace, and Richardson are fond of a "present-tense manner of writing," it is still a "manner"—an act of artifice designed to engage the reader. Clarissa's narrative begins in the moment when she casts her eye back over the events of the previous days or hours. She must grasp a capsule of time as "past" before re-creating it as "present." Then the past can be presented so its shape seems pre-ordained and its meaning subdued to the ends of the subject who directs the narrative. In the "real" scene Clarissa describes, she apparently was subject to the uncertain contingencies swirling through the moment; but in her narrative, that past has become her "sub-ject"—now "subject" to her activity as a ruling "subject."

This sequence repeats itself in the meditations where Clarissa entertains the possibility that her adversity is evidence of God's judgment against her (more fully analyzed in chapter 1). In this moment of anxiety, Clarissa is suddenly aware of another subject, a master-subject, hovering over her and making her *His* object. She feels abject and helpless. But here Clarissa does something cunning and important. She assumes God's position, casts her eye over her own past, and discovers a punishable sin: "I was the pride of all my friends, proud *myself* of *their* pride, and glorying in my standing" (I,419). Now, in reading the traditional meditations of the Renais-sance period, like Donne's *Devotions*, all the drama comes from our sense of the vast distance between man and God. The meditation begins with an acute sense of the disparity between man's perverse will and God's will, and only arrives at an exalted sense of the realignment of those wills through the work of the meditation itself (man's suffering, a confession of weakness, momentary backsliding) and God's gratuitous act of grace (in offering man Christ, in giving the meditator new hope).

But what is the relationship between Clarissa and God in her meditation? Clarissa ends the meditation reconciled with God, but one wonders if they have ever been separated. Maybe Clarissa (a significant but limited subject) and "God" (the Super-Subject) are not independent agents, but exist in a suspicious complicity with one another. We shall consider this possibility later, when more evidence is in. But we can see now that Clarissa gains a broader, more comprehensive grasp of time by considering her life as an integrated temporal unit (with pride to be purged), and she does this by imitating God's power to subject all of human history to His act of Judgment by miming this act in her own meditation. Clarissa's subject has been enlarged and its dominion expanded by her cooperation with God-as-subject.

Building the Book, 1: A New Body for Clarissa

The rape violates the forms that have mediated Clarissa's presence before others—the body, the "self." The subject that had invested itself in these forms is for a moment bewildered: wandering astray and lost, it knows not how to act or what to be. Thus, after the rape Clarissa feels shame, self-hatred, and an urgent desire to be hidden from the eyes of others. She begs Lovelace to send her to Bedlam. Then, fearing she might be recognized there, Clarissa suggests "a private madhouse where nobody comes" (III,212). But Clarissa does not maintain a stance of radical self-abnegation for very long. By the time Clarissa escapes from Sinclair's, a significant alternative has developed.

In her first letter to Anna, the rape is still presented in terms of loss: "O MY DEAREST MISS HOWE!—Once more have I escaped— but, alas, *I*, my *best self*, have *not* escaped! Oh, your poor Clarissa Harlowe! *You* also will hate me, I fear! Yet you won't, when you know all! But no more of my self! my *lost* self" (III,321). There is an equivocation in this passage which gives us a clue about how Clarissa has chosen to meet her crisis. She declares the loss of her "self," accepts the loss of her old friendship, and goes one better on any reproach Anna might direct at her. But simultaneously she points backward to the story of her fall, and there she finds an opening for self-justification: "You also will hate me . . . Yet you won't when you know all! . . . What a tale I have to unfold!" When Mrs. Howe intercepts this letter and replies harshly, Clarissa is more assertive about her chosen strategy: "My story is a dismal story. It has circumstances in it that would engage pity, and possibly a judgment not altogether unfavourable, were those circumstances known" (III,323).

What is Clarissa doing? In the interval between her rape and the escape from Sinclair's, Clarissa finds a new form in which to embody the subject—the story she will eventually have cast into a book. Even in the first papers written after the rape, Clarissa makes primitive efforts to give her life some fictional form: she tells the story of the lady and the lion (paper 3), she casts Lovelace as a series of insects that despoil the garden (paper 8), and she displaces her situation into a series of quotations (paper 10) (III,209). But as usual, it is the need to continue the struggle with Lovelace that teaches Clarissa the potential power of a verbal repetition of recent events.

For since something genuinely arresting has happened to Clarissa, a skillful presentation of her drugging and rape allows her to dominate Lovelace and his allies in the pen-knife scene. Clarissa finds the story of her whole life has taken on new vividness and form. The magnitude of her fall imbues all the details of her past with new interest. A narrative of events has always been an adjunct of Clarissa's representation of her life. But now hierarchies are inverted so the whole pathos of her present life gains its importance from the frame it offers for her story. The story and the book become the sole forms to embody Clarissa's subject, and sacrificing the old "self," the old virgin body, and any future as a living subject, are the necessary preliminary steps in the institution of the book called "The History of Clarissa Harlowe."

It is not surprising that Clarissa's anguished letter to Anna and Mrs. Howe should stir up a good deal of interest. Anna remarks that her mother "could not but have a great curiosity to know the occasion of so sad a situation as your melancholy letter shows you to be in" (III,347). So Anna urges Clarissa to communicate the *"particulars at large of your sad story"* (III,349). Clarissa now takes a series of steps to organize and disseminate her story. First she writes to Lady Betty Lawrance and her uncle's housekeeper to determine the extent of Lovelace's deception (III,331–35). This is the equivalent of doing background research for her book. She gives Lady Betty hints of the darkest parts of her story to validate her accusations against Lovelace (III,336). This helps to put him on the defensive in his family and keep him at a distance while she arranges her affairs. She gives a detailed account of the catastrophe of her story (the rape) to Anna and a more cursory one to Mr. and Mrs. Smith and Mrs. Lovick. Finally, and most crucially, Clarissa makes Belford her executor, and bequeathes him letters that will allow him to "do [her] character justice" and be "the protector of [her] memory" (IV,78).

Clarissa shows her daring and intelligence as an author by the way she brings her book into existence. Instead of writing the long first-person narrative she once planned, she chooses to become the dominant member in a collaboration. She lets Anna initiate the idea for a narrative of her story; Belford is to join Anna in editing the two sets of correspondence into one account; and, most boldly of all, Lovelace is to be given "equal time" with Clarissa's own letters. Clarissa understands the wonderful efficacy of incorporating Lovelace's private correspondence in the construction of her book:

> It will be an honour to my memory, with all those who shall know, that I was so well satisfied of my innocence that, having not time to write my own story, I could entrust it to the relation which the destroyer of my fame and fortunes has given it.
> [IV,79]

Of course, there are very real risks in making use of Lovelace's correspondence. Lovelace's letters invite the reader to think and feel the novel's action in a wildly divergent manner from what Clarissa's correspondence has accustomed us to. Clarissa finds ways to "tame" Lovelace's "otherness," however, so that his letters become a valuable adjunct to a presentation of her self. Firstly, the presumption of Clarissa's possession of the action gains authority by keeping the fact of her suffering and redemption in view and predominant. If this fact dominates the novel—and Clarissa and Richardson are sure that it does—then Lovelace's "otherness" can be given a modifying critique so that it serves Clarissa's story. So asides in which Clarissa formally judges Lovelace are strategically placed throughout her letters to teach the reader of the novel how to "read" Lovelace's character.

Lovelace's role-playing and parodies are not a counterattack to and displacement of the values Clarissa asserts; they are signs of a "bad heart," one unable to deal honestly and forthrightly with an open heart like Clarissa's (III,464). Lovelace's elaboration of artful means of deceit are not the improvisations of one who enjoys a shifting performance; they are the dangerous machinations of one bent on destroying Clarissa. Even Lovelace's most innocent playfulness and fun become, in Clarissa's eyes, discouraging evidence of his lack of "seriousness" (IV,175). By incorporating her opponent's letters, Clarissa puts Lovelace's "otherness" to work for her. It becomes a key element in her staging, with his "otherness" casting back images of her nature. Thus Lovelace's perversity mirrors Clarissa's good and his artifices illustrate her truth. When Clarissa's suffering and death are made radically central—by placing her upstage in a blaze of lights—Lovelace's "otherness" takes on the appearance of "evil" and, of course, this "evil" becomes the most useful possible foil to Clarissa's "virtue." By teaching the reader how to interpret Lovelace's letters, Clarissa hopes to subject Lovelace and his letters to her authorial design.

There is interesting evidence that Richardson altered prepublication versions of the novel so as to obscure Clarissa's initiative in organizing the book. The novel's first title begins, "The Lady's Legacy" and ends with this sentence: "Published in compliance with the Lady's order on her death-bed, as a warning to unguarded, vain, or credulous innocence." This makes Clarissa directly responsible for the final publication of a book edited by others. But by a year before publication of the first edition, Richardson has changed things, as he explains to Aaron Hill, so as to make "Sollicitude for the Publication to be rather Miss Howe's than Clarissa's" (*Letters*, 77).

Why does Richardson make this change? It is in keeping with Clarissa's decision to produce her book by means of collaboration. Clarissa and Richardson know that urgent first-person attempts at self-justification often lead to the most strident and dubious forms of discourse. If they can disperse the responsibility for this book into several hands, if they can create the impression that it is an objectlike assemblage of letters, they can remove Clarissa from the fray of authorship and assertion. Then this book will seem "unmotivated." It will seem to stand outside, or at least have an even-handed relationship, with the struggle it records. But, in fact, it is Clarissa's climactic move in that struggle. For, with this final act of composition, Clarissa tries to incorporate and control her friends and adversaries so they all contribute to the construction of the book that embodies one person and one subject: Clarissa Harlowe.

Clarissa's organization of her book as a collaboration helps to conceal the self-interested subject hovering behind the book. The book also helps to explain the pose adopted by Clarissa in the weeks before her death—one of disinterested tranquility and sweet-souled resignation. This is the best possible screen for a book which labors so mightily to exalt Clarissa over her adversaires. But the book also makes this sublime calmness possible. Clarissa's transition from open confrontation (the pen-knife scene), to bitter recriminations against

Lovelace and her family, to a benign acceptance of her lot, can be understood in terms of a progressive movement away from earthly concerns toward heavenly ones.

But this progression also reflects the way in which the book she is preparing takes on the tasks of justification and revenge, so she can desist from strident self-assertion. Right after Clarissa's detailed narrative of her rape, an account that plays a crucial part in the book she constructs, Clarissa begs Anna to keep Lovelace's use of the potions a secret, professes to have given up all hopes for her public "character," and adds something strangely at odds with her own extensive compositional efforts: "let me slide quietly into my grave; and let [my life] not be remembered, except by one friendly tear" (III,374). Clarissa can "slide quietly" toward the grave, for her book will remain behind, to speak for her in a voice that is loud and clear.

Building the Book, 2: Subjecting the Reader to Personal Correspondence

Clarissa smartly enhances the credibility of her account by incorporating Lovelace's correspondence into her book. There are other forces at work that help to subject the reader to Clarissa's story: through her exchanges with Lovelace, Clarissa learns how to solicit reader interest in story-telling; and Clarissa's use of "familiar letters" is designed to make a sympathetic "friend" of every reader. It will not do to have a reader who comes to the book with icy indifference or keen skepticism. Lovelace is a skilled story-teller and shows how an auditor may be drawn willingly into a story-teller's fiction. At Hampstead he sits Mrs. Moore and Miss Rawlins down to hear the "whole story" of his relationship with Clarissa, lying only in claiming to be married. Lovelace entertains Belford (and us) with the tension evident in Moore and Rawlins between a censoring mechanism that shuns any improprieties, and an avid curiosity that wants all the details. The "story" he narrates, of a frustrated husband's problems with a headstrong wife, wins ready acceptance because it panders so well to the listeners' sexual curiosity and romantic sentimentality. In a similar vein, the intense interest manifest in Lovelace's story at Lord H.'s house mitigates the moral force of the disapprobation he meets. Lovelace notes that Lord H. continually returns "with a new appetite to my stories" and though his cousins "pretend to blame me sometimes for the *facts,* they praise my manner, my inventions, my intrepidity" (III,389). Thus an eager listener or reader becomes an unwitting collaborator, who gives a tacit approval to every turn of the fiction each time he asks himself "what next?" Clarissa harnesses the sexual and romantic dimensions of her affair with Lovelace in her letters to his family and in her brief narrative to Mrs. Lovick and the Smiths. She also tames her reader by using a medium, familiar letters written between intimates, that encourages every reader to become her sympathetic "friend." If the reader is not an Anna or a Belford, she hopes he will at least read over their shoulders, identifying intuitively with Clarissa's feelings and situation.

Lovelace praises "familiar letter writing" between friends with strong emotional ties, in words that explain the reasons why "fa " iar" correspondence should earn this kind of sympathy. He is explaining his attachment to this form of writing to Clarissa:

> I proceeded, therefore,—That I loved familiar letter-writing, as I had more than once told her, above all the species of writing: it was writing from the heart (without the fetters prescribed by method or study), as the very word *correspondence* implied. Not the heart only; the *soul* was in it. Nothing of body, when friend writes to friend; the mind impelling sovereignly the vassal-fingers. It was, in short, friendship recorded; friendship given under hand and seal; demonstrating that the parties were under no apprehension of changing from time or accident, when they so liberally gave testimonies, which would always be ready, on failure or infidelity, to be turned against them. For my own part it was the principal diversion I had in her absence: but for this innocent amusement, the distance she frequently kept me at, would have been intolerable. [II,431]

The special claims for "familiar letter-writing" come in part from what it is *not.* It does not employ lofty diction and formal rhetoric so as to persuade a skeptical adversary. The writer does not assume a stiff public persona or observe a rigid system of decorum. Here, the supposition is that we have a radical honesty, with no subtle use of language to conceal real intentions or feign false ones. To explain how this happens, Lovelace embraces a false etymology. He derives "correspondence" from the Latin word *cor, cordis* to show that familiar letter-writing gives us words directly from the heart. This

kind of writing involves an intricate transaction. By writing, one
friend opens the innermost part of the self, the "heart," to another
friend—one assumed to be actively sympathetic. Familiar letter-
writing becomes the channel between them, where the writer bends
to express and describe while the reader bends to apprehend and be
"impressed" with the other's words. The two work in concert to
write and read a shared world, and it is in the earnest glow of the
concourse between these two subjects that the cool doubt of a skeptical reader becomes unthinkable.

Lovelace's language indicates another reason why Clarissa (and
Richardson) prefer to use familiar letters to compose the book. Lovelace insists "the *soul* was" in these letters: "Nothing of body, when
friend writes to friend; the mind impelling sovereignly the vassal-
fingers." This sovereignty of mind over body allows the familiar letter
to become more than a stay against time. Within a familiar correspondence, all the "subjects" of communication become "subject" to
the tides of affect that sweep between two kindred corresponding
spirits. Richardson's extraordinary praise of familiar letter-writing, in
a letter to Sara Westcomb, explains how this is said to happen. Sara
has been reticent about writing to the famous author, appealing to
her own lack of talent and a general dearth of good topics. Richardson
urges Sara to correspondence in the way he glorifies intimate letters
between friends. He says it is the way to "continue" and even
"perpetuate" "innocent pleasures that flow from social love, from
hearts united by the same laudable ties":

> I make no scruple to aver, that a correspondence by letters,
> written on occasions of necessary absence, and which leaves a
> higher joy still in hope, which presence takes away, gives the most
> desirable opportunities of displaying the force of friendship, that
> can be wished for by a friendly heart. This correspondence is,
> indeed, the cement of friendship: it is friendship avowed under
> hand and seal: friendship upon bond, as I may say: more pure,
> yet more ardent, and less broken in upon, than personal con-
> versation can be even amongst the most pure, because of the
> deliberation it allows, from the very preparation to, and action of
> writing. [*Letters,* 65]

Richardson finds a vivid instance of this kind of power in the very
letter he now has before him—Sara's latest:

While I read it, I have you before me in person: I converse with you, and your dear Anna, as arm-in-arm you traverse the happy terrace: kept myself at humble distance, more by my own true respect for you both, than by your swimming robes. . . . I see you, I sit with you, I talk with you, I read to you, I stop to hear your sentiments, in the summer-house: your smiling obligingness, your polite and easy expression, even your undue diffidence, are all in my eye and my ear as I read.—Who then shall decline the converse of the pen? The pen that makes distance, presence; and brings back to sweet remembrance all the delights of presence; which makes even presence but body, while absence becomes the soul; and leaves no room for the intrusion of breakfast-calls, or dinner or supper direction, which often broke in upon us. [*Letters*, 65]

Familiar letters may enable the writer to transcend the physical presence of the human body, but they also constitute a new kind of body—one made of words, paper, and letters. Richardson describes an ideal setting for letter-writing as he promotes this activity for a woman like Sara:

Retired, the modest Lady, happy in herself, happy in the Choice she makes of the Correspondent of her own Sex (for ours are too generally Designers); uninterrupted, her Closet her Paradise, her Company, herself, and ideally the beloved Absent; there she can distinguish Her Self: By this means she can assert and vindicate her Claim to Sense and Meaning.—And shall a modest Lady then refuse to write? . . . A virtuous and innocent heart to be afraid of having its Impulses *embody'd*, as I may say? [*Letters*, 68]

Familiar letter writing begins with the isolation of the writer from the mundane world, with its random interruptions, so all attention can be concentrated on the self and the "beloved Absent" who is addressed. The writer's closet becomes a kind of tranquil "Paradise" where ordinary life is spiritualized and a prelapsarian innocence can be reconstituted. In this keenly personal space, one's own feelings take on vivid importance, coloring every perception and shaping every communication. The delicious intimacy of these letters demands a scrupulous secrecy and helps to explain why Clarissa and Anna guard their letters with the same fervor as they protect their bodies.

Clarissa initially refuses a private correspondence with Lovelace, and only accepts his descriptions of his Grand Tour on the premise that they may be read to the whole family. When events give this correspondence a private turn, the results are dire. The course of events establishes an exact parallelism between Lovelace's violation of Clarissa's correspondence and his violation of her body (II,272, 279). Thus, early on, Anna promises Clarissa to look "narrowly into the sealings of your letters. If, as you say, he be base in that point, he will be so in everything" (II,201).

The conditions of familiar letter writing make the expression of desire one of the incessant themes of these letters. The writer resorts to language because of a twofold separation: separation from the world outside, and separation from the friend addressed. Writing becomes an effort to overcome these separations, at the same time blending in the writer's desire for another object presently beyond his reach. Thus, Richardson's vivid apostrophe to familiar corre-spondence has an ulterior motive—he hopes to stimulate Sara's interest in letter writing. The familiar writing Richardson analyzes is supposed to take place between two female friends. But, significantly, Richard-son makes himself an exception to his general warning against females taking male correspondents. Thus he warns, "our [sex] are too generally designers," but describes himself as "a plain writer; a sincere well-wisher: an undesigning scribbler" (*Letters,* 68, 66). Be this as it may, the fervor of Richardson's affection for the young Sara is only faintly veiled in the excited, imaginary description of his following Sara and her friend Anna at a "humble distance" on the "happy terrace:" "I see you, I sit with you, I talk with you . . . your smiling obligingness, your polite and easy expression, even your undue diffidence, are all in my eye and my ear as I read."

A close analysis of Richardson's account to Sara Westcomb of the act of representation in the familiar letter will allow us to grasp the surprising powers this act is supposed to confer. Richardson begins with a conventional assumption. When "necessary absence" or "the demands of an indulgent parent, deprive [a girl] of the person of her charming friend," the familiar letter allows the girl to "continue" the "pleasures" of "social love." Here the letter is an inferior supplement to, and temporary substitute for, direct social intercourse. But almost immediately Richardson suggests something very different. Letters stimulate warm expectations for reunion, thereby leaving "a higher joy still in hope, which presence takes away." Beyond this, familiar letters are the best form for "displaying the force of friendship": "more pure, yet more ardent, and less broken in upon, than personal conversation can be even amongst the most pure."

Richardson repeats the same shift—from a presumption of the inferiority of letters to an assertion of their superiority—in still more vivid terms, in the next long paragraph of his letter to Sara. He begins by assuming that writing strives to simulate the direct "presence" separated friends have lost: "Who then shall decline the converse of the pen? The pen that makes distance, presence; and brings back to sweet remembrance all the delights of presence." But suddenly there is an inversion of the hierarchy of values: "and brings back to sweet remembrance all the delights of presence; which makes even presence but body, while absence becomes the soul." How can the "absence" associated with writing be superior to the "presence" that writing repeats? In the first paragraph Richardson attributes this superiority to the "deliberation" and "preparation" connected with "the action of writing." In the second paragraph Richardson's explanation seems still more inadequate. He reminds Sara that familiar writing "leaves no room for the intrusion of breakfast-calls, or dinner or supper direction, which often broke in upon us."

The last image gives us the best clue to what is happening. The familiar letter lets the writer formulate his experience within the stable, inviolate boundaries of a private correspondence. Anything outside these boundaries of use to the writer is purified and abstracted as it passes into language. Conversely, anything too inert and physical, anything that is resistant to the subject, is filtered out by the process of writing as being inferior. Thus writing "makes even presence but body, while absence becomes the soul." On a foundation of this absence, a repetition in language of an improved world is possible. Every-"thing" in familiar letters can then become rarefied, saturated with affect and purpose. The superiority of this method of representation is a result of the subject's supposed sovereignty over the whole proceeding. The subject-as-writer can mandate a coherence for an account which re-presents the subject-as-topic (tells his story) and, in turn, serves and excites the complicitous "friend" who is the subject-as-reader.

We shall consider the efficacy of this powerful little "circuit of subjects" at greater length below. Little wonder that, in the third

paragraph quoted above, Richardson praises familiar letter writing
as the way a "modest lady" may "distinguish her self." Because this
activity allows one to transpose the given world into something
controlled and spiritual, it quite literally allows the writer to "assert
and vindicate her Claim to Sense and Meaning." It is easy to imagine
the usefulness of "familiar letter writing" for the construction of a
book like Clarissa's. There, it will enable Clarissa to do what Richardson recommends to Sara—it allows a "virtuous and innocent heart"
to be, not only represented, but even *"embody'd."* The book recon-
stitutes the violated virgin body by giving Clarissa a new life in the
body of her book.

Building the Book, 3: The Incorporation of the "Other"

There is little doubt that after the rape, Clarissa feels used—by her
family's financial schemes, by Lovelace's fictional machinery. She
responds by making *use* of others, by incorporating them into her
book. In one respect she has little choice. She does not represent
herself as a timeless essence but as the central actor in a series of
encounters. She will need to give an account of others in order to tell
her story. But in doing so, she must not let so much of the world—
with its worldly wisdom—into her account that her life appears to be
nothing more than the seduction and death of yet another inexpe-
rienced young girl. How can Clarissa take the numberless interstices of
life—the people, the places, the moments, with all their formless
profusion and "otherness"—and make them hers? Her solution is to
incorporate them into her narrative, thereby giving them a subordinate role in the vast act of explanation that her crisis necessitates.

For Clarissa urgently needs to reconcile her adversity with her own
sense of inner virtue. As she explains to Anna: "I am . . . a poor lost
creature: and yet cannot charge myself with one criminal or faulty
inclination. Do you know, my dear, how this can be?" If, like Job,
she remains mystified as to the "why" of her trials, she can tell Anna
"how" they happened, and the metaphorical language Clarissa
employs to describe her crisis indicates one way in which she patterns
her own experience:

One devious step at setting out!—that must be it—which pursued,
has led me so far out of my path, that I am in a wilderness of

doubt and error; and never, never, shall find my way out of it: for, although but one pace awry at first, it has led me hundreds and hundreds of miles out of my path: and the poor estray has not one kind friend, nor has met with one directing passenger, to help her to recover it. [II,262–63]

In analyzing Clarissa's use of the myth of the Fall, we notice that even the gloomiest interpretations of her situation are often calculated to solicit more favorable prospects (see above, chapter 3). Thus, after her first escape from Sinclair's, her earthly hopes are at low ebb, and she wonders "what I had done that [Lovelace] should be let loose particularly upon me!" But she quiets this "murmuring question" with a reflection:

And who knows but that this very path into which my inconsideration has thrown me, strewed as it is with briers and thorns which tear in pieces my gaudier trappings, may not be the right path to lead me into the great road to my future happiness? [III,18]

Clarissa, like most of us, would like to think she is on a journey; but often she wonders if she is not wandering in a "wilderness of doubt and error." In interrogating her own past for the grounds of her error, she discovers something akin to "false fires," "fens," and "quagmires" (II,263). She confronts great expanses of the inert, the mute, the banal—the whole vast, vague tendency of life to spin into a heap of random discrete moments. The quirks and details of the past tease their interpreter with a compliant assimilation to his meaning, only, in a second instant, to lapse tenaciously back into being nothing more than random moments. Even the events of our own life, even our own actions, can, over time, take on an unsettling opaqueness—an air of mystery that balks the keenest analysis.

Thus Clarissa focuses on the correspondence with Lovelace, and her meeting with him, as the crucial errors that have led her out of her path (I,486). To explain these errors she castigates herself with accusations of "pride" and hidden "love." She finds herself prideful in refusing to submit to parental authority and in exhibiting too much confidence in her own ability to control Lovelace. Late in her transactions with Lovelace, she also finds a hidden "love" that probably encouraged her to deal directly with Lovelace early in their relationship. But this analysis does not overcome Clarissa's crisis. By applying the words *pride* and *love* to herself, Clarissa does not really explain anything, or remove the danger of continued wanderings and error. They are merely the indices Clarissa uses to point to the strange confluence of motive and circumstance that has marked her crisis. No amount of analysis can make us (or her) really sure that Clarissa's life is a purposeful journey rather than aimless wandering. None knows her actual destination (if there is one), though Clarissa gives a brave appearance to her death, assuring all around her that she is close to arrival in Heaven.

But she does more. In losing her "path" through life, Clarissa tells us she is bothered by *ignis fatuus*, the illusory "fool's fire" that "plays around" her and frustrates attempts to know things as they are (II,263). By building a book, Clarissa responds to this disorienting experience by orchestrating an illusion for herself and her reader. She arranges for an account of her wanderings which give them the aspect of a journey—a record of her life with all the cohesiveness and direction of a story. But Clarissa's life does not *begin* as a story, and we must look into the quantities of clever shaping that make it look like one.

Clarissa's eager acceptance of death takes her a long way toward turning a very amorphous entity (her life) into a form—a story with a beginning and an end whose written record will fill out a book. See what her death does. Death as an ending makes the apparent cause of death—the rape—the climax and center of the story. Now a plausible beginning offers itself. The duel begins the crisis in Clarissa's family which results in her flight with Lovelace, so it is fitting that Clarissa's book and story begin with an account of the duel, and Anna's subsequent request for a brief narrative of the events that precipitated the duel (Lovelace's introduction into the family, his falling out with Bella, James's return from Scotland).

There are several things to notice about the way Clarissa (and Richardson) have marked the limits, and imposed a center, on her life story. First, the rape is not the inevitable center of a preexistent form. If, as Lovelace and Lady Bradshaigh wished, Clarissa had rushed to Lovelace's side when he fell ill, then this illness would have become the crucial moment of a story ending in reconciliation. If Clarissa had said "yes" to any of Lovelace's proposals, that moment would have become the center of a story with a very different shape.

Secondly, once given its definition, Clarissa and Richardson must take certain steps to protect the boundaries of this story. Clarissa works feverishly to remain separated from Lovelace after her second escape from Sinclair's, for, beyond the anger or embarrassment he causes her, she must make sure that their story does not reopen onto a new and uncertain future. Richardson keeps Clarissa an isolated and suffering adjunct to a heinous crime, so as to keep the center of the story, the rape, continuously in view.

This requires a lot of circumstantial gimmickry: Hannah too sick to join Clarissa; Mrs. Norton caring for her ill son, and then forbidden to visit Clarissa by family order; Cousin Morden in Florence until Clarissa is nearly dead; and Anna visiting relatives on the Isle of Wight. Finally, delimiting the boundaries of Clarissa's life involves an enormous increase in intelligibility. As long as it seems to touch too many things to talk about, it leaves one with an excess of meanings that induces silence. But when a life like Clarissa's winds down toward death, it begins to look like one single thing instead of many. It then invites someone to convert a multitude of curiously related happenings into a narrative that tells a lucid story.

Thus Coleridge wrote to Joseph Cottle, in 1815, "The common end of all *narrative* . . . is to convert a series into a *Whole*: to make those events, which in real or imagined History move on in a *strait* line, assume to our Understandings a *circular* motion—the snake with its Tail in its Mouth."[3] Clarissa uses this device, the *ouroboros*, on her coffin as an emblem of her movement beyond life and time toward God and eternity. But if, near death, Clarissa gains access to a godlike control over her life and its meaning, she does so by shaping that life into the material for a story and a book.

Clarissa's definition of the boundaries and center to her life is the crucial preparatory step, the bold act of simplification, that allows her to catch a glimpse of her life "whole." It extends the benefits which accrued to the earlier activities of narrative and meditation. All are formal means of allowing the subject to seem to hover outside and above its own life. All that "happens" within the narrative letter, the meditation, or the life recorded as story, takes on an air of

---

3. Samuel T. Coleridge, as quoted by M. H. Abrams in his essay on the romantic lyric, in *From Sensibility to Romanticism*, ed. Frederick Hilles and Harold Bloom (London: Oxford University Press, 1965), p. 532.

inevitability and necessity, because it is asserted to be part of something which seems past and complete. We may liken the benefits of these ways of mediating experience to the "lift" which comes to a traveler when his ship pulls away from the crowded pier of a great city. There is a delicious moment of separation, when the noises of the shore are still heard but are growing mute, and the memory of personal struggles in this place are vivid but now inexplicably unreal. An emotional constriction is superseded by a sense of autonomy, release, and accessibility: a riot of urban shapes are suddenly distinct as forms grasped at a distance over water. Aided by an abrupt reduction of the scene to a serene triad of sky, land, and water, the traveler can know the city (the place of contention and desire) as a simple silhouette.

Clarissa is, as we have seen, someone quite comfortable with the idea of her life as a journey, and she hopes to extend this kind of calm control over her own experience through the organization of her life as a story. But is is not enough to establish boundaries for her life: she must also integrate every significant event of that life into one logically unfolding sequence. There must be nothing in her story that is simply "other" than Clarissa; everything must crackle with meanings that seem to be aimed particularly at *her*.

How can this be done? We can give this question better focus, and get a clearer picture of how Clarissa shapes and manipulates her experience, by looking at how she discusses the letter she receives from Cousin Morden warning her about the dangers of libertine husbands:

> It is now in vain to wish [the letter] had come sooner. But if it *had*, I might perhaps have been so rash as to give Mr. Lovelace the *fatal meeting*, as I little thought of going away with him. But I should hardly have given him the *expectation* of so doing, previous to meeting, which made him come prepared. . . .
>
> Persecuted as I was . . . it is, however, hard to say what I should not have done as to *meeting him*, had it come in time: but this effect I verily believe it would have had—to have made me insist with all my might on going over, out of all their ways, to the kind writer of the instructive letter, and made a father (a protector, as well as a friend) of a kinsman, who is one of my trustees. . . .
>
> But I *was to be* unhappy . . . That a man of a character which

ever was my abhorrence [a libertine] should fall to my lot! But depending on my own strength . . . I too little perhaps cast up my eyes to the Supreme Director: in whom, mistrusting myself, I ought to have placed my whole confidence. . . .

Inexperience and presumption, with the help of a brother and sister who have low ends to answer in my disgrace, have been my *ruin*! [II,261–63]

Clarissa's broodings about this letter are carried on within the general context of her anxiety about the adverse turn her life has taken. She chafes and suffers helplessly before the incongruity of being consigned, by a kind of arbitrary fatality, to marriage with a "man of a character which ever was my abhorrence." She begins to wonder how all might have been different if this letter had arrived earlier. Perhaps she wouldn't have met Lovelace or, even if she had, he wouldn't have expected her to go with him or, at least, she would have insisted on going off to Cousin Morden. Being unable to use one significant detail—the timing of this letter—to evade her predicament, Clarissa reasserts the inevitability of her fate ("I *was to be* unhappy") and then solicits the reasons for her fall: she depended too much on her own strength and looked too little to God.

Clarissa ends her speculations, and some of the anxiety concomitant with them, with a carefully stated analysis of the causes for her crises: "Inexperience and presumption, with the help of a brother and sister who have low ends to answer to my disgrace, have been my *ruin*!" This whole passage is curious in the way it blends gloomy speculations with a more confident determination of the causes of her difficulties. But in the very next letter Clarissa reaches a more optimistic note by quoting lines of a poem. Here her own errors are seen, with some qualifications, in the light of an overarching providential design ("Impute my error to your own decree: My FEET are guilty; but my HEART is free" (II,266)). Clarissa's speculations about her cousin's letter, and this poem, taken together, repeat a progression commonly enacted by Clarissa in her letters. She starts with a gloomy awareness of a hostile fate, interrogates the arbitrary details that seem to compose that fate, then uncovers a logical cause-effect concatenation which orders these details, and finally feels an exultant acceptance of a divine Providence that glorifies her. What drives this progression? What enables Clarissa to assimilate apparently arbitrary events into a life-pattern redolent with meaning and value? For the purpose of analysis, and by referring to other appropriate passages in the text, we can schematize this progression into four discrete "moments."

First moment: The moment of anxiety and "fate." This is the constantly recurrent moment in the novel, when Clarissa is seized by the incongruity between her sense of personal virtue and the adversity she experiences. This moment is effectively symbolized by her rape—it is the moment of loss and anxiety which catalyzes all Clarissa's creative activity. It is from the standpoint of this moment that Clarissa interrogates her life with Job's question: why has this happened to *me*? To the extent that she can rationalize her crisis, she feels a hostile force has swept through her life. She calls this force "fate," and insists upon its mysterious quality by coupling it with the word *strange*. Early in her trials she writes Anna, "Oh, my dear! how wise have I endeavoured to be! how anxious to choose and to avoid everything, *precautiously,* as I may say, that might make me happy or unhappy: yet all my wisdom now, by a strange fatality, likely to become foolishness!" (I,291). Just before she is tricked away from Harlowe Place, Clarissa contemplates her family's behavior in this way: "*Strange* . . . that we seem all to be *impelled*, as it were by a perverse fate which none of us is able to resist?" (I,419). Even when Clarissa blames Lovelace as the "author of my calamities," she finds something fateful about the "strange concurrence of unhappy causes" which allowed him to seduce her from home (IV,251).

Second moment: The moment of the arbitrary event. As she contemplates her own difficulties, many of the events and circumstances of her life—even trivial ones—take on new importance because of her crisis. She cannot resist wondering how much better everything might have been if this or that had been different. In this second moment, Clarissa feels the separateness and arbitrariness of the many circumstances of her life, and she begins to prod and manipulate them with the little question "what if?". Thus, early in the story she wonders: "How happy might I have been with any other brother in the world but James Harlowe, and with any other sister but *his* sister!" (I,38). After Lovelace slights Bella and begins to court Clarissa, James counters by advancing Solmes as Clarissa's suitor.

Clarissa broods: "were ours a Roman Catholic family how much happier for me, that they thought a nunnery would answer all their views! How happy, had not a certain person slighted somebody! All then would have been probably concluded on between them before my brother had arrived to thwart the match; then had I had a sister, which now I have not, and two brothers" (I,62).

Finally, after Clarissa has been tricked away from Harlowe Place, she tells Anna her thoughts on waiting for Lovelace at the ivy summer-house. She thinks about the dreadful final meeting planned with her family concerning marriage to Solmes. Clarissa resolves on certain strong appeals she will make, and then more and more begins to fear seeing Lovelace. She comments to Anna: "on what a point of time may one's worldly happiness depend! Had I had but two hours more to consider of the matter . . ." she thinks she might not have met Lovelace (I,475).

These speculations follow a common pattern. Clarissa looks into her own past and finds a circumstance magnified in importance by a meditation which says—"if only this one thing had been different, all would have been well." Clarissa's language makes us feel the resistant, objectlike quality of each of these details. For Clarissa, these circumstances no longer seem "natural," "right," or her "own"—they seem strange, arbitrary, and perverse. James being her brother, Bella her sister, Lovelace insulting Bella, and Lovelace arriving at the garden gate when he does—all these circumstances are like so many hostile objects. They are attached to her life in the most significant way, but they mock her interrogation of them with their obliviousness to her will and desire. Like the "fate" that has transformed her life, these objects are saturated with "otherness." Each object is so much itself, it seems to have no value for Clarissa.

Third moment: The moment of cause and effect. But notice. With a slight shift in perspective these objectlike circumstances seem to turn toward Clarissa; they even seem *aimed* at her. Clarissa's questions have given these "objects" a certain life; they suddenly seem to be acting on Clarissa as the "causes" of her crisis. How does this happen? Clarissa's crisis leads her to assume the centrality and importance of her suffering. Everything in her life begins to take on its value in relation to this suffering. The rhetorical form of Clarissa's speculations—if this object had been different I might have been happy—animates the object. It appears to have a perverse will or intention. It seems to *want* Clarissa's suffering; it "causes" her suffering. This suspicion is confirmed by the particular objects and circumstances Clarissa chooses to speculate about. Clarissa does not ask "what if" Lovelace had never heard of the Harlowe family; nor does she wonder "what if" she had accepted one of her earlier suitors. Near each object Clarissa contemplates there is a malevolent subject that wishes her ill.

Thus Clarissa's passing desire that her family had been Roman Catholic seems like a plausible suggestion. Then Clarissa could have left the family wealth to her siblings and embraced the single life she now desires. But this wish reminds us of her actual family, and the perverse way they have paired a Protestant bias in favor of marriage with their own boundless ambition to advance the family's social standing. Clarissa's speculation about the effect of a different brother or sister, or the effect of Lovelace's not insulting Bella, have the same tendency: they remind the reader of the hostile figures (James, Bella, Lovelace) who have worked for Clarissa's undoing. Even the way Clarissa wishes that Cousin Morden's letter had arrived earlier has the effect of foregrounding her family's harshness. Thus she writes, "persecuted as [she] was" she might still have met Lovelace, but she would have been sure to have "insisted with all [her] might on going over, out of all their ways, to the kind writer of the instructive letter, and made a father (a protector, as well as a friend) of a kinsman, who is one of my trustees."

In each case, Clarissa's speculation is a way of countering the malevolent subject with a wish that often has an aggressive content of its own. Thus, wishing James and Bella out of existence as her brother and sister is not generous of Clarissa, and even wanting her cousin's letter to arrive at an earlier date involves her in a flight away from a "father" who has failed in his task as her "protector." Now we can see why these objectlike circumstances of Clarissa's life—which she solicits with her questions—seem to point toward her, seem to exist for her. Near each hovers one of the antagonists of Clarissa's struggle.

Clarissa's meditations on the reasons for her fall have taken her opening question—"Why has this happened to *me*?"—and shifted it to the more pointed one, "*Who* has done this to me?" This does not only manifest an incipient paranoia, or a penchant for treating inanimate objects as if they concealed malicious little spirits. It is characteristic of the whole tendency of Clarissa's analysis and description of her life: she hopes to find the "causes" of her fall in the intelligible and ultimately controllable domain of the subject. But the causes of Clarissa's tragedy are neither simply arbitrary, object-like facts, nor the wills or intentions of a subject. The "cause" rests in a zone between the arbitrary event and the subject, and it partakes of the objective resilience of the first and the motivated, directional tendency of the second.

Remember, we are sketching Clarissa's progression toward a mean-ing-full control of her life as a story. The progression need not be logically consistent, if it works for her. Thus, quite surprisingly, when Clarissa moves from seeing fragments of her past as arbitrary events (second moment) to seeing those same moments as "causes" of her fall (third moment), the second moment is never "lost." The event keeps its objectlike quality at the same time that it expresses wills and intentions which make plausible an organization of past events into patterns of cause and effect. This "double nature" of the event is logically contradictory, but it is absolutely crucial to the way it func-tions in Clarissa's story and book. For the "event" must stand in for "real," objectlike, substantial facts of the past, at the same time that they open onto and articulate a meaning for the subject. Although Clarissa assimilates and sustains the second moment of the progression as she moves on to the third, one essential change has taken place. In the second moment the arbitrary event seems to exist for itself, beyond the range or the control of the subject (Clarissa). But in the third moment this "event" is converted to the "cause" of an "effect" —and a subordination has taken place. Now the objective entity faces toward Clarissa, it serves her, it becomes the means to a greater end (the cause of an effect). Retrospectively, all the obstinate circum-stances of Clarissa's life join together and form a concatenation of causes and effects, so as to actualize an over-riding purpose. The larger purpose is Clarissa—the working out of her life as a movement through adversity toward triumph.

Fourth moment: The moment of achieved meaning. Once Clarissa has arrived at the fourth moment of this progression, everything looks different, and a geometric clarity overtakes her past. Now a once hostile "fate" becomes animated with human concern as "Provi-dence"—the instrument of a kindly master subject and mathematician who takes the sum of the wills of all the "causes" of Clarissa's life-story so as to tally His will and purpose. Now the events of Clarissa's life seem to have "arranged themselves" (as if anything ever arranged itself!) into an eloquent and objective-looking paradigm that actualizes a precise message: Clarissa must fall so that virtue may be tested and finally reign triumphant.

But Clarissa does not just communicate her meaning—she forces all to do homage to that meaning. There is no better way to do this than to get everyone thinking he may be to blame, might be a "cause" of Clarissa's death. We can see this most dramatically by noticing that Clarissa's death is the one event in the novel that evades the cause-effect pattern that dominates so much of the book. For right at the point in the action where we expect to find a cause for a subsequent effect (Clarissa's death), we find her imprisonment. Before her imprisonment, Clarissa has escaped from Sinclair's and is writing vigorously to Lovelace's relatives and to Anna. Her position is combative, and there is no mention of Clarissa's being in bad health. She even speaks of going to live in Pennsylvania! After her humiliating arrest and imprisonment, Clarissa has moved onto her deathbed, and all efforts at reconciliation appear too late.

The imprisonment is partly an outcome of Lovelace's sustained attack on Clarissa (the women think they are doing what he would want), partly an expression of their malicious hatred of Clarissa, and partly mere chance (they happen to see her going to church). In other words, responsibility is diffused in such a way that Clarissa in prison is somewhat isolated from what comes before. In fact, imprisonment is greeted and approved by Clarissa as a proper emblem of her situation. Thus she refuses to move from her prison-room when her keepers urge her to take their bed. She asks, "Was she not a prisoner? . . . Let her have the prisoner's room" (III,431). Clarissa urges Sinclair to sell all her worldly goods to pay her supposed "debts." Wanting "no surplus," Clarissa adds: "Let my ruin . . . be LARGE! Let it be COMPLETE, *in this life*! For a *composition*, let it be COMPLETE!" (III,441). Rather paradoxically, this imprisonment somehow functions as a symbolic "cause" of Clarissa's death, though as a real cause imprisonment is incommensurate with the effect, her death. For who dies from being locked up in a dingy room? Most importantly, Richardson uses this specious cause (imprisonment) to resist designating a "real" cause for death—such as pregnancy ("Lovelace killed her"), or illness ("chance or fate killed her"), or poverty ("her family's neglect of her killed her"), or the drug ("Sinclair killed her with an overdose").

The very absence of any pointed natural cause for Clarissa's death means that none of these is true, while *all* can be true and all are thought of in the interpretive groping that attempts to explain and blame others for the loss of Clarissa. This sets up a situation of general guilt and mutual recrimination from which even Belford and Cousin Morden cannot escape. Morden reproaches himself for having stayed in Florence so long; Belford blames himself for standing by while Lovelace executed his plots against Clarissa. By dying without any explicit "cause" for doing so, Clarissa allows blame for her death to spread and infect everyone who has touched her life. Everybody becomes a subordinate "cause," in the orchestration of one great "effect"—the death of Clarissa Harlowe.

Book-Builder as Con-Artist or, Clarissa Goes to a Country Fair

Are you suffering from suffocation or claustrophobia? The recital of all the ways in which Clarissa shapes, tames, and controls her world can induce anger and irritation—and a profound itch for an entirely new wave of sentiment. A history of Clarissa's life, compiled from two correspondences, *seems* to be life recorded. It proceeds with the same elegant autonomy we associate with our own experience. But it's difficult to shake the suspicion that we've been tricked out of the genuine openendedness and excitement we expected. What's missing is the "play" in a system that allows things to go "either way." Clarissa's way of representing her life has taken all the risk out of these proceedings. Two things take place simultaneously: all that's happened to Clarissa suddenly looks inevitable, and for some reason Clarissa *can't lose.* Why is this so?

Clarissa makes her life look like a series of genuine transactions—with all the give and take and bluster of her encounters with Lovelace. These transactions take place between Clarissa, as the experiencing subject, and a series of "others": (1) the arbitrary event in her own past (like the late arrival of Cousin Morden's letter); (2) other people, with a widely divergent way of experiencing things (most notably, Lovelace); (3) God as a taxing critic and judge of her life; and (4) the reader (of letters, and later of her book), who is capable of a skeptical response to her story. As long as we accept the notion that Clarissa's book is merely reporting these transactions, we will be duped. Instead, her book is the instrument by which the subject incorporates the "other" into its dominion, so the "other" may be repeated as an adjunct of the subject, and in the process be shorn of any "otherness." Within the illusion-engendering confines of the book Clarissa constructs, the "other" becomes the "subject's subject"— subjugated by the representational system that gives it form and presence.

We have seen the many ways in which Clarissa makes her own subject the model for the representation of the "other." The arbitrary event in her past is imbued with a subjectlike aspect of motivation and purposiveness by linking it with the hostile will of her adversary, and then by incorporating it into a pattern of causes and effects that complete Clarissa's story. By making use of Lovelace's correspondence to tell her story, an-"other" person like Lovelace is made to look like a negative version of Clarissa—and his mendacity and cruelty become a way of illustrating the inner virtues of truthfulness and goodness in the novel's dominant subject, Clarissa. Clarissa tells us there is a God who stands apart from and above her life and submits that life to judgment. But this "God" turns out to be an abstract version of Clarissa, for he judges *with* Clarissa, validates her judgments of others, and gives Clarissa definitive assurances of her coming salvation (by the ease of her death and the smile on her corpse).

Finally, Clarissa works hard to make the reader her friend—by admitting him into her private correspondence, and by writing in a pathetic and sentimental mode that invites an immediate, intuitive identification with her. In each case, Clarissa uses crafty representations and seductive rhetoric to transform what is "other" than Clarissa into her loyal subject. The arbitrary event becomes the "cause" of Clarissa's tragedy; God, a celestial assistant who validates Clarissa's design; and the reader, a sympathetic friend. In this way Clarissa reduplicates and disseminates her own subject, in different forms, throughout the book so as to constitute an interlocking circuit of subjects that can control the life sequence they represent. There is no genuine "play" between these elements of the book because Clarissa, as the master-subject, controls their interaction to produce a "plot" of her own liking.

The plot is no longer just the form of one completed action, with a natural-looking beginning and end, and a decisive climax or turning-point somewhere in between. The plot is also a design against the credulity of the reader, part of a "con game," that passes itself off as a chancy moment of genuine play so as to conceal the extent to which the whole structure of the book is the result of force applied by the subject in order to gain a godlike authority over its world. As a subject, Clarissa hopes to win the same relationship to her book as the Christian God has to His universe—being everywhere and nowhere, the whole procession of history moves toward an incarnation of His/her presence and meaning.

Someone might ask: if Clarissa is such an effective illusionist, if on the way to representing her own past in a "book" she is able to change genuine transactions into the carefully choreographed dance of complicitous subjects, then how can we even "see" this act as duplicitous? If an illusion is effective, nobody will see it as illusion. But there are forces at work that can circumvent even the subtlest illusions. For one thing, readers demonstrate the perverse habit of bringing their own interests, assertions, and desires to bear on every text (more on this later.) But beyond open insurrection by the reader, it is important to note that Clarissa's possession of this text as "her" book depends on our taking all of its pages as an illustration of her history, her suffering, her tragedy, and her virtue. If our attention wanders, even for a moment, the text becomes more than her "book"; it seems to contain "other" things. Thus we have seen that there is much in these letters which opens onto comedy, and, at least at one moment, it takes very little imagination to link these obstinate lovers with the one word *yes*. No amount of solemn, retrospective, cause-effect plotting can efface this opening toward mirth and love.

But I hear some skeptics chafing in the corner: "It's all well and good to talk about what might have been. But what's happened has happened. Clarissa and Lovelace never get together, and they both die. Clarissa's book is a report on how this happens. O.K., so her account is distorted here and there, whose isn't? How would *you* tell the events of her life and death?"

Luckily, there is no need to speculate on what a fundamental retelling of Clarissa's story might be. Lovelace offers a direct challenge to the authority of Clarissa's version of her life. It is found in the text called *Clarissa*, but it functions as a kind of antidote to the emotional tonalities and logic of the "book" Clarissa has constructed. When her death begins to appear likely, Lovelace writes his friend Belford this rendering of Clarissa's story:

It is certainly as much my misfortune to have fallen in with Miss Clarissa Harlowe, were I to have valued my reputation or ease, as it is that of Miss Harlowe to have been acquainted with me. And, after all, what have I done more than prosecute the maxims by which thou and I and every rake are governed by, and which, before I knew this lady, we have pursued from pretty girl to pretty girl, as fast as we have set one down, taking another up; just as the fellows do with the flying coaches and flying horses at a country fair, with a *Who rides next! Who rides next!*

But here, in the present case, to carry on the volant metaphor (for I must either be merry, or mad), is a pretty little miss just come out of her hanging-sleeve coat, brought to buy a pretty little fairing; for the world, Jack, is but a great fair, thou knowest; and, to give thee serious reflection for serious, all its toys but tinselled hobby-horses, gilt gingerbread, squeaking trumpets, painted drums, and so forth.

Now behold this pretty little miss skimming from booth to booth, in a very pretty manner. One pretty little fellow called Wyerley perhaps; another jiggeting rascal called Biron, a third simpering varlet of the name of Symmes, and a more hideous villain than any of the rest, with a long bag under his arm, and parchment settlements tagged to his heels, ycleped Solmes; pursue her from raree-show to raree-show, shouldering upon one another at every turning, stopping when she stops, and set a spinning again when she moves. And thus dangled after, but still in the eye of her watchful guardians, traverses the pretty little miss through the whole fair, equally delighted and delighting; till at last, taken with the invitation of the *laced-hat orator*, and seeing several pretty little bib-wearers stuck together in the flying coaches, cutting safely the yielding air, in the one go-up the other go-down picture-of-the-world vehicle, and all with as little fear as wit, is tempted to ride next.

In then suppose she slyly pops, when *none of her friends are near her*: and if, after two or three ups and downs, her pretty head turns giddy, and she throws herself out of the coach when at its elevation, and so dashes out her pretty little brains, who can help it? And would you hang the poor fellow whose *professed trade* it was to set the pretty little creatures a-flying?

'Tis true, this pretty little miss, being a *very* pretty little miss, being a *very much-admired* little miss, being a very *good* little miss, who always minded her book, and had passed through her sampler doctrine with high applause; had even stitched out in gaudy propriety of colours, an Abraham offering up Isaac, a Samson and the Philistines, and flowers, and knots, and trees, and the sun and the moon, and the seven stars, all hung up in frames with glasses before them, for the admiration of her future grandchildren: who likewise was entitled to a very pretty little estate: who was descended from a pretty little family upwards of one hundred years' gentility; which lived in a very pretty little manner, respected a very little on their own accounts, a great deal on hers:—

For such a pretty little miss as this to come to so great a misfortune, must be a very sad thing: but, tell me, would not the losing of any ordinary child, of any other less considerable family, of less shining or amiable qualities, have been as great and as heavy a loss to that family, as the losing this pretty little miss could be to hers? [III,316–17]

Lovelace acknowledges that this version of Clarissa's story is a kind of therapy for the loss of Clarissa ("for I must either be merry, or mad"). It eases the weightiness of their difficult transactions by engaging in an amusing parody, not a faithful report. The leitmotif in this tour de force—"pretty little miss"—is a habitual reminder that this is a playful, self-conscious performance which Lovelace enjoys indulging in and which is intended to entertain his reader. This little story is also casuistical in its force, because it defends Lovelace against the charge that he has ruined Clarissa. But beyond this, Lovelace's displacement has the power to develop a deconstructive counterforce to the story and book Clarissa has constructed. It does this by placing in question those fictions—the subject, the cause-effect plotting of events, the paragon of virtue—that give Clarissa's "book" its structural cohesiveness and authority.

The Olympian perspective assumed by the narrator to describe the country fair is justified by the *contemptus mundi* theme announced at the beginning: "for the world, Jack, is but a great fair . . . and . . . all its toys but tinselled hobby-horses." From this standpoint nothing that could happen to this "pretty little miss" will be very important. It has happened before, it will happen again. In the transitory world of appearances that is a country fair, the passing of one little girl seems quite "natural." And the narrator puts us at such a distance from the actors of this scene, that it seems quite pointless to wonder what their little wills and passions and petty awarenesses might be.

There is a remarkable absence of agency in this story full of action. People assume roles and move through the scene, but actions are not focused by an originating intention or explained by motive. Thus, the story is introduced by Lovelace to explain an action (the rape) by refusing to explain it. In his dealings with Clarissa he has done no more than "prosecute the maxims by which . . . every rake [is] governed." All the characters in this story act in the mechanical fashion of automatons. Lovelace's action is as mechanical as "the fellow" at the fair whose "professed trade it [is] to set the pretty creatures flying." Even the pretty little miss has come to embark on a series of transactions that look automatic: she's come to "buy a pretty little fairing," and in doing so takes risks and spends money in hope of some fun. Her crucial "act"—riding the eighteenth-century equivalent of the ferris wheel—is represented in phrases that are neatly ambiguous as to agency: "till at last, taken with the invitation of the *laced-hat orator* . . . [she] is tempted to ride next." The passive voice used in the final phrase (she "is tempted"), like the passive voice used in speaking of the maxims rakes "are governed" by, leaves responsibility for these actions sliding between the little miss and the orator, the rake and his maxims.

Not only are the successive events in this account denied the aspect of agency, they are also not connected in any logical way with each other. Thus the little miss is tempted to ride with the laced-hat orator after being followed by Solmes and watched by her "guardians," but not *because* of Solmes's chase or her family's watchfulness. These three events do not exist in a causal relationship with one another as they do in Clarissa's story; they are just three elements in a series. And the series is the key rhetorical trope used by Lovelace to shape this passage. It begins with the assertion that rakes go "from pretty girl to pretty girl" just the way the fellows at the fair give rides by asking, "Who rides next! Who rides next!" And the passage is laced with elements presented in series: the world's "toys" are likened to a list of children's toys found at the fair; the "little miss" is followed by a series of suitors and she pursues a succession of different activities; finally, the "little miss" is praised through a listing of her achievements in needlepoint. The series is dogmatic in its simplicity. It lists and parades elements in succession and does not require that there be a logical order to what it presents. This is quite apt for describing a fair, because the country fair is a multitudinous display of riches that has a semblance of untidy randomness, an excess of the world that discourages organization.

Since every event in this story is just part of a series, it is appropriate that even the climactic death of the "little miss" is presented as arbitrary and devoid of meaning: "her pretty head turns giddy, and she throws herself out of the coach when at its elevation, and dashes out her pretty little brains." This descriptive sequence has an obstinate simplicity and descends to a ludicrous use of "pretty" and "little," applied not to "miss," but to the miss's "brains." The whole description is set in connective particles that emphatically separate the "little miss's" death from all that came before: ("and if . . . she throws herself out . . . who can help it?"). If there is any logic to the passing of this young thing, it comes from the emblematic associations of the "ferris wheel." She does not die in accord with the complex calculus of the Christian providential system Clarissa invokes, but through the grim economy of the wheel of fortune: some prosper, some are destroyed, with no rhyme or reason evident to man.[4]

Now we are in a better position to apprehend how Lovelace's parody undoes the logic of Clarissa's story. Within the broad outlines of her life, he engages in an aggressive impoverishment of the subject. Here, there is no awareness, no suffering, and no self-consciousness. The pretty miss seems to be having a fine time until her "head turns giddy." Since there is no sense of loss, there's no need to brood about the past—to engage in all the meditation that goes along with tragedy. Everything that happens in this account is foregrounded as radically "present-tense." Thus the paragraphs begin, "But here . . .

4. Margaret Doody includes copies of a Dutch print in her book to demonstrate that Lovelace's image of the eighteenth-century equivalent of the "Ferris wheel" is often used in the eighteenth century as an emblem of the wheel of fortune. See *A Natural Passion*, pl. 4 and pp. 223–25.

is a pretty little miss"; "Now behold this pretty little miss"; "In then suppose." With each event present, eccentric, and gratuitous, it takes a place in a series of moments that resist arrangement into some larger pattern that doubles back on itself and holds a meaning over time. Since there is no central subject, the subject cannot read itself into the past as a "cause" which points toward a fulfillment of its present, and it cannot join hands with a complicitous master-subject (a God) that broods over all life and time. With no central subject, and no meaning-full personal history, how can there be a book to embody that subject or record that history? How can there be a book, if there is no image of a person truly special and truly superior, whose life and death sweep toward the revelation of some precise meaning, something communicating the imperishable value of virtue?

And another difficulty is evident: Lovelace does not even grace his account with the *name* of this "pretty little miss." There is no name like "Clarissa," no seed of specificity, no vivid phonetic axis around which a book and its account might turn. Her achievements are repeated in language that mocks the very idea of real personal distinction, the very possibility of an exemplary paragon of virtue. But, what is most difficult of all, this death is asserted to be no different, in essentials, than the death of innumerable other young girls. At the conclusion of the story, the teller has the temerity to insist that "his" pretty little heroine is, after all, quite commonplace, and her story carries no distinctive meaning or value.[5]

---

5. In these paragraphs I am employing a distinction that will be developed more explicitly in the second part of this study: although Clarissa hopes she has constucted a "book"—a consistent self-identical entity composed of self-present meanings—Lovelace's little narrative shows that we have a striated "text," where different meanings and versions of the same story converge and contend. On the difference between the "book" and the "text," see chapter 1 of Derrida's *Of Grammatology*, trans. Gayatri Spivak (Baltimore: The Johns Hopkins Press, 1974).

PART II

THE RECEPTION OF *CLARISSA*:
A CASE HISTORY OF INTERPRETATION

5: Richardson as Author: Gamester and Master

Richardson's debate with his readers about the true meaning of *Clarissa*, and the proper ending for the story, is one of the truly bizarre episodes in the annals of the English literary tradition. These debates provide historical evidence for something we have already noticed about the text—its openness to divergent interpretations. Why does this text incite such diverse interpretations? An answer emerges from a consideration of Richardson's aesthetic—his stated intentions in writing *Clarissa*, and the steps he takes to realize those intentions. A shorthand formulation of this aesthetic might go this way: Richardson has a design upon his readers. He wishes to re-form them so they will embrace the Christian ideals of virtue that a wayward age has forgotten (IV,553). The first step is to engage the reader in the story as powerfully as possible. Richardson does this by working to give his fiction all the immediacy, suspense, and presentness of a game. Then, with the reader caught in the coils of the fiction, Richardson plans to make his story swerve toward virtue, and carry the reader with him irresistibly.

During her long, formal character-sketch of Clarissa, Anna Howe tells an anecdote about her friend which helps to show how this kind of aesthetic might work:

Once I remember, in a large circle of ladies, every one of which (I among the rest) having censured a generally reported indiscretion in a young lady—Come, my Miss Howe, said [Clarissa] . . . let me be Miss Fanny Darlington. Then removing out of the circle, and standing up, Here I stand, unworthy of a seat with the rest of the company till I have cleared myself. And now, suppose me to be her, let *me* hear your charge, and do *you* hear what the poor culprit can say to it in her own defence. And then answering the *conjectural* and *unproved* circumstances, by circumstances as *fairly* to be supposed *favourable*, she brought off triumphantly the censured lady; and so much to every one's satisfaction that she was led to her chair, and voted a double rank in the circle— as the reinstated Miss Fanny Darlington, and as Miss Clarissa

Harlowe. "Very few persons, she used to say, would be condemned, or even accused, in the circles of ladies, were they
present: it is generous, therefore, nay, it is but just, said she, to
take the part of the absent, if not flagrantly culpable." [IV,492–
93]

How does Clarissa's artifice function? Clarissa creates a game to
effect a discrete purpose. She feels Miss Darlington has been treated
unjustly, so Clarissa acts according to the general principle of fair-
ness she enunciates after the game—"it is but just to take the part of
the absent, if not flagrantly culpable." Now it is the special virtue of
Clarissa's little game that it wins the company over to a just treatment
of Miss Darlington without apparent force. Once Clarissa has engaged
in role playing, everyone eagerly restores Miss Darlington and Clarissa
to their rightful place in the group. But it is worth taking note of two
details of this anecdote. First, the game involves a certain risk for the
artist—Clarissa makes a barter to engage everyone's interest, by
assuming the position of the outcast. If she cannot clear Miss Darlington, Clarissa expects to share her fate, ostracizing from the group.
Secondly, the whole moral value of Clarissa's artifice comes from her
ability to put a bit of untruth (her own "act") at the service of truth
(winning justice for Miss Darlington). If the game had gone out of
control, if Clarissa had become involved in the fun of being Miss
Darlington for its own sake, or if she had failed to win over her
friends, the value of the artifice would have vanished.

How does Richardson's practice with *Clarissa* compare with this
account of Clarissa's use of art? Can Richardson win the ultimate
control over his readers which this anecdote posits for Clarissa? If
anything, Richardson's actual experience with *Clarissa* argues the
opposite—it proves easier to provoke a reader's perverse independence
than to win his docile compliance. Also, the position of this anecdote
in the text of *Clarissa* should make us suspicious. Anna's formal
characterization of Clarissa was greatly enlarged in the third edition
as part of an attempt to silence critics of the heroine. It is designed as
a formal panegyric of Clarissa. Richardson used Clarissa's status as an
example to postulate general ideals in almost every area of womanly
endeavor. It is entirely appropriate that, while he works to assert
control over the reception of his own work of art, Richardson gives
us a version of art's operation which dramatizes its radical subordina-

tion to an artist's moral intention. This picture of Clarissa as an ethical artist is more an expression of Richardson's aspiration for his own art than a faithful record of his practice. To the more uncertain cross-currents of that practice we now turn.

In writing *Clarissa*, Richardson took a calculated risk. Each move to enhance the immediacy and power of his fiction also threatened to undermine his own authority. Here is a list of several steps Richardson took in shaping *Clarissa*. Notice how each augments the power of Richardson's work by engaging the interest of the reader, *at the same time* that it disengages the work from Richardson's direct control:

1. Richardson publishes *Clarissa* in three installments over the period of one year. This stimulates the reader's curiosity and invites him to develop his own scenarios for the story's ending.
2. Richardson effaces his own presence in the text by adopting the low-profile role of an editor. At the same time he enhances the importance of each letter-writer's momentary presentation of events. In this way the reader gains the illusion of an unmediated experience of the major character and his or her unfolding predicament.
3. Richardson tells a story of romantic love to encourage reader identification and . . .
4. the story of a daughter's fateful disobedience to her father, in order to trigger debates about the propriety of her conduct.

With these techniques Richardson tosses his work into the neutral space that exists between an author and his readers. *Clarissa* seems to become the reader's plaything. And yet, Richardson cannot forget that it is *he* who started this game, that the book is after all "his" toy, and that the game is designed to be controlled by a higher purpose (reforming the reader). With the debates that begin around *Clarissa* "control" becomes the problem of this text; "control" becomes its question: how is control asserted and relinquished? what are the limits of that control for both the author and the interpreter of the text?

The Umbrage of Editor

Richardson's authorial control over *Clarissa* is put into question by the novel's central fictional presupposition: the notion that Clarissa and Lovelace are "real people," and that their letters have an independent existence as the written records of their lives. Even when Richardson acknowledges the fictionality of his characters, he never tires of insisting that his account is "taken from nature," or is, as we would say, "true to life." *Clarissa*, like all realistic fiction, invites the reader to test the extent to which the text corresponds to the "reality" we are assumed to share. This "reality" is the ultimate source of any authority the text may have. In this situation, the visibility of an author can be an embarrassment. His position is most problematic: he even begins to look like an unwelcome interloper.

For, to the extent that we accept the "reality" of Clarissa, Lovelace, and their story, the "author" as the creative genius who spins all of the book out of his mind (or borrows it from somewhere else) must discreetly withdraw from view. What we see instead is the dutiful editor—a trustworthy assembler of letters taken to have a prior existence as the "actual" correspondence of "real" persons. To sustain this illusion, it is important that there be no author around to take responsibility for the existence of this artifice—which explains Richardson's uneasiness with the preface Warburton offered him for the second installment of *Clarissa*.

Richardson was flattered by the attentions of this famous and learned man, but the preface alludes quite openly to Richardson as the gifted author of *Pamela* and *Clarissa*. Richardson's articulation of his misgivings about the preface, in a letter to Warburton, describes the subtle balance he wants *Clarissa* to maintain. It must seem real to the reader at the very same moment that it is understood to be fictional:

> Will you, good sir, allow me to mention, that I could wish that the *Air* of Genuineness had been kept up, tho' I want not the letters to be *thought* genuine; only so far kept up, I mean, as that they should not prefatically be owned *not* to be genuine: and this for fear of weakening their Influence where any of them are aimed to be exemplary; as well as to avoid hurting that kind of Historical Faith which Fiction itself is generally read with, tho' we know it to be Fiction. [*Letters*, 85; April 19, 1748]

Richardson understands that the power of his fictional illusion, and the moral program linked to this fiction, are contingent upon the absence of a visible author or narrator. In place of the dominant author, we get a tactful and low-profile editor. Thus Richardson is blocked from extensive intervention in the fiction by the limits of the role of editor he has assumed.

In spite of the limits of this role, playing the editor gives Richardson important power, which he exercises with a good deal of astuteness. A letter to Aaron Hill allows us to step behind the scenes to watch Richardson making editorial decisions that modulate the power relationship between Clarissa and Lovelace. In the first drafts of the novel, Richardson had Clarissa and Lovelace give independent narratives of the big scenes where they encounter each other. While shortening the novel for publication, Richardson decided to abridge some of these duplicate narratives and quickly discovered the importance of *how* this is done. Thus he writes to Aaron Hill that he started by cutting Lovelace's accounts and putting the most interesting of his comments in the form of footnotes to Clarissa's account. But because these notes broke "in upon the Narration, and his wicked levity turning into a kind of unintended Ridicule half the serious and melancholy Reflections, which she makes on her Situation: So I alter'd them back" (*Letters*, 71; October 29, 1746).

Richardson, acting as editor, finds an alternative to protect Clarissa's sentiment from the force of Lovelace's raillery. He gives Clarissa the dominant role as narrator and supplements her account with connective summaries of his letters, "preserving only those Places in his, where his Humour, and his Character are shown, and his Designs open'd, [and I] have put many others, into a merely Narrative Form, referring for the Facts to hers, so of some of hers, vice-versa" (*Letters*, 71; Oct. 29, 1746).

If one follows the editorial interventions over the course of the novel, an interesting pattern emerges. The pendulum swing of power —from Clarissa, to Lovelace, and back to Clarissa—is faithfully reflected in which character delivers the central narrative of events. Thus, at St. Albans at the beginning of her stay at Sinclair's, Clarissa's letters are inviolate, while Lovelace's letters are subjected to summary (II,96–97; 207–09; 212; 213). As the action proceeds, Lovelace gains more and more of the narrative, until his first physical attempt on Clarissa, where his correspondence begins to overshadow Clarissa's in a most decisive fashion (II,379). From there on, until Clarissa's final escape from Sinclair's after the fire scene, Clarissa has only two complete letters totaling six pages, compared to almost five hundred pages of text written by Lovelace.

During this central segment of the novel, the editor will sometimes give segments of Clarissa's letters within Lovelace's letters. Some of her letters are intercepted by Lovelace, others are forged by Lovelace to deceive Anna. Clarissa's correspondence loses its autonomy as she loses control of her body. At one point, extraordinary circumstances are contrived to keep the narrative with Lovelace. Clarissa has escaped from Sinclair's and wanders around Hampstead, lonely and frightened, until she finds her way to Mrs. Moore's. We do not get an account of these events in a letter from Clarissa to Anna, as might be expected. Instead, Lovelace reconstructs her movements through the eye-witness accounts of a servant hired by complete strangers to follow the movements of this mysterious woman (III,28).

What is the logic behind these shifts in the location of the narrative? They are not arbitrary steps taken by Richardson to manipulate our sympathy. Nor do they depend very much on Clarissa's inability to write Anna at certain points in the action—for this is only the case between her rape and her final escape from Lovelace. We get a clue to the answer to this question when Lovelace's authority begins to ebb. In working to subdue Clarissa after the rape, he tries to lure her into an attempted escape from Sinclair's with the assistance of Dorcas. For some reason, Clarissa senses a trick and refuses to fall for the ruse. The editor breaks into Lovelace's narrative with these words:

> Mr. Lovelace gives here a very circumstantial relation of all that passed between the lady and Dorcas. But as he could only guess at her motives for refusing to go off . . . it is thought proper to omit his relation, and to supply it by some memoranda of the lady's. [III,255–56]

Now we can understand the constraints which govern the editor's procedure. The editor shifts to Clarissa's account, and unveils her "book of memoranda," at the very point when Clarissa begins to regain control over the action. This is appropriate, for the editor must select an account that will give the reader the fullest possible understanding of how and why events are unfolding the way they are. In practice, this involves giving the narrative to the character who has the most initiatory power over the action. An author may favor one character over another, as Richardson favors Clarissa over Lovelace, but once he has assumed the role of editor "his" behavior is sharply circumscribed. Thus, on the vital matter of which character will deliver the narrative to the reader, the editor's moves become a function of all the other positions of the text: Clarissa, Lovelace, and the flow of power and awareness from one character to the next.

Our discussion of the author-as-editor has emphasized the limits Richardson accepts through the way he constructs his fiction. But when the novel becomes engulfed in controversy, Richardson steps forward as the staunch defender of the moral program of his art: in *Clarissa*, he has given the world an example of virtue. In this polemical moment, the role of editor is viewed as a temporary sleight of hand—a convenient fiction to enable the author to steal into the hearts of the unsuspecting readers. So, in the postscript to *Clarissa*, greatly lengthened for the third edition (1751), Richardson adds this passage to explain his own intentions and methods:

> It will be seen by this time that the author had a great end in view. He has lived to see scepticism and infidelity openly avowed . . . and a taste even to wantonness for outdoor pleasure and luxury, to the general exclusion of domestic as well as public virtue, industriously promoted among all ranks and degrees of people. . . . He imagined, that, in an age given up to diversion and entertainment, he could steal in as may be said, and investigate the great doctrines of Christianity under the fashionable guise of an amusement. [IV,553]

By introducing the higher purpose of the artwork, Richardson can claim that the role of the editor is just a means to an end, not a way in which he "lets go" of the work, but a cunning method of disguising the ultimate control of an author who exercises his authority indirectly and at a distance. Thus Richardson explains to Aaron Hill that he can write an "assuming and very impudent preface" to *Pamela*, making great claims for his art, because he has "the umbrage of the editor's character to screen myself behind" (*Letters*, 42; 1741).

Does the role of editor disengage the text from authorial control, or merely give an inviting illusion of reader and character freedom from author manipulation? While we must defer our response to this question, we should note that Richardson's description of his art, as a means to steal into the reader's heart, coincides with a much more aggressive use of the role of editor in the second and third editions of *Clarissa*. For now the editor is no longer the benign and docile figure who invites the reader to judge and compare the rival claims of the protagonists. Instead he enters the text with an army of footnotes and textual addenda designed to expose Lovelace's plots and tip the scales of justice in favor of his heroine, Clarissa. Perhaps the role of editor always concealed the dual possibilities of dispassionate judge and manipulative prosecutor. By the third edition, Richardson has exploited both of these contradictory possibilities.

The Character: The Author's Impersonator (and/or) His Trope

If the role of editor offers a most uncertain vehicle for Richardson's control of the fiction, perhaps his characters—the children of his imagination who loom so large in the spectacle that is *Clarissa*—perhaps these characters will allow Richardson to direct the fiction toward its "proper" destination. Richardson has two ways of talking about his characters. Sometimes they are the people he loses himself in becoming; sometimes they are the rhetorical tropes he stands outside to manipulate. In the first case, Richardson emphasizes a movement beyond himself, toward something distinctly different from his self. Thus, to a Frenchman he describes his balanced treatment of the Catholics and Protestants in *Sir Charles Grandison*, and attributes this to an act of impersonation he undertakes during the process of writing: "in short, this Part is one of those that I value myself most upon, having been as zealous a Catholic when I was to personate the Lady, and her Catholic Friends, as a Protestant, when I was the Gentleman" (*Letters*, 238; July 5, 1753).[1]

In another letter, Richardson offers a careful description of what happens when he writes or speaks for a character. Lady Bradshaigh has reproached him for having Charlotte Grandison tease Aunt Nell, or allowing Aunt Nell to wear the pink and yellow ribbons that make her worthy of ridicule:

> Was it *I* that dressed Aunt Nell? Fie upon me: I ought *never to be forgiven*—Only I know I did it not so much for Ridicule Sake as

---

1. The *OED* shows that the word *personate* carries all the several meanings of the modern term *impersonate*: (1) assume a mask, act a part; (2) deceive by pretending to be a person you are not; (3) to cheat someone in this way.

to give occasion to correct the Ridiculer. . . . But how can it be said I and not Charlotte dressed Aunt Nell?—here I sit down to form characters. One I intend to be all goodness. All goodness he is. . . . Another Lady G——ish; All Lady G——ish is she. I am all the while absorbed in the character. It is not fair to say—I, identically I, am anywhere, while I keep within the character. And if I have done so, why say you, madam, that *I* dressed Aunt Nell? [*Letters,* 286; Feb. 14, 1754] [2]

In this playful response to Lady Bradshaigh, Richardson reminds one of Lovelace, by offering an elegant alibi to separate himself from all the particular consequences of his artifices. But in doing this, Richardson also gives us a valuable analysis of his own practice. Richardson begins as removed from his fiction and in control of its unfolding. He writes the scene not to ridicule, but "to give occasion to correct the Ridiculer." He sits down "to form characters," and in every instance they mirror that intention. But during the process of writing, something new happens. Richardson as a separate entity disappears: "I am all the while absorbed in the character." It is in reference to this moment that Richardson offers his most radical formulation: "It is not fair to say—I, identically I—am anywhere, while I keep within the character."

Richardson-as-author is lost "within" his character, because the act of writing has displaced Richardson from the position of a firm public persona to that of a character who writes a letter. In this situation, Richardson cannot be held responsible for what a character does—for, to the extent that the character "is," the author as a separate controlling agent simply "is not." Richardson presumes that this process will also enfold the reader and prevent a reader's reproach of the author. To Mrs. Watts, Richardson wrote, "I am apt to be absorbed in my characters when I write for them, and the reader that is not, as he or she reads, must be too often alarmed, I doubt, especially by the things put into the mouths of the freer characters."[3] In spite of these warnings, Richardson cannot prevent critics of the tragic ending from insisting on his responsibility as the "author" of the novel. Richardson responds, in a letter to Lady

2. The *OED* shows that the appropriate meaning for *identically* is "the very same."
3. This is quoted from MSS of the correspondence of April 9, 1755, in T. C. Duncan Eaves and Ben D. Kimpel, *Samuel Richardson: A Biography* (Oxford: Oxford University Press, 1971), p. 590.

Bradshaigh, by sharing responsibility with his characters: "if the
Author rather than the *Characters* in his story must be considered, I
only hope to be weighed in an equal Balance" (*Letters,* 316; October
10, 1754).

Richardson's effort to conceal the author's presence in the fiction
is not simply a function of strategy. It also responds to his most
personal needs. When Harriet Mulso asks about his health, Richardson
responds: "I write, I do anything I am able to do, on purpose to carry
myself out of myself: and am not quite so happy when tired of my
peregrinations, I am obliged to return home. Put me not therefore in
mind of myself" (*Corr.,* III,190–91; Sept. 10, 1751). Writing does
more than take Richardson away from his chronic illness. It helps to
overcome the shyness and "bashfulness" Richardson customarily felt
when he appeared in public. This shyness came in part from his
modest origins and in part from his scanty formal education.[4] We get
a vivid glimpse of Richardson's feelings of inferiority, and the concomitant uses of his art, in a letter sent to Lady Bradshaigh. An
admirer of Richardson's novels has visited the author, but then failed
to write a follow-up note:

> He has not written to me since he left London. I suppose I
> answered not, on a personal Acquaintance, the *too* high ideas he
> had of me from what I had published. I am always jealous of
> suffering in the Opinion of my Readers, when we come into
> personal Conversation—And why?—Because the simplicity of my
> Character (I hope I may say so) and the Frankness of my
> Communicativeness, lay me open all at once, and must convince
> the new Acquaintance that they had thought too highly of me,
> by their Reading. I design not either Affectation or Reserve; and
> if I appear to have Shyness, it is owing more to my native
> Awkwardness, than to Design. Let me own to you, that I never
> paid my personal Duty to your Ladyship, but I came away half
> dissatisfied with myself, from Diffidence I have mentioned; and
> glad at my Heart was I, when the next Visit from your Lady-
> ship, or Command to attend you, gave me Hope, that your
> Goodness had not permitted me to sink in your Favour. In

---

4. Richardson often describes himself as "bashful" in public encounters. The accounts of
others confirm this characterization. See ibid., p. 520.

writing, I own, I was always an impudent Man. But need I tell your Ladyship that? [*Letters*, 318–19; August 13, 1755]

Here is a Richardson who is both self-conscious and ineffectual, making a confession that is difficult to read over two centuries after it was written. Little wonder friends reported that Richardson was quiet in public and only eager or confident in discussing his own books. Little wonder, too, that he should choose to win laurels and importance by effacing a public persona felt to be inadequate. Instead, Richardson displaces himself into characters that give free rein to an "impudence," assertiveness, and fantasy-life otherwise inaccessible to this awkward old printer.[5]

But, if Richardson is absent from the work of art because he has been "absorbed" into the characters, how can he hope to control the work so that it serves a useful moral purpose? Richardson's answer comes in the debates which follow publication of the novel. For Richardson, Clarissa is not just one character among many, she is an exemplar of virtue who excels all those around her. For this reason, any thoughtful and judicious reader should grant her priority over her adversaries. At least one prominent reader, Samuel Johnson, felt that it was Richardson's distinctive virtue as an artist to give us a picture of vice in Lovelace that would stimulate some admiration but ultimately draw a negative judgment. Johnson compares Richardson's treatment of Lovelace to Rowe's treatment of his rake, Lothario, in *The Fair Penitent*:

> Lothario, with gaiety which cannot be hated, and bravery which cannot be despised, retains too much of the spectator's Kindness. It was in the power of Richardson alone, to teach us at once esteem and detestation; to make virtuous resentment overpower all the benevolence which wit, and elegance, and courage, naturally excite; and to lose at last the hero in the villain.[6]

In *Rambler* Number 4, Johnson rejects the notion of mixed character advanced by Fielding and makes the idea of the moral exemplar, as

---

5. Richardson's very first letter to Lady Bradshaigh is quite explicit about the gratification he feels when his artwork functions as an effective surrogate in stimulating intercourse with others. Richardson urges her not to be ashamed of the fervor of her opinions: "Indeed I admire it; and have reason to plume *my self* upon the interest you have in my story" (*Letters*, 89; October 26, 1748; Richardson's emphasis).

6. From Johnson's *Rowe*, in *Lives of the Most Eminent English Poets* (1779–81).

used by Richardson, the keystone of his fictional program.[7] Richardson's practice in designing his novel—effacing himself and putting an exemplary character before the reader—will only lead to a predictable reader response if the reader feels the aspiration toward virtue shared by Richardson and Clarissa, and described so vividly by Johnson:

> In narratives, where historical veracity has no place, I cannot discover why there should not be exhibited the most perfect idea of virtue; of virtue not angelical, nor above probability, for what we cannot credit we shall never imitate, but the highest and purest that humanity can reach, which, exercised in such trials as the various revolutions of things shall bring upon it, may, by conquering some calamities, and enduring others, teach us what we may may hope, and what we can perform.[8]

When we descend from the high ground of prescriptive aesthetics to the more mundane terrain of actual reader response, we shall find that many do not share Johnson's judgment of Lovelace, Richardson's evaluation of Clarissa, or either author's concern with virtue. To describe Clarissa as an elaborate trope—an exemplar for the reader—

---

7. A consideration of the moral programs advanced for the new prose fiction of the 1740s and 1750s might place these texts together: Richardson's practice in *Pamela* and *Clarissa*; Fielding's rejection of "models of perfection" and his preference for the efficacy of moving readers with "mixed characters," as explained in the first chapter of Book 10 of *Tom Jones*; Johnson's *Rambler* No. 4; and Richardson's *Sir Charles Grandison*, where the use of a moral exemplar is carried to an untenable extreme, and defended in "A Concluding Note by the Editor" in language which echoes Johnson's position (just as Johnson had earlier implicitly praised Richardson's practice). In this convergence of texts, *Rambler* No. 4 is the best systematic defense of Richardson's moral program for fiction. The briefest summary will show why this is so: Johnson opens with a comparison of the new fiction with romance that is strongly favorable to fiction "drawn from real life." Examples in this fiction have greater power over their readers—and this offers danger and opportunity for the author. The author must choose and describe his characters so the reader feels an appropriate attraction to virtue and disgust for vice. In advising an author how to guide his reader toward virtue, Johnson makes several related points: (1) Just because something exists in nature does not mean it should be drawn. (2) He explicitly rejects the notion of the "mixed character," for this tends to confound virtue and vice. (3) He insists that man may consult reason so as to choose between "gratitude" and "resentment," even if they "arise from the same constitution of the passions." (4) Art should offer an ideal of virtue to draw the reader toward virtue and away from vice—and the priority of virtue must be constantly maintained. A consideration of Johnson's central ideas and a close analysis of his language show that he is making a case for the vigilant assertion of virtue over vice in every phase of a novel's production. It is the difficulty of Richardson's doing just that in his actual writing of *Clarissa* that concerns me at this juncture.

8. *Rambler* No. 4, in *Samuel Johnson: Essays from the Rambler, Adventurer, and Idler*, ed. W. J. Bate (New Haven: Yale University Press, 1968), pp. 14–15.

subdues the novel to the original intentions of the author who manipulates that trope.

But this also does a good deal of violence to the illusion that the novel is designed to sustain. If instead we are dutiful readers, and embrace the terms of this illusion, the characters of *Clarissa* take on a life of their own within our reading. When Richardson "meets" these characters, and he does so in the correspondence which follows the publication of *Clarissa*, they will look somewhat strange to their author. They may stand opposite Richardson in the very way wayward teenagers stand opposite a parent. He knows he participated, in the most direct possible way, in their passage into this world, but he is not quite sure how they came to be what they are, and he has moments of uneasiness when he contemplates the discrepancy between his original intentions and the very independent existence they have come to assume. He still calls them "my" children, but he does so under protest.

The Uses of Love: To Interest (and/or) to Instruct

When Richardson tells his readers that he has presented *Clarissa* under "the guise of an entertainment" in order "to investigate the great doctrines of Christianity," he is invoking the oldest and most pervasive dictum of Western aesthetics: the notion that art should both entertain and instruct.[9] Richardson's *way* of describing his own practice in this postscript to *Clarissa* serves as a heavy-handed reminder to wayward readers that instruction is more valuable and important than entertainment. This reminder is only necessary because many readers have gotten too "caught up" in the entertainment, and seem to want nothing more from this novel than the happy culmination of a story of love.

But the reader should not be blamed for this. For it is Richardson who has scattered the sweet and heady elixir of love through his fiction. *He* invents an immaculate and incorruptible heroine and then allows her to be raped. *He* presents Lovelace as a master of the art of seduction—a hero who engages the mystique of an irresistible male physical presence that can arouse the passions of every woman but Clarissa. To acknowledge the sexuality of this novel, one does not

9. See Horace, *Ars Poetica.*

need to marshal all the sexual symbols together, the way Dorothy Van Ghent does; nor must one agree with D. H. Lawrence that "Boccaccio at his hottest seems to me less pornographical than *Pamela* or *Clarissa Harlowe*."[10] Just look at the descriptions Clarissa and Anna offer of Lovelace's physical charms, and the effect on women of his winning arrogance and cool command (IV,18–26).

And when one has read how Lovelace disarms the ladies at the ball, ladies who all know of his cruel treatment of Clarissa, then turn to the very different description of the "rake" we find in Jane Austen's unfinished novel *Sanditon*. The narrator explains:

> Sir Edward's great object in life was to be seductive. . . . He regarded it as his duty—He felt that he was formed to be a dangerous man—quite in the line of the Lovelaces.—The very name of Sir Edward he thought, carried some degree of fascination with it . . . but it was Clara alone on whom he had serious designs; it was Clara whom he meant to seduce. He had . . . been long trying with cautious assiduity to make an impression on her heart, and to undermine her principles.—Clara saw through him, and had not the least intention of being seduced.

The simple finality of Clara's understanding and resistance brings the whole intricate sequence of seduction to an abrupt close. To have a story involving seduction, Clara would have to have some belief in Sir Edward's power. The clear style and good sense of the Austen narrator will not admit of mysteries about male potency. Here Austen does to Lovelace what Lovelace has done to others so often and so well. The rake's mastery is subjected to merciless formalization, so all Lovelace's enterprise and energy become stylized gestures—the delusions of the fatuous Sir Edward. One is not surprised to discover that a very mundane lack of funds delivers the final blow to Sir Edward's ambitions: if a forced abduction becomes necessary "he knew his business . . . he must naturally wish to strike out something new, to exceed those who had gone before him . . . but the expense alas! of measures in that masterly style was ill suited to his purse."[11] Austen's

---

10. See Dorothy Van Ghent, *The English Novel: Form and Function* (New York: Harper & Row, 1953), pp. 60–83. Lawrence is quoted in Philip Stevick's edition of *Clarissa* (San Francisco: Rinehart Press, 1971), p. xxvii.

11. Jane Austen, *Sanditon*, ed. Margaret Drabble (Harmondsworth: Penguin, 1974), pp. 191–92. All quotations are from these pages.

heroines are seldom in danger of seduction. When Anne Eliot and Fanny Price encounter suitors like Mr. Eliot and Henry Crawford, their "danger" arises from the possibility that they will be drawn into a dreary marriage with confirmed egotists.

The very idea of the rake cannot long survive the kind of laughter Austen develops at Sir Edward's expense. Reading *Sanditon* on the "rake" places the enabling fictions of *Clarissa* in sharp relief. For a novel to revolve around an act of seduction, we must have the shared acceptance, by all the major characters, of a group of related fictions: the virgin's purity, the man's potency, and the woman's constant danger. The characters of *Clarissa* accept these notions with dire earnestness, and every reader is invited to entertain these fictions as the conditions of the possibility for his imaginative participation in the life of this novel. But if the reader drinks the rich potion of love and seduction, will he be ready to return with the author at story's end to a spartan diet of moral instruction?

Some of Richardson's most avid readers had grave doubts. In the fall of 1755, Lady Echlin, the serious elder sister of Lady Bradshaigh, had read all three of Richardson's novels, and felt his collection of moral maxims to be "the pith and marrow of nineteen volumes." She calls herself an "old fashioned matron . . . better pleased with musty morals than a pretty love-story." For his next story she hopes Richardson will, as she writes, "disappoint your amorous readers, by not making the passion of love their entertainment." She adds:

> Allow me to say, the finest lessons you have written, and the best instruction you can give, blended with love intrigues, will never answer your good intention. I wish to see an exemplary widow drop from your pen. [*Corr.*, V,54; Sept. 2, 1755]

Richardson's response is significant. He says, in effect, "I have no choice"—"I am afraid, Instruction without Entertainment . . . would have but few Readers." And then he offers a celebrated formulation:

> Instruction, Madam, is the Pill; Amusement is the Gilding. Writings that do not touch the Passions of the Light and Airy, will hardly ever reach the heart. [*Letters*, 322; Sept. 22, 1755]

Another letter, this one to his doctor and friend, George Cheyne, helps us to understand Richardson's metaphor for his art. Dr. Cheyne worries that there is too much "fondling" and kissing between

Pamela and Mr. B. after their engagement. Richardson explains his
purposes:

> I am endeavouring to write a story, which shall catch young and
> airy Minds, and when Passions run high in them, to shew how
> they may be directed to Laudable Meanings and Purposes, in
> order to decry such Novels and Romances, as have a Tendency to
> inflame and corrupt: And if I were to be too spiritual, I doubt I
> should catch none but Grandmothers, for the Granddaughters
> would put my girl indeed in better company, such as that of
> the grave Writers, and *there* they would leave her; but would still
> pursue those stories, that pleased their Imaginations without
> informing their Judgments. . . .
>
> There is a Time of Life, in which the passions will predominate;
> and Ladies, any more than Men, will not be kept in Ignorance; and
> if we can properly mingle Instruction with Entertainment, so as
> to make the latter *seemingly* the *view*, while the former is *really*
> the End, I imagine it will be doing a great deal. [*Letters*, 46–47;
> August 13, 1741]

Richardson proceeds through a long analysis to demonstrate how
every expression of physical affection between Pamela and Mr. B. is
subtly paired with "some laudable Behavior or Conduct; *Benevolence*
on *his* Side, which obliges her, or *Gratitude* on her's."

In these letters, Richardson makes extraordinary claims for his art
by organizing an alliance with the very romances he scorns. He does
not just acquiesce in the use of a story of love; through a calculated
deception, he wraps instruction in love. The patient is drawn by the
sweet gilding on the surface of the pill, but he is renewed by the
bitter medicine within. In a similar way, young readers come to
Richardson's novels to satisfy their sexual curiosity, only to be
carried away on a swerve toward virtue. Has Richardson found a way
to submit the reader's passions to the author's control? This is the
megalomaniac dream of Richardson's art—he wishes to make his book
the drug which induces a permanently altered state of consciousness.
Young people with "light and airy minds" will be drawn to Richardson's story, hoping for the excitement of novels and romances rife
with love; but unbeknownst to them, their hearts will be changed as
their passions are linked to the purposes, meanings, and moral
examples Richardson proposes for their reformation.

This kind of authorial control is implied in eighteenth-century descriptions of Richardson as the "master of the heart" and the "Shakespeare of the heart." Johnson's concise tribute, in introducing Richardson to the readers of *Rambler* Number 97, says it best: Richardson is the author "who has enlarged the Knowledge of Human Nature, and Taught the Passions to move at the Command of Virtue."[12] Some of Richardson's readers accepted these extravagant claims of authorial control quite literally. A clergyman named Phillip Skelton wrote Richardson that *Clarissa* was not a "novel," but "a system of religious and moral Precepts and Examples, planned on an entertaining Story, which stands or goes forward, as the excellent Design of the Author requires."[13]

But there were always critics ready to be skeptical about the actual tendency of Richardson's art. In a pamphlet entitled "Critical Remarks on Sir Charles Grandison, Clarissa, and Pamela," published in 1754 by someone calling himself "A Lover of Virtue," Richardson is accused of stimulating the passions by making "Love eternal Love . . . the subject [and] burden of all your writings."[14] After an allegorical reading of the story of the Fall—with Adam, reason, Eve, "outward sense," and the serpent, "lust or pleasure"—this critic declares that Richardson's volumes

contain nothing else but a minute and circumstantial detail of the most shocking vices and villainous contrivances, transacted in the most infamous characters, and all to satisfy the brutal and sensual appetite. Thus you act the part of the serpent, and not only throw out to men the tempting suggestions of lust and pleasure, but likewise instruct the weak head and the corrupt heart in the methods how to proceed to their gratification. That is, you tempt them to swallow the forbidden fruit of the tree which they were commanded not to eat. [p. 43]

The author of this pamphlet offers a vivid picture of the likely fate of one of the readers of *Clarissa*:

12. As quoted by Eaves and Kimpel, *Samuel Richardson*, p. 333.

13. *Preface, Hints of Prefaces, and Postscript*, intro. R. F. Brissenden, The Augustan Reprint Society pub. no. 103 (Los Angeles: Clark Memorial Library, 1964), pp. 8-9.

14. The following quotations from this rare pamphlet by an unknown author are taken from the copy in the Houghton Library at Harvard University.

Accordingly our amorous youth sallies forth, fully bent to enjoy Clarissa in imagination; but before he has got halfway to mother Sinclair's, he meets a pretty girl in the streets, who invites him to a glass of wine, and the next tavern stands open for their reception. This is the natural catastrophe of a serious perusal of the fire-adventure. [p. 47]

There is no record of Richardson's response to this pamphlet. But in the spring of 1749 he wrote his own pamphlet defending the "fire scene" against charges of indecency. He cannot believe the scene can be inflaming; in writing it

> the passion I found strongest in me, whenever I suppose myself a Reader only, and the Story real, was *Anger,* or *Indignation*: I had too great an Aversion to the intended Violator of the honour of a CLARISSA, to suffer anything but alternate Admiration and Pity of her, and Resentment against him, to take place in my Mind, on the Occasion.[15]

Here we find Richardson imagining himself the reader of his own book, and then describing a response to the fire scene which he hopes will be normative. In this way, Richardson acknowledges an embarrassing fact. The reader had never relinquished his sloppy independence and impudent right to bring his own will and interest to bear on every text he reads. By entering into a dialogue with his readers, Richardson is no longer the artist with pharmacological control over the heart. He has reentered a political and transactional relationship with the reader.

When we examine many of Richardson's artistic decisions in this light, a very different image of the artist emerges. Now Richardson seems like a clever side-show director, who never takes his eyes off his audience, and never stops seeking just the right "mix" of entertainment and instruction to arrive at the response he desires. When the Abbé Prévost cut much of the moral instruction out of his French translation of *Clarissa,* Richardson complained that the translation departed from "the very motive with me, of the story's being written at all" (*Letters,* 224; February 24, 1753 to Lady B.). But

---

15. This is quoted from the above pamphlet by Eaves and Kimpel in *Samuel Richardson,* p. 290.

when the didactic strain of the final installment—with Clarissa's slow death and Belford's interminable narratives—threatened to submerge the pathos and excitement of the protagonist's death, Richardson himself omitted large quantities of this material: Clarissa's reflections upon "transitory life," most of her formal meditations, Belford's meditations on death, and his "very serious answer" to Lovelace's letter implicating Belford in the plot to rape Clarissa (IV,458).[16]

Richardson always felt that Clarissa should be an instructive example to his readers. So when some of them are too critical of her and seem to have missed the point, he adds a paragraph to the preface in the third edition explaining her exemplary status. On the other side of this issue, the critic of the *Gentleman's Magazine* essay wants a flawless heroine, so Clarissa is criticized by him for disobedience to her father, disrespect to Solmes, and running off with Lovelace.[17] Now, part of the interest of Clarissa's position in the first installment arises from the way she is entangled in a situation where there is simply no morally sanctified position, so casuistical debate becomes inevitable. But this invites the kind of heated reader debates which insure interest. Richardson playfully explains this to Lady Bradshaigh, in a letter about *Sir Charles Grandison*:

> The whole story abounds with Situations and Circumstances debatable. It is not an unartful Management to interest the Readers so much in the Story, as to make them differ in Opinion as to the Capital Articles, and by leading one to espouse one, another, another Opinion, make them all, if not Authors, Carpers. [*Letters*, 296; February 25, 1754]

When the debates about *Clarissa* begin in earnest, Richardson soon gives up playing with his readers in this spirit. Like a cranky old schoolteacher, he loses interest in motivating his readers and tries to subject them to a solemn interpretive discipline.

The attempt to balance entertainment and instruction in *Clarissa* carries certain risks. For when Richardson blends love into his moral design, he risks losing ethics in eros. This repeats a pattern we have

---

16. See Eaves and Kimpel, "The Composition of *Clarissa* and Its Revision before Publication," *PMLA* 83 (1968): 427. Richardson wrote Lady Bradshaigh that he cut many of Clarissa's meditations for the first edition.

17. *Gentleman's Magazine* (June and August 1749), pp. 245–46, 345–49.

found elsewhere. To the extent that Richardson adopts the role of editor, he can't be the deity presiding over *Clarissa*; to the extent that he "speaks" in the voices of the characters, he effaces his own presence. *Clarissa* invites divergent interpretive response because it is a stratified text carrying these contradictory tendencies within itself. Sometimes its author acts like Clarissa—asserting identities, fixing boundaries, defining the "true" nature and meaning of the book; but sometimes Richardson reminds us of Lovelace: concealing himself behind a multitude of contradictory roles, he alienates the text from himself so as to initiate a game that will involve every reader.

6: The Struggles of Interpretation

One man, Pygmalion, who had seen these women
Leading their shameful lives, shocked at the vices
Nature has given the female disposition
Only too often, chose to live alone,
To have no woman in his bed. But meanwhile
He made, with marvelous art, an ivory statue,
As white as snow, and gave it greater beauty
Than any girl could have, and fell in love
With his own workmanship. The image seemed
That of a virgin, truly, almost living,
And willing, save that modesty prevented,
To take on movement. The best art, they say,
Is that which conceals art, and so Pygmalion
Marvels, and loves the body he has fashioned.
He would often move his hand to test and touch it,
Could this be flesh, or was it ivory only?
No, it could not be ivory.
His kisses, he fancies, she returns; he speaks to her,
Holds her, believes his fingers almost leave
An imprint on her limbs, and fears to bruise her.
He pays her compliments, and brings her presents
Such as girls love, smooth pebbles, winding shells,
Little pet birds, flowers with a thousand colors,
Lilies, and painted balls, and lump of amber.
He decks her limbs with dresses, and her fingers
Wear rings which he puts on, and he brings a necklace,
And earrings, and a ribbon for her bosom,
And all of these become her, but she seems
Even more lovely naked, and he spreads
A crimson coverlet for her to lie on,
Takes her to bed, puts a soft pillow under
Her head, as if she felt it, calls her Darling,
My darling love!
        And Venus' holiday
Came round, and all the people of the island
Were holding festival, and snow-white heifers,
Their horns all tipped with gold, stood at the altars,
Where incense burned, and timidly, Pygmalion
Made offering, and prayed: "If you can give
All things, O gods, I pray my wife may be—
(He almost said, My ivory girl, but dared not)—

One like my ivory girl." And golden Venus
Was there, and understood the prayer's intention,
And showed her presence, with the bright flame leaping
Thrice on the altar, and Pygmalion came
Back where the maiden lay, and lay beside her,
And kissed her, and she seemed to glow, and kissed her,
And stroked her breast, and felt the ivory soften
Under his fingers, as wax grows soft in sunshine,
Made pliable by handling. And Pygmalion
Wonders, and doubts, is dubious and happy,
Plays lover again, and over and over touches
The body with his hand. It is a body!
The veins throb under the thumb. And oh, Pygmalion
Is lavish in his prayer and praise to Venus,
No words are good enough. The lips he kisses
Are real indeed, the ivory girl can feel them,
And blushes and responds, and the eyes open
At once on lover and heaven, and Venus blesses
The marriage she has made. The crescent moon
Fills to full orb, nine times, and wanes again,
And then a daughter is born, a girl named Paphos,
From whom the island later takes its name.

Ovid, Metamorphoses *X. 243–97*

While Heraclitus' imagination was eyeing the never-ceasing motion of the cos-
mos, this "actuality," like a blissful spectator who is watching innumerable pairs
of contestants wrestling in joyous combat and refereed by stern judges, a still
greater intuition overtook him. He could no longer see the contesting pairs and
their referees as separate; the judges themselves seemed to be striving in the con-
test and the contestants seemed to be judging them.

Nietzsche, Philosophy in the Tragic Age of the Greeks

Those who claim to know *Clarissa* keep attending to the edges, the margins, the surfaces of the body of this text. It is on the interface between reader and text that rival interpretations are mustered and the battle to control *Clarissa* unfolds. In 1744 the first handwritten copy of *Clarissa* was sent to Aaron Hill. It was interlayered with blank sheets which Richardson had placed between his own writing in order to receive Hill's corrections, revisions, and addenda.[1] Eighteen years later, just before his death, Richardson devoted his last days to reading the marginalia Lady Bradshaigh had written in her personal copy of *Clarissa*. Richardson examined this borrowed copy

---

1. Eaves and Kimpel, "Composition of *Clarissa*," p. 417.

carefully, and added his own responses to her notes.[2] But beyond writing in the margins of actual copies of *Clarissa*, much of Richardson's vast correspondence is best understood as existing in the interface, or margin, between the novels and their readers. Its preservation resulted from Richardson's emergence as a prominent novelist. Mrs. Barbauld, the author's early biographer, tells us that Richardson did not transcribe his correspondence until the publication of *Pamela*.[3] *Pamela* brought fame, correspondence with persons of rank and importance, and a stagey, quasi-public status for Richardson's letters. *Sir Charles Grandison* grew out of the debates and exigencies of the correspondence, and it never lost contact with this matrix. Richardson, at one point, half-seriously contends that the novel belongs to Lady Bradshaigh (*Letters*, 182; 1751).

But it is not just that Richardson's novels stimulated letter writing which then affected production of the novels. In most of these letters, *Clarissa* and the other novels become the locus of value and medium of exchange for both correspondents. Thus the proximity of the novels establishes eccentric forms of correspondence. Richardson frequently brags that he uses the responses to the novels as a touchstone to look into the heart of the reader and judge his character (*Letters*, 143). In debates on a range of everyday subjects—from women's education to parental authority—Richardson often bolsters his own position by quoting from the novels, as though they were the scripture of this epistolary dominion (*Letters*, 184; 1751). For instance, in one of the first letters to Lady Bradshaigh, Richardson sends a copy of volume 5 "courting" her "acceptance and perusal," just as Lovelace courts Clarissa. When he wishes to compliment her on the sweet vivacity of her response to *Clarissa*, Richardson writes: "I love Miss Howe next to Clarissa; And I see very evidently in your letters, that you are the twin-sister of that Lady; tho' I never before knew that she had a Sister" (*Letters*, 116; December 15, 1748; also 96; October 26, 1748). Lady Bradshaigh tells Richardson of a forced marriage, like the one planned between Clarissa and Solmes, which ends unhappily (*Corr.*, VI, 99–100). Richardson was one of the founders, and on the board of directors, of an institution called Magdalen House. It was a hospital for repentant prostitutes—women

---

2. Eaves and Kimpel, *Samuel Richardson*, p. 234.
3. Anna Barbauld, *The Correspondence of Samuel Richardson* (London, 1804), I, cxc–cxci.

whose trials ended less happily than Pamela's, who wished to mend their ways.[4]

Why is Richardson so addicted to this artful play around his novels? Of course, it must have been flattering to discuss his own work at such length. Also, disagreements lengthened correspondence and allowed him to trade on his fame as an author, in order to gain an intimate acquaintance with young ladies of fashion. At times he seeks advice and information about manners in high life. But why does he pry criticism out of reluctant friends, like Sara Westcomb and Aaron Hill, both before and after publication of the first installment? And why encourage Lady Bradshaigh to expatiate on her objections to the tragic ending, when the third installment had, by that time, gone to press? Richardson knows that the efficacy of his moral program depends on modulating reader response to his novel. Sometimes he uses the authority gained from his position as author to teach readers how to read his book. At moments this is done in a playful manner. When one correspondent accuses Clarissa of being a "coquet," and another takes her to task for being a "prude," Richardson answers both by sending each the other's letter (*Letters*, 178; 1751).

But Richardson does more. He encourages those debates to build up in the margin of the text, and then, in the second and third editions, he adds footnotes, a longer preface, an index, and a conclusion to anticipate and deflect the criticism and misreadings of *Clarissa*. Now the debates which have unfolded in the interface between text and reader have become a protective shield. Like the "mantle of integrity" Clarissa throws around her shoulders in moments of distress, they assert and guarantee the integrity of body of the text. It is as if Richardson welcomed the disease of misreading so he might fortify the text with antibodies against its recurrence.

If we *do* look into the margins of *Clarissa* at the debates between Richardson and his readers, we discover interpretive positions that have a twofold significance. When considered with Richardson's addenda to *Clarissa*, these debates lay down the dominant critical positions taken on the novel from Richardson's day to the present. But despite their "marginal" status, these debates do something more. They also replay the interpretive struggle within the novel

4. Eaves and Kimpel, *Samuel Richardson*, pp. 463–65.

between Clarissa and Lovelace, and deepen our understanding of the sources and significance of that struggle.

Late in life, Richardson realized the importance of this correspondence. In 1758 he wrote Lady Bradshaigh that he had been reperusing their early debates on the ending of *Clarissa*, and wondered if she would permit publication, in some form, after his death. He has shown their letters to "select Friends," who, he says, "admired greatly the charming spirit of your Ladyship's Part in the correspondence, and declared, that together it would make the best Commentary that could be written on the History of Clarissa" (*Letters*, 336; November 19, 1757). Of course, Richardson is only too happy to show his friends entertaining debates about *Clarissa*. He is confident they have become a compliant commentary on his novel, because he is quite sure that he has won these debates with Lady Bradshaigh. Since we have doubts about Richardson's victory, we have different motives for looking into these letters. We are interested in discovering what kind of interpretive struggle it could be that no one can win.

The Virgin Text

We will consider three interpretive positions on *Clarissa*. Each suggests the appropriate way to know, control, and complete the text. The first position, championed by Joseph Spence, says, "do nothing" —the text is virgin and pure as it is; the second, advanced by Aaron Hill, finds ways to modify the characters of Clarissa and Lovelace so as to perfect the story; and the third, articulated most strongly by Lady Bradshaigh using the pseudonym "Belfour," urges a happy ending to the story. Like all interpreters, these three readers feel that *their* position is true to the text in its essence. None are more sure of this than Joseph Spence. On reading the first installment of *Clarissa*, and a long summary of the remainder of the novel lent him by Richardson, Spence writes the author to express his intense admiration. Spence has heard of the torrent of contrary advice Richardson has received, and he knows how the author frets about it. Spence himself is worried that Richardson will do injury to his own work by attempting to satisfy his critics. So Spence urges Richardson to "take up a resolution of neither trusting others, nor distrusting yourself, too much." Two important reasons are offered for doing so. He explains,

Even the opinions of good judges, in general, when they come
to decide about particulars in your Clarissa, are most to be suspected. Do they know the connections and dependencies of one
part upon another? Are they acquainted with your various ends
in writing it; your unravellings of the story; and your winding up
of the whole? Without these lights, a very good judge may give a
very wrong opinion about the parts that compose it. Another de-
fect in those that are called the best judges is, that they generally
go by rules of art; whereas your's is absolutely a work of nature.
Nature, I think, you have followed more variously, and at the
same time more closely, than any one I know. For Heaven's sake,
let not those sworn enemies of all good works (the critics) destroy
the beauties you have created. If you indulge them all in their
wicked will, they will cut every tree in your garden into a bird or
a beast. What I have just said will hold stronger against lopping.
You love the Scriptures. There, you know, a good man is said to
be like a tree by the rivers of water. You are, as yet, flourishing
in all your verdure; for God's sake, don't let them make a pollard
of you!

To drive his point home, Spence tells a story of his going to a
coffee-room near Buckinghamgate to read *Clarissa*. He falls asleep
"to the hum of three or four critics, who were gravely debating over
their coffee, on the other side of the room." He dreams:

I found myself again walking by the side of the Mall. . . . There was
one lady, whom I had never seen there, I think, before, and who
soon engaged all my attention. She was tall; of an easy air, and
noble deportment; with a face more charming than one of Gui-
do's angels. There was grace in all her looks and motions; her
dress was rather negligent than set; she had very little head-dress,
and her hair fell in easy ringlets down to her shoulders; her bosom
was shaded with lawn, but not imprisoned in stays, as one could
discern through her long robe of white satin, which was collected
there, though it flowed all loose, and at its full liberty, behind
her. As I and several others were admiring her (for no man could
look steadily on her without admiring her) a little, pert, busy
woman, with much of the air of a French milliner came tripping
to her, and cried (half out of breath) "O! Ma'am, I'm most extremely glad of having the pleasure of meeting your ladyship

here! but, for God's sake, who dressed you today? Never did
Heaven give so many beauties to any one person to be so hide-
ously neglected as your ladyship's are. Those beautiful auburn
ringlets to be suffered to run to all that wildness! why, they wan-
der at least three fingers-breadth lower than they ought to do!
Then these wide unmanaged sleeves! and that intolerable length
of your robe, that hides the prettiest feet in the universe! That
length of robe is what I can't nor won't bear with!" As everything she said was accompanied with much action, these last
words were followed by a very violent one; for just as she had
finished them, she applied a pair of scissors (which she had till
then concealed) to the robe, which had so much offended her,
and running them along with the greatest impetuosity, in a moment as it were, divided all the lower half of it from the upper.

A gentleman standing by is incensed at the indignity suffered by such
a "noble" lady at the hands of such a "mean" one. He then explains
to the narrator that these are allegorical ladies: "That fine lady (says
he) with so free and graceful an air, is NATURE: and that little busy
French milliner, who has cut off the most flowing part of her robe
(perhaps only to make pincushions and patchwork of it at home) is
ART." Before Spence and this bystander can fly after the two women—"to catch that wretch, and conduct the noble sufferer out of
this crowd"—Spence is awakened "by a sudden quarrel that had
arisen between critics in the coffee-room:"

It seems they had taken up your book, which I had dropped
heedlessly on the table. Three of them maintained, with great
clamour, that it ought to be reduced to half its bulk; that a story
ought to be short and quick, and the events crowding in upon
one another; that a giant novel was a monster in nature; and
several other things that put me in mind of the restraining character of the Milliner in my dream. I could not help smiling a
little to myself. I put your book into my pocket, which they had
flung down again upon the table, in the impetuosity of their arguments; and left them to debate over a point, which they seemed
very little to understand. [*Corr.*, 320-27]

Spence develops his allegory with a good deal of precision. The
text of *Clarissa* (and the author) are aligned with the beautiful

lady, Nature; the "false critic," who would trim the text, is aligned
with the milliner. Less explicitly, Spence as dreamer and letter-writer
is the true critic, who seeks to protect the text-lady from an attack
by the critic-milliner. This kind of stance, when assumed by a critic,
develops into a general interdiction against interpretation. Readers
who want to argue a point or alter the work are reduced to carpers
deserving a condescending dismissal. Then what does this critic do?
Spence shows us quite vividly. He is *conservative* in every sense: he
protects the text, resists change, and affirms the prior authority of
the text.

To argue for the privileged position of the text, Spence draws on a
familiar two-part Aristotelian conception of the work of art. A work
of art is a subtle coordination of parts into one harmonious whole;
and in this way, it is a living thing—like the trees of the garden threatened with fashionable trimming, or like the "good man" Scripture
compares to "a tree by the rivers of water." But this metaphoric substitution (living thing for artwork) does not simply illustrate an idea
(the interrelation of parts in the whole); it also makes the text seem
mysteriously powerful and inviolate. In other words, it confers a
certain "virtue" on the text, and prepares for the likening of the text
to a beautiful lady. Now, if we recall that Belford and Lovelace describe Clarissa as an image of overpowering beauty—one that can reconcile opposites in a whole—then it should not surprise us that the
work of art gains in purity by becoming an object of desire. Thus
Spence's description of the lady (or text) is quite sexual in content.
Her ringlets and robe flow to generous length; her dress is "negligent,"
and her air "easy." The speaker is not over nice in his observations:
he notes that "one could discern through her long robe" that "her
bosom was not imprisoned in stays."

From this perspective the "false critic"-milliner has a contradictory status. She is both the prude who reigns in the easy negligence
of this beauty, and the rival admirer who violates the lady. In each
case she is hated for removing the object of desire. The milliner's
presence is made jolting to the reader through the contrast of language in this passage. The speaker's description of Nature is adula-
tory and subtly arousing. It builds gradually, and flows through a long
graceful period: "there was one lady . . . she was tall . . . there was
grace in all her looks and motions; her dress was rather negligent . . .
it flowed all loose, and at full liberty, behind her." The milliner

violates this moment of gentle appreciation by repeating the description of the lady, now in clipped emphatic phrases, studded with exclamations. This has the effect of terminating the illusion so carefully contrived by the describer of the dream.

Now we can see that the broad outlines of Spence's allegory constitute a displaced repetition of *Clarissa*: the "action" of the allegory—a public indignity suffered by a noble person at the hands of rascals—strangely resembles the scene of Clarissa's arrest (III,426–28). The lady/the text is the virgin beauty Clarissa; the milliner/the "false critic" is a reduced and trivialized version of Lovelace; and the dreamer/the "true critic" is Belford—the person who acts too late (in both stories) to prevent the violation of the lady, but compensates for this failing by becoming one who knows and proclaims her true value.

We have now isolated the position of the "true critic," and touched on the contradiction which besets him. The true critic effaces himself before the text. He elevates the text to a position of preeminent authority, and lays down an interdiction against touching her. But his relationship with the text is one of desire, so that—like Spence—he constantly dreams the violation of the very object he holds sacred. Belford himself is not free from difficulties raised by this kind of contradiction. All through the novel, Belford has a most problematic relationship with Clarissa's suffering and death. He knows of Lovelace's plans from the very beginning. On meeting Clarissa, his response is extravagant: he describes her as "all mind," and wonders if "such an angel of a woman should marry." In our detailed analysis above, we connected Belford's adoration of Clarissa with the processes of art (see chapter 2). This establishes the correct context for understanding why Belford does nothing to help the woman he worships.

However much it later galls him, Belford is implicated in the rape of Clarissa. As an avid reader of this story, an eager observer of the unfolding show, Belford must patiently watch the test of Clarissa's virtue. In this trial of innocence, Belford is the voyeur—the one who watches patiently, comes as close as he can, but never touches. After the rape, when Belford heaps abuse on his friend, Lovelace (and Clarissa) give Belford some awkward moments by reminding him of the many opportunities he had to disrupt Lovelace's plottings. Thus, when the blame for Clarissa's rape and death is distributed, he too must come in for a share. Belford responds to any guilt he may feel by increasing the vehemence of his panegyrics to the dying Clarissa. His narratives wipe clean the stains of her past, delicately separate her from her mundane surroundings, and purify this frail human object. Little wonder that he surreptitiously renews Clarissa's lost virginity, while describing the way she asks her doctor and pharmacist to predict the length of time she has to live: "each sweet hand pressing upon the arm of each gentleman, with that mingled freedom and reserve which *virgin* modesty, mixed with conscious dignity, can only express" (IV,179; emphasis added).

In a manner reminiscent of Belford, Spence tries to be the text's true friend. He warns Richardson against following the advice of others and tells an allegorical story about the text's violation by the critics, only to awaken and rescue his own copy of *Clarissa* from the carpers at the coffee-house. Belford and Spence gain a kind of self-righteous strength from the suspicion that *they* are among the precious few who give the object of their concern the veneration that is its due. In working to protect this novel, Spence gives the text a particular definition: it is separate from its reader and possesses a subtle interrelation of parts to the whole; these qualities make it what it is— pure, virgin, and to be protected by the "true critic" as, simply and invitingly, itself. Spence claims for the body of the text the position of awe, respect, and integrity Belford labors to earn the dying Clarissa. In Chapter 7, below, we shall find that the "humanist" critics of *Clarissa* repeat all these ways of knowing *Clarissa*.

While the idea of the "virgin" text is implicit in Spence's story, it becomes quite explicit when Aaron Hill returns the two vellum volumes of the 1774 hand-copied *Clarissa*. Hill has left their white inter-layered sheets white:

> I have (in weighed and oft-repeated readings), found your blank leaves doomed to an unspotted virgin purity. I must not, I dare not, think of violating them. Indeed, I see no modest possibility of doing it; since precision, in so natural a flow of drapery, would only serve to stiffen what you bid me shorten. [*Corr.*, 100]

Hill makes use of this elegant conceit—the text as virgin—to refuse Richardson the detailed criticism he has invited. In this way Hill anticipates the idea of the text's purity, naturalness, and prior authority which Spence expresses through allegory.

Sometimes Richardson seems to accept this way of thinking about his works. He justifies writing a continuation of *Pamela* because he has heard others are engaged in the project: "I was resolved . . . to do it myself, rather than my Plan should be basely Ravished out of my Hands, and probably my Characters depreciated and debased, by those who knew nothing of the Story" (*Letters*, 43; August 1741). But, as we have seen, Richardson himself usually courts the criticism that seems to others like a violation. Thus he finally overcomes Hill's reticence and obtains detailed criticism of *Clarissa* from him in the fall and winter of 1746.

Hill's criticism takes two forms: general suggestions for handling the novel's opening situation, and a sample seven-letter abridgment designed to help Richardson shorten the novel. Hill modifies the story in three basic ways: (1) *He makes the story more romantic.* Now the duel between James and Lovelace arises from Lovelace's forbidden correspondence with Clarissa. Hill's way of suggesting this change shows how he enhances the romantic connection between Clarissa and Lovelace:

> The Ground-work of the Duel might, with a considerable heightening to Clarissa's Character, derive itself from Mr. Harlowe's forcing it on Lovelace, for persisting in his Correspondence after Prohibition by the Family.—And, am I in the wrong, to wish the Lady to have been, before, in downright Love?—For then how irresistibly must she be hurried, by a new Increase of Passion, on her Lover's being forced into such Hazard of his Life, for her sake only—(Whereas now the Motive of the Quarrel is quite foreign as to *her*) and then behaving with such Manly Courage in it—Yet declining to make use of his Advantage when 'twas gained —and parting from an Adversary, fallen, disarmed, and in his Power—with some genteel impressive compliment—from his respect to, and Remembrance of, *her* Influence. [*Letters*, 70; Hill to Richardson October 23, 1746]

(2) *Hill makes Lovelace a more delicate character.* Hill wishes to make Clarissa's attraction to Lovelace more plausible, so he gives Lovelace a role in this duel which appears very gallant. Now Lovelace opens the secret correspondence with Clarissa in a delicate manner—by sending his first letter through Mrs. Howe, who passes the letter on to Clarissa. Hill repeatedly insists that Lovelace must

not be made too dark, "since no young lady will think herself in danger of a wretch—each will think *her* Lovelace too different."[5] (3) *Hill gives Clarissa much of the blame for her tragedy.* He wants Clarissa to be "downright in love with Lovelace"—only this will explain Clarissa's "rash Elopement with a man . . . [her] running away from her Father's House, with a worse man than Solmes, of her own choosing." Clarissa's culpability in running away is one reason Hill feels Richardson shouldn't entitle this novel *Clarissa*, for then people will think Richardson "intended her for an example," instead of simply a "warning."

This was *not* the kind of criticism Richardson had expected. A slight adjustment of the Clarissa-Lovelace configuration by Hill brought a small but decisive shift away from Richardson's conception of the novel. The author was appalled. It must be remembered that Aaron Hill was Richardson's closest friend and literary advisor, a man of genuine intellectual attainment, whom Richardson greatly admired. Hill was also enthusiastically committed to Richardson's general project—a story of love ending in tragedy, as a warning to the unguarded. These factors make Richardson's distress all the more acute.

Richardson felt compelled to reject most of Hill's advice. He did use the duel to drive hero and heroine together, but he resisted making Lovelace so very noble with James, or so delicate as to send his first letter after the duel to Mrs. Howe rather than to Clarissa. In the character of Lovelace, Richardson departs from the rake of Restoration comedy Hill tries to make him, and aims at an "uncommon though not unnatural character." He is opposed to Clarissa's being "downright in love," because the ground for a tragic ending must be prepared (*Letters*, 76). Thus, Richardson explains that he would have love "imputed to Clarissa, by her penetrating friend" Anna, so that Clarissa may later subdue her love with "prudence" and, after the rape, rather choose to "refuge her self in the Arms of Death, than in Lovelace's" (*Letters,* 73, 72). Finally, though Richardson is willing to acknowledge that Clarissa errs, he still "intended" her to be an example, so he calls the novel that tells her story, *Clarissa* (*Letters*, 83).

But Richardson is not simply disturbed because Hill's advice proves

5. As paraphrased by a letter from Hill to Richardson, by Eaves and Kimpel, "Composition of *Clarissa*," p. 424.

unuseful. To Richardson, Hill's whole way of thinking the story, of judging the moral disposition of the heroine, and of reading the novel's lesson, seems flawed. It is flawed in such a way that Richardson's personal confidence as an author who can modulate the reader's experience is deeply shaken. This fact emerges from Richardson's vehement defense of Clarissa against the charge of "eloping" with a rake:

> But I am very greatly mortified, that what I have so much laboured, as to make it manifest, that Clarissa, tho' provoked as she was by a disgraceful confinement; by her Brother's and Sister's *permitted* Insults; tho' threatened to be *forced* into the Arms of a Man she abhorred; tho' thus provoked, I say, to *promise* to go off; yet repenting, and resolving *not* to go off, only to meet him, in order to let him know as much; and to re-assure him personally (for fear of Mischief), that, although she would stay, she would die rather than be compelled to be the Man's Wife she hated; That this should be called, by such a clear Discerner; *a rash Elopement with a Man*; and that your reasoning in this material Place, is built upon the Supposition of her voluntarily *running away from her Father's House, with a worse Man than Solmes of her own choosing!* I am very unfortunate, good Sir, let me say, to be so ill-understood; To have *given Reason, I should say*, to be so little understood; And how can I but doubt my own conduct in this Story, when, if I did not, I must question your attention to it, in the most material Point of all, respecting my Heroine's Character, and, as I may say, one of the principal Morals that I proposed to be drawn from my Story? [*Letters*, 82; January 26, 1746/7]

Richardson has expended a lot of ingenuity in contriving elaborate machinery to get Clarissa abducted from Harlowe Place, so she does not look like "any giddy girl who runs away with her father's footman."[6] Richardson not only explains all this in his long letter to Hill, he also quotes a testimonial by two ladies, who, after reading the piece, said, "*having met him*, they should not, in their cases, have been able . . . to avoid being carried off (tricked off)" by Lovelace (*Letters*, 83).

6. Paraphrased from Richardson's letter (Forester MS, XIII, 3, fols. 59–62) by Eaves and Kimpel, ibid., p. 420.

Hill's revisions of *Clarissa* point beyond the author's handling of one important scene. They open up the whole problematic of the power relations and balance between Clarissa and Lovelace. This problematic can be viewed from two sides: the plot which brings hero and heroine together, and the control of reader sympathy. Hill's response to Clarissa forces Richardson to re-pose basic compositional questions: How can virtue love evil and remain virtuous? How can an exemplary heroine become entangled with a potentially evil hero (and this while she disobeys parental commands) without a good deal of blame accruing to her behavior? How can Clarissa's involvement with Lovelace seem both probable and not exceedingly culpable, at the same time that Lovelace's final assault on Clarissa (and the whole tragic turn to the action) is properly anticipated?

But the elegance and romance of Lovelace's behavior in Hill's version indicates another still more fundamental side of the Clarissa/Lovelace problematic. Lovelace has obviously won a good deal of Hill's admiration and sympathy. Lovelace's wit, his command, his easy honesty, and his self-deprecations endeared him to many of the novel's first readers. Once a reader extends sympathy to Lovelace, Lovelace provides ways to interpret the action which undermine Clarissa's perspectives. He invites the reader to see his plots of seduction under the rubric of play, and if this is done, Clarissa's tacit cooperation may be attributed to an unconscious love for the hero. This implicates her in all of the action, and the final catastrophe.

Of course, Richardson is usually quite confident he can modulate the reader's sympathy for Clarissa and Lovelace. Hill's "errors" in reading disturb this confidence so much that he suspends the whole procedure of soliciting advice from friends, and returns to the drawing board to carry out one more extensive revision of the novel.[7] A Lovelace that is too dark makes Clarissa's trust of him, however slight, seem culpable. So Richardson must articulate Lovelace's evil more clearly for the reader but keep it hidden from Clarissa. The author hopes this will increase respect for the heroine while it curtails sympathy for Lovelace.

    7. There is an eight-month hiatus in the Richardson-Hill correspondence, perhaps reflecting a quarrel. A year later, when the novel was finally published, Richardson confessed to Edward Young, "What contentions, what disputes have I involved myself in with poor Clarissa, through my own diffidence, and for want of a will. I wish I had never consulted anyone but Dr. Young" (*Letters*, 84; November 19, 1747). For a moment, Richardson sounds like a battle-weary Clarissa!

One passage from a letter of Richardson's gives us evidence of the decisive change that has been worked in Lovelace's character. During the Hill-Richardson debates, Richardson had explained Lovelace's honorable intentions in first courting Clarissa: "And in his first Letter to his Friend, he acknowledges honourable love; and has no Intention of other, till he finds [Clarissa] in his Power. . . . At the time of his courting her . . . he *meant* her no Evil" (*Letters*, 81–82; January 26, 1746/7). After a year of revision, Lovelace's first letter to Belford tells of his determination to pursue Clarissa until he has seduced her to "MATRIMONIAL, or EQUAL intimacies" (I,150). This change allows Richardson to answer one admirer of Lovelace and advocate of a happy ending, "And did you not perceive, that in the very first Letter of Lovelace all those Seeds of Wickedness were thick sown which sprouted up into Action afterwards in his Character?—Pride, Revenge, a Love of Intrigue, Plot, Contrivance!" (*Letters*, 92; October 26, 1748). It is difficult to underestimate the importance of this revision of Lovelace's character. Behind this change, with our knowledge of the first edition, we can catch the outlines of a very different story of Lovelace and Clarissa: one where Lovelace intends "honourable love" when he first courts Clarissa, is frustrated in his marriage proposals by Clarissa's family, only conceives the idea to "test" Clarissa's virtue after the abduction, and frequently lapses away from this plan by proposing quite honestly. He is finally driven to more and more violent means of seduction by the momentum of their struggle.

This hypothetical early version would have been Lovelace's "tragedy" as much as Clarissa's. It would have disclosed a more volatile notion of events and a more fluid conception of character. That story would have been everywhere much more like the proposal scenes and three melodramatic scenes as analyzed above, where we get a sense of genuine play, moments that can go "either way." Richardson's revision of Lovelace's character has the effect of taming this radical contingency. Now the final catastrophe of the rape has its origin in Lovelace's initial designs on Clarissa. What finally happens is now made to appear preordained. We shall see, in more extended analysis below, that this is the logic which underlies Richardson's additions to the text in the second and third editions.

Now we are in a position to see how Aaron Hill's suggestions during composition, and Richardson's revisions, put in question the whole perspective on the text asserted by Spence—the whole possibility of a virgin text, one that might stand apart from the vulgar assertions of readers and authors, and simply fulfill a self-identical presence, a disciplined whole that magically reconciles its divergent parts into one essential, inevitable object. The very idea of a virgin text depends upon drawing a boundary between the inside of the text, the text in itself, and all that is outside of the text, and then keeping this boundary secure and inviolate. But if Richardson modifies his own text to meet the problems raised by Hill's suggestions, then Hill's response, and Richardson's counter-response, invade the text and become part of *Clarissa*. Even if we knew the novel as it was in October 1746, we would not have a text untouched by "extrinsic" concerns such as the reader's reception of the story. For Richardson tells Hill of changes he made to darken Lovelace even *before* Hill's suggestions:

> I once read to a young lady Part of his Character, and then his End; and upon her pitying him, and wishing he had been rather a Penitent, than to be killed, I made him still more odious, by his heighten'd Arrogance and Triumph, as well as by Vile Actions. [*Letters*, 73; October 29, 1746]

Sometimes it seems that Richardson was never *not* doing battle with anticipated misreadings. Even if we were to get back to the very first draft of *Clarissa*, we would not have effaced the presence of a potential reader and his response. Thus Richardson never tired of telling Hill, Lady Bradshaigh, and others that, in composing this piece, he was always determined to "explode . . . that pernicious Notion" now too much abroad, "that a Reformed Rake . . . makes the best Husband" (*Letters*, 73; October 29, 1746). Spence's advice to keep the text unviolated by the responses of readers and suggestions of critics is perhaps well intentioned—but it comes too late, and to the wrong author.

The Reader as Pygmalion

In the fall of 1748, a woman unknown to Richardson wrote him *incognita* under the name of "Belfour." This began a remarkable epistolary debate over the ending of *Clarissa*. Near the beginning of his third letter to her, Richardson describes the special circumstances that triggered this debate:

You and others . . . by Reason of the distant Publication of two Volumes, and two Volumes, have formed from the Four a Catastrophe of your own; and are therefore the more unwilling to part with it, in favour of that which I think from the Premises the only natural one. [*Letters*, 103; December 15, 1748]

Richardson's publication of the novel in widely spaced installments encouraged every reader to imagine himself the author and invent an ending of his own. The second installment takes the reader down to the fire scene, Clarissa's escape from Sinclair's, and Lovelace's discovery of her whereabouts. Between April 1748, when the second installment was published, and October 10, 1748, when "Belfour" writes Richardson, Lady Bradshaigh and other readers were busy imagining ways this story of Lovelace and Clarissa might end. Rumors of a tragic ending reached Belfour and led her to write to the author.

Lady Bradshaigh was an attractive woman of about forty whose letters display warmth, charm, and intelligence. She felt justified in intervening in the compositional process by the sheer magnitude of her imaginative participation in the fiction. This led the nineteenth-century editor of Richardson's correspondence, Laetitia Barbauld, to comment that Belfour carried her "passionate interest" in the story to a "whimsical excess." Barbauld adds, "She seems to have considered Clarissa and Lovelace as real beings, whose fate the writer held in his hands."[8] This remark is apt. Belfour sustains a sense of these characters' reality for her as reader at the same time that she acknowledges their absolute dependency on the will and verdict of Richardson as author. This is why her letters give us unusual access to the authorial position behind the text of *Clarissa*. In writing to Richardson, Belfour declines to be the docile and respectful reader. She wishes to intervene in the compositional process and become a coauthor of the novel—or if not a coauthor, at least a respected literary advisor. In her first letter, she excuses herself with winning charm for infringing on the author's accustomed authority:

Now, Sir, I must inform you, that I do blush most immoderately . . . for I must be mistress of a consummate assurance, in offering to put words in the mouth of the ingenious Mr. Richardson without a blush of the deepest dye. [*Corr.*, IV, 180]

8. Barbauld, *Correspondence*, I, ccvi–ccvii.

Belfour finds an ingenious way of participating in the compositional process. She just joins her voice to a debate assumed to be already in progress:

> I have heard that some of your advisors, who delight in horror, (detestable wretches!) insisted upon rapes, ruin, and destruction; others, who feel for the virtuous in distress (blessings for ever attend them!) pleaded the contrary.

Richardson could have given a speedy term to Belfour's appeal by invoking his prerogatives as author, or informing her that the third installment had already gone to press (for this was the case). In other words, he could have immediately closed the space for debate and interplay which Belfour's letter opened behind the half-published novel. Instead, Richardson answers her objections point by point and encourages continuing correspondence and debate. An unspoken premise gives these exchanges their vitality: that *Clarissa* is a text which might be written with either a "happy" or a "sad" ending. Richardson even admits that "invention was at liberty," and "Lovelace might have been drawn a Penitent" (*Letters*, 115; December 15, 1748). After the whole novel is out, Belfour suspects that she never could have had an effect on Richardson, and she sounds a little hurt and betrayed for having been misled:

> I am humble enough to own my want of power, I have only aimed at moving you by intreaties to compassion. You say it was impossible to be otherwise, and I must try to believe you. Had you told me so at first, it would have saved you an immense deal of trouble. [*Corr.*, IV, 214]

Sometimes the Belfour-Richardson debates take on all the playfulness of a game. Near the end of her first letter, Belfour adds a warning "curse" which neatly consigns Richardson to the company a moral author should have:

> If you disappoint me, attend to my curse:—May the hatred of all the young, beautiful, and virtuous, for ever be your portion! and may your eyes never behold anything but age and deformity! may you meet with applause only from envious old maids, surly bachelors, and tyrannical parents! may you be doomed to the company of such! and, after death, may their ugly souls haunt

you! Now make Lovelace and Clarissa unhappy if you dare. [*Corr.,* IV, 181; October 10, 1748]

But at times Belfour is graciously appreciative of the bother she might have become to the busy author. When she writes one letter immediately after another, she imitates Richardson's annoyance: "What! every post! No respite! No quiet! No hopes of being relieved from the persecutions of this troublesome woman!" (*Corr.,* IV, 202; November 20, 1748). She even offers a coy apology for refusing to grant Richardson's request that she abandon her pseudonym "Belfour" (*Corr.,* IV, 199). However earnest her argument becomes, this artful woman can modulate from an urgent seriousness to endearing raillery. Belfour has accused Richardson of sadistically enjoying the "destruction" of Lovelace, and then adds,

> After all, I believe you are of a cruel disposition; just now is one of those times I hate you, and I want to say something still more spiteful. But why should I add venom to my pen? I can plague you enough without that. [*Corr.,* IV, 244–45]

Belfour is always acutely aware of how little leverage she has in her attempts to influence Richardson. She goads him to accept her revision with a threat and a promise. If Richardson goes the path of "rape" and "ruin," she threatens to break the reader contract and never finish his book (*Corr.,* IV, 198). Richardson is disturbed enough by this to send Belfour a copy of the fifth volume, at the same time frequently urging her to continue her reading (*Letters,* 105). If Richardson will "make Clarissa and Lovelace happy," Belfour makes a solemn promise: "I will promise to read your history over, at least once in two years, as long as I live" (*Corr.,* IV, 184).

Repeated reading gives this final interpretation and rendering of the story Belfour's endorsement. The novel would then gain the authority and status of personal scripture. When she's disappointed by the author, she condemns him for destroying "the amusement of her life" (*Corr.,* IV, 207). Even when she does read the ending, she keeps clearly in mind the blissful happiness she had promised the two lovers and herself, and repudiates Richardson's (authoritative) version of the story, by refusing to ever look on this book again: "I will suppose it buried with my beloved Clarissa at the feet of her grandfather." She adds this taunt for Richardson: "It might have been otherwise; it might have been that some one of the volumes would for my life have adorned my toilet" (*Corr.,* IV, 253).

Belfour may be engaged in a playful debate with Richardson, but her stake in proceedings is real, and her attachment to the characters profound. Her ending for the novel—the reform of Lovelace and his marriage to Clarissa—is shaped to save the characters she adores. Thus she confesses to Richardson:

> You must know . . . that if I was to die for it, I cannot help being fond of Lovelace. A sad dog! why would you make him so wicked, and yet so agreeable? He says, sometime or other he designs being a good man, from which words I have great hopes; and, in excuse for my liking him, I must say, I have made him so, up to my heart's wish; a faultless husband have I made him, even without danger of a relapse. [*Corr.,* IV, 180–81; October 10, 1748]

Here Belfour is quite open in acknowledging that she has engaged in a fictional elaboration and completion of character. Thus she changes Lovelace "up to my heart's wish," so the work of art will meet her felt need, and Lovelace and Clarissa will be "hers." This leaves Belfour extremely vulnerable to the direction Richardson chooses to take with the artifice. When the novel's action turns against her, Belfour is taken through an involuntary sequence: anxiety for "her" characters as she awaits Richardson's verdict; a frantically proffered "revision" she hopes can reverse their fortunes; and a manner of suffering the loss of "her" characters which looks a lot like mourning.

After the first letter to Richardson and while waiting for the novel to be published, Belfour describes herself as alternating anxiously between "a faint glimmering of hope" and "despair" (*Corr.,* IV, 182). Her second letter has very little to say, but she finds that "write I must, or die, for I can neither eat or sleep till I am disburdened of my load" (*Corr.,* IV, 183). When she receives and reads volume 5, the rape has occurred. Belfour's sufferings intensify, and she gropes irrationally for a way out of this impasse: "Dear Sir, if it be possible—yet recall the dreadful sentence; bring it as near as you please, but prevent it. . . . Blot out but one night, and the villainous laudanum, and all may be well again."

Three days later, on November 17, 1748, Belfour has found a way to save Clarissa and Lovelace, even though the rape has occurred. She presents Richardson with her idea for an ending in three-page summary. This ending has the effect of "blotting out" the violent memory of the rape by making it part of the succession of trials which precede the reconciliation of hero and heroine. But once again Richardson follows his own lights in shaping his story. The tears and suffering Belfour experiences while reading the final two volumes are described with extravagant hyperbole. Even after finishing the novel her trial is not over: "My spirits are strangely seized, my sleep is disturbed; waking in the night, I burst into a passion of crying; so I did at breakfast this morning, and just now again" (*Corr.*, IV, 242).

We do not need to doubt the sincerity of these responses of Belfour's in order to notice a certain artfulness about them. For these displays of passion gain added resonance and authority from the example the novel provides. Belfour's reading experience imitates Clarissa's passion. Her initial anxiety is like Clarissa's fearful wait the night of the rape. After reading about the rape, Belfour writes, "I am mad as the poor injured Clarissa." The ending she sends frantically to Richardson works to blot out catastrophe, as Clarissa's papers written in "madness" displace her loss into more bearable fictional forms. Finally, Belfour enhances the authority of her sufferings through explicit comparison with the ways Belford and Lovelace mourn the death of Clarissa (*Corr.*, IV, 241, 243).

When Belfour had read the fifth volume it did not take much imagination to see that Richardson was guiding his story toward a tragic conclusion. Belfour is shocked by the rape, but she quickly rallies to offer Richardson her revision of the anticipated ending. This ingenious piece of composition would save Lovelace and Clarissa from the disaster the rape seems to portend:

Suppose Clarissa, after having been brought to the verge of the grave by the ill treatment she has received; suppose she should, by using proper means, assisted by her own divine reflections, and a consciousness of her innocence, so far compose her mind, that she is in a great measure restored to her former state of health, but still steady in her refusal of Lovelace; upon which, he, being overwhelmed with grief, remorse, and self condemnation, is thrown into a dangerous fever, or any other illness, so as to make his life despaired of. At the desire of a dying man, the good Dr. Lewen intreats and prevails with compassionate Clarissa to make him a visit, as a charitable act. (What an interesting scene

might you there introduce!) He endeavours to excite her pity
and forgiveness. She promises him her prayers, and a second visit;
when we will suppose him given over by his physicians, and in all
appearance very near his end; and, after receiving the communion
together, as a token of their perfect charity to each other, would
the following request be inconsistent with his present circumstances? That she would condescend, in her great charity and
goodness, to suffer Dr. Lewen to join their hands, that he might
have the blessing and satisfaction of dying her husband; which
would enable him to bear with greater resignation, the tremen-
dous change just now commencing; and, as he should think himself united to her spotless soul, he might hope, as a part of it, to
be admitted into the awful presence of the great God, whom for
some time past he has worshipped with as much zeal, as she once
kindly wished him to do. Might not this move her to comply, at
least to a promise of marriage in case of his recovery? From which
promise, by proper care and application, his disorder may take an
unexpected turn, and he be restored to life, to health, and to Clarissa. What joy must she feel to have so much good in her power,
to perform at her will!

Methinks I see her as his wife, or wife elect, kindly attending
and administering means for his recovery, (which we will imagine
for some time doubtful); he eagerly receiving it, as draughts of
life from her hands. This goodness is accompanied with her constant and fervent prayers for the success of such means, which, if
they prove effectual, may establish them in mutual and uninterrupted happiness; I see her resentment over, her stifled love returning with double force; with the addition of an esteem for
him, to which, from his former demerits, she was before a strang-
er. [*Corr.*, IV, 205]

Belfour's suggested ending is not only outrageously sentimental; it is
also an ingenious way to undo the damage of the rape, return the
story to the comic-romantic possibilities of the proposal scenes, and
then exploit those possibilities (see above, pp. 81ff.). By slipping
to the verge of death and then recovering her health, Clarissa could
not regain her lost virginity, but she would earn back a semblance of
wholeness and purity. Lovelace's illness is a penalty for his evil deeds,
and a way to do penance for them. Dr. Lewen's appeal, Clarissa's

Christian charity, and Lovelace's weakened state combine to bring the estranged lovers together on his deathbed. By taking communion with Clarissa, Lovelace acknowledges the power of religion. This represents a victory for the values Clarissa has always championed, and shows that he has finally embarked on the journey toward reformation she had always planned for him.

At this point in the story, Belfour shows herself to be a mistress of sentimental invention. She uses the chief obstacle to reformation—the evil of the rape—to add poignancy to Lovelace's request that she marry him on his deathbed. For only with Clarissa as his mediator with God can he have hopes of heaven. When his health takes "an unexpected turn" for the better, Lovelace is "restored to life, to health, and to Clarissa." But something very important has changed. Power relations are completely inverted from what they were before the rape. Clarissa is no longer an encircled victim. She is a gentle but masterful physician who labours to heal Lovelace's body and soul. He is "eagerly receiving" her care, "as draughts of life from her hands." Clarissa is safe to feel redoubled "love" and a new "esteem," because she has become the angelic guarantor of Lovelace's permanent reformation. The resolution of tensions between hero and heroine is complete; all struggle has ended.

What does Belfour's ending do to the text? While Belfour was writing this letter, the sixth and seventh volumes were moving through the presses. In those volumes Clarissa is busy perfecting a very different design. We have seen that Clarissa's acceptance of death, and her construction of a book around the event, enables her to confer a special value on all the earlier events of her life. Now the rape is the decisive center of her story, and all the events before the rape take their value, as causes and effects, in relation to the rape. Belfour has worked in a very similar way. By contriving to marry Lovelace and Clarissa, the rape does not become a critical event in Clarissa's life. Instead, it is merely the last in a long succession of trials, building toward a climactic reversal in the protagonist's deathbed marriage.

In designing things this way, Belfour merely reactivates the comic strata of the text that Clarissa worked to put out of play: the romantic evocations of the initial situation, the battle of the sexes, and the openings toward love and marriage. Belfour also offers resistance to Clarissa's willingness to die, her melancholy tendency to find a "strange fatality" in her life, and the whole pattern of meaning and virtue she uncovers there. Belfour ends on the same side of this issue as characters like Anna, Belford, Lovelace, and others, who labor to win a reconciliation through marriage. All were perfectly aware that marriage was the one event which could atone for the violence of the rape. Ironically, Lovelace wishfully imagines something very close to Belfour's resolution—Clarissa rushing back to him during his serious illness (IV, 297).

Belfour was not the only reader of the novel who felt the story could and should end in marriage. Colley Cibber and Henry Fielding are only the most distinguished of a host of readers who advised Richardson to end the novel happily. Nor was Belfour alone in supplying a new ending to the novel. Quite independently, Belfour's older sister, Lady Echlin, was disturbed enough by the rape of Clarissa and the death of the protagonists that she composed a new 166-page conclusion to the novel. In this version, Clarissa is never raped and Lovelace dies a penitent, perfectly reconciled to the dying Clarissa.[9]

In writing her suggested ending to the story, Belfour feels she is offering Richardson a way to perfect his own work. Belfour communicates this idea with firmness and grace in the paragraphs that follow her suggested ending. The metaphor and myth she employs to explain the artist's activity will give us a deeper understanding of Belfour's response to *Clarissa*:

> I know not whether the above scheme be new or not, but it appears to me very delightful. I said before, I did believe you had a noble one within you; I wish you would produce it, though sure I am it would make all I have produced appear like nothing. You are in love with your image as it is, and you will be more so, by giving it additional and enlivening graces. A picture, by being touched and retouched by an unskillful hand, might be defaced and spoiled; but a master must, by each stroke, add a new beauty, and heighten his piece.
>
> Can you be in love, and be pleased with the death of what you love? It is not in nature; nor can you be a *perfect Pygmalion* without giving *life* to your image. [*Corr.*, IV, 206]

9. This manuscript, in the Berg Collection of The New York Public Library, makes very amusing reading. Richardson was also amused, and wonders why Lady Echlin must kill Clarissa and Lovelace, since the rape never occurs. He playfully suggests that Lady Echlin might have left Lovelace "shining as a governor of one of the American colonies." See Eaves and Kimpel, *Samuel Richardson*, pp. 448–49.

Now we can see the subtlety of what Belfour has done. She offers a revised ending of *Clarissa*—one that is comic, affirmative, and conciliatory—and then she gently backs off, giving Richardson back his brush, as if to say, "But really, I've just been showing you one way to save Clarissa and Lovelace—it is you, the 'master,' who must add new touches to your portrait so as to complete your own scheme."

Belfour assumes the role of a solicitous advisor, who sees that Richardson has a "noble" design "within" him, but fears he is in danger of losing it. She tempts and woos Richardson toward a revised ending by comparing him to a master painter. He must add brush-strokes to retouch and "heighten" an image that is almost complete. The analogy is significant, because the very slightness of brush strokes makes this activity seem innocent. Belfour has offered an imperfect model for a new ending. If done properly, a new ending will not deface but enliven. It will be a supplement which will complete or perfect the image Richardson has *already* sketched.

This helps us to reassess the meaning of Belfour's proposed ending. It is less a plausible conclusion to the story than an interpretation of the text. Thus Belfour claims to understand, and wishes to determine what the text "is." She has read the first five volumes with consummate attention. She feels that the love, marriage, and good feelings invoked by the novel are more important than the violence and ill will that add shades of darkness to the story—so, she constructs her ending accordingly. Belfour looks upon this ending the way Richardson looks at his—it is "from the Premises the only natural one!" Like most interpreters, she pretends not to have added anything to the text that is not, in some sense, already there. Of course, Richardson and Belfour are both keenly aware of the importance of winning this struggle. Both expect their ending to be a crucial increment—one which will have the power to control the meaning of the whole text.

But why do Belfour and Richardson expend so much energy in an effort to control the text that lies between them? And what kind of relationship does each hope to win with *Clarissa*? When Belfour, in her first letter to the author, accuses Richardson of undue cruelty to his own heroine, Richardson pleads that he too is sensitive to Clarissa's suffering. He adds, "Nor can I go through some of the Scenes myself without being sensibly touched (Did I not say, that I was another Pygmalion?)" (*Letters*, 90; October 26, 1748). By comparing himself to Pygmalion, Richardson confesses to having fallen in love with his own creation. Belfour turns this allusion against him by asking, rhetorically, if it can be nature to be "pleased with the death of what you love." She adds, "nor can you be a *perfect Pygmalion* without giving *life* to your image." That Belfour and Richardson both invoke the Pygmalion myth to bolster their positions is significant. Each hopes to play Pygmalion to *Clarissa*; each strives to get the text to turn his or her way, to come alive, and exist as his or her very own private possession. If we read the Pygmalion myth with attention, we shall be able to gauge the discrepancy between the version of the reader's role it implies and the actual situation common to Belfour and Richardson. In other words, this myth, inscribed as an exergue to this chapter, will allow us to interpret the interpreters of *Clarissa*.

Pygmalion escapes from the profane public world of "shameful" prostitutes into the private world of his own art. Here he can create an image of woman that has hyperbolic beauty and purity. This initiates a time of fantasy play with this "ivory girl." She has a boundary status: neither person nor statue, Pygmalion is puzzled by his own illusion and wonders if she might be real. He asks, "Could this be flesh, or was it ivory only?" He answers 'no,' but treats her as if she were real. He brings her gifts, drapes her body with clothes, and takes her to bed with him. But this situation proves ultimately unsatisfactory. Either the illusion is transient, or it does not have the satisfaction that comes with possessing a "real" girl. Thus Pygmalion returns to the public sphere he once abandoned. Here, praying at the altar of Venus on a festival day, Pygmalion's fantasy world seems less authentic than before, so he phrases his wish in a disguised form: "I pray my wife may be," not "My ivory girl," but "one like my ivory girl." Venus gratifies Pygmalion's quest to have his fondest wish in actuality. He returns home to find his "own workmanship" a real woman, and his to enjoy.

In the context of Belfour's debate with Richardson, it is not difficult to see the special appeal this story must have had for Belfour. The story of Pygmalion can serve as a model for a *Clarissa* she could live with. Not only does the heroine go from "death" to life, but all ends in the idyllic union Belfour wants for Clarissa and Lovelace. But more significantly, the Pygmalion story articulates the kind of relationship Belfour, as a reader, seeks with the text of *Clarissa*. She too has removed herself from the mundane world to enter the fantasy life of art. In embracing this fictional illusion, Belfour is just as active as the Pygmalion who shapes his idea of perfection into an "ivory girl" he can love; all the time that she reads, Belfour builds her story (of love, reformation, and marriage) into the novel Richardson is writing. When this story is threatened by a tragic ending, Belfour becomes the suppliant praying before the temple of Venus. If Richardson will only accept her idea for a happy ending, then Belfour will have achieved something as wonderful as Pygmalion's return to his "ivory girl." For Belfour, this miraculous coming to life would correspond to the moment when the text is "real" for her as reader, because her interpretation—what she takes the text to be—enlivens, that is, breathes (her) life and desire into the text. Now she will see her idea in the text; the text will mirror this idea back to her. Interpretation and text will seem to achieve closure with one another. As with the union of Pygmalion and his "ivory girl," no one will question the authority (i.e. the reality) of this marriage.

A full understanding of Richardson's interpretations of *Clarissa* will only be possible after an analysis of his responses to Belfour. But it is already easy to see why the Pygmalion story can also serve him. By invoking Pygmalion, Richardson makes himself the adoring artist-creator of his "ivory girl," Clarissa. In such an alignment, Lovelace is a rival for Clarissa's attentions who must be kept separate from the divine Clarissa. By contrast, Belfour can enjoy Lovelace in fantasy through Clarissa. For both Belfour and Richardson, the struggles of interpretation around *Clarissa* raise a similar problem. If Richardson is going to enjoy full control and possession of the novel he has conceived, then he must win public acceptance for *his* interpretation of this story. Now Richardson will no longer be Venus to Belfour's Pygmalion; he is a Pygmalion who approaches the altar, hoping for sympathy and understanding from this divinity, the reader.

There are two reasons why the Pygmalion story offers a flawed (or wishful and deluded) picture of the reader-interpreter's relationship to *Clarissa*. First, the "ivory girl" sustains an almost complete passivity in relationship to Pygmalion. Thus she is created by and for her maker's pleasure; she has no name, and speaks no words. Secondly, Pygmalion's story unfolds in a world almost entirely insulated from any social or political transactions. For one brief moment (in going to Venus with his prayer), Pygmalion ventures into a public sphere

where give-and-take and compromise might be in the offing. But
there he simply wins full confirmation of his fantasy life. In marshal-
ling their interpretations of *Clarissa*, Belfour and Richardson take
particular steps to render the text passive and other readers quiescent.

We have seen that Joseph Spence interprets the text as virgin in its
purity by exalting Belford's position in the novel until it seems to
control the whole text. In a very similar fashion, Belfour seeks to
control the story for a conciliatory marriage by adopting Anna
Howe's practical and worldly perspective on Clarissa's situation.
Although Belfour is usually more romantic and sentimental than
Anna, Belfour harbors the same secret admiration for Lovelace, and
she contrives an ending which fulfills Anna's dream of female dominance over the male, by assimilating Lovelace's roguery to Clarissa's
connubial bliss.

But the text of *Clarissa* is never as compliant as Pygmalion's "ivory
girl." It offers myriad forms of resistance to the future Belfour
would impose on the protagonists. Thus, after the rape, Lovelace
offers a parodic version of Belfour's wish when he mocks Clarissa for
having "formed pretty notions of how charming it would look to
have a penitent of her own making dangling at her side to church
thro' an applauding neighborhood" (III,316). The idea clearly does
not appeal to Lovelace. In a more serious moment, he worries about
how drab and ordinary his relationship with Clarissa might become if
all the conflict and passion of their ongoing adventure were con-
tracted to a permanent condition (see above, chapter 2). But Belfour
also contravenes the will of the very heroine she would make happy.
Thus marriage with Lovelace would impose a series of actions on
Clarissa: it would mean accepting compromise with all her adversaries, forging a composition with her past failings, and ending the
dream of establishing herself (through her death and the book) on
the high ground of a truly distinctive personal merit and virtue.

Precisely because Richardson wrote this novel, the text does not
spare its author the same kind of resistances it develops against Belfour. We have seen the kinds of disputes the novel stimulated upon
publication. When these debates threatened to go out of control,
Richardson developed an interpretation of his own novel which
worked to return the text to some of the simplicity and discipline
it seemed to have lost. Richardson did this by giving a more and

more insistent emphasis to Clarissa's role as an exemplar of virtue. But this could only be done by stilling the voices of those, like Bella, James, and Lovelace, who had always questioned Clarissa's motives in wanting to be a paragon.

Now we can see that the readers of *Clarissa* we have studied (Spence, Belfour, Richardson) seek to master the text by subordinating all of the text to one moment or position of the text. This creates the illusion of the text's passivity which, in turn, lends credence to their interpretive mastery of *Clarissa*. This helps to advance another activity—the effort to depoliticize the community of readers (of course, such effort is itself political). Since these readers want us to believe the text simply "is" what they interpret it to be, there is no need for disagreement about the novel. Thus, each of these readers finds a way to tame or discredit debate. Spence scorns as mere "carpers" the rival readers and critics who would change the shape, length, and boundary of *Clarissa*. He also asserts the prior authority of the author's design (which, of course, Richardson never stops modifying). Belfour tries to charm and cajole Richardson into accepting an ending she avows "all" her friends also desire. And finally, while he encourages debate for a time, Richardson soon begins to make his text something of a heavily defended fortress—one that will anticipate every attack by the design of its outer perimeter. When hardpressed, Richardson even stoops to rudely revoking his reader's freedom and asserting his special prerogative as author.

We may summarize our discussion of the way the text of *Clarissa* is depicted and her readers behave by posing an alternative. If the text is represented so that the whole is subordinated to one of its moments, positions, or characters, it may act like an "ivory girl" and passively assimilate itself to its reader's desire. Then a closure of meaning among the text, the reader, and a community of readers is possible. In other words, things may end as the story of Pygmalion ends. But if *Clarissa* operates as a succession of shifting positions in a relationship of struggle and tension with one another, then the history of its reading will be just as turbulent, and a closure of meaning may never occur.

Richardson's Defense of Clarissa, *1: The Position of Judgment*

In defending his ending of *Clarissa*, Richardson asks Belfour if she has not seen, "from infancy," "in Lovelace the early libertine, in [Clarissa] the early Saint?—the one in a manner calling out for Punishment—the other for a heavenly crown?" (*Letters*, 94). These words give us a clue to Richardson's mode of participation in *Clarissa*. He assumes the role of a judge—both in the determination of Clarissa's and Lovelace's fate, and in his defense of that determination through his letters to Belfour. He outlines his position to Belfour with an impressive display of rationality.

Since *Clarissa* is a work in which he proposes to "follow Nature," Richardson must shape the action so that it conveys a plausible picture of the ways of the world. Thus there are many factors militating against the quick reformation of a man such as Lovelace: "Reformation is not . . . a sudden thing, in a Man long immersed in Vice—The temptations to it, as from sex to sex, so natural; constitution, as in such a character as Lovelace, so promotive, a love of intrigue so predominant—so great a self admirer—so supposedly admired by others" (*Letters*, 94). In ending the story as he has, Richardson has delivered his judgment on Lovelace's character *and* the character of an actual public type—the libertine Lovelace represents. In a similar way, Richardson justifies the plausibility of the tragic ending by appealing to the inevitable trials of real life. Thus he tells of the long succession of deaths in his own family and insists that a "writer who follows nature . . . cannot make a heaven in this world for his favorites" (*Letters*, 109–10, 108).

But the novel's ending must not only correspond with Richardson's sense of the world; it must also be compatible with the other parts of itself. So Richardson represents this ending as an act of artistic judgment which is consonant with the nature of the characters and action, and the way they combine to form one harmonious whole. This allows Richardson to tease Belfour with the incongruity of making Clarissa an efficient producer of babies: "Let us attend Clarissa in the Issue of her supposed Nuptials. We will imagine her to have repeatedly escaped the perils of Child birth. How many children shall we give her? Five? Six? Seven? How many, Madam? Not less I hope" (*Letters*, 107). By emphasizing one aspect of the happy ending Belfour advocates—Clarissa's role as a mother—Richardson makes this ending seem grotesque and implausible. Clarissa as the mother of seven babies diverges rather wildly from the refined and ardent young woman who battles Lovelace to protect her physical integrity.

Sometimes Richardson goes so far as to assert that the course of the action fulfills a natural entelechy, which makes his ending not only just and likely but even inevitable. Thus Richardson offers Belfour this explanation for Lovelace's evil: "Mr. Lovelace's Mother is often hinted at in the Progress of the story, as having by her faulty indulgence to him in his early youth, been the occasion of that uncontrolableness of will, which proved so fatal to many innocents and in the end to himself" (*Letters*, 116). Richardson often blamed his readers for missing these details, and he praises Lady Bradshaigh, late in their correspondence, for the repeated readings of his novels that allow her "to examine into the unjustness or justness of a novel's several parts, as they contribute to make one whole" (*Letters*, 289; February 14, 1754).

This phase of Richardson's defense of *Clarissa* rests on a two-part argument: an argument from "nature" (the ending is plausible given the nature of the characters, and the world they represent); and an argument from the form of the work of art (the ending is necessary given the relationship of the parts to the whole). The first presents an author who is sage in his knowledge of the world; the second, one who shapes and unifies his work with adroitness. Both these arguments emerge from the intrinsic qualities of *Clarissa*—what *Clarissa* is in itself, and as a mirror of the world.

But Richardson also develops a defense of *Clarissa* which argues from extrinsic factors, such as the experience he wishes to orchestrate for his reader—the suffering he would cause, and the values he wishes to instil. Thus Belford carries out a full comparison of Clarissa and Calista, the heroine of Rowe's *The Fair Penitent*. He demonstrates the ways in which Clarissa is a true tragic heroine who displays real penitence and piety, while Calista is a flawed heroine: "She has no virtue; is all pride; and her devil is as much *within* her as *without* her" (IV,118–20). By invoking *The Fair Penitent* within the novel, Belford and Richardson establish a context within which *Clarissa* should be read. Since Rowe has failed to give the world a fair penitent, Richardson will. *Clarissa* is also written against the context established by Richardson's earlier novel, *Pamela*. Richardson discredits Belfour's idea for a worldly triumph by Clarissa, asking:

Had I drawn my Heroine reconciled to Relations unworthy of her, nobly resisting the attacks of an intrepid Lover; overcoming

her Persecutors; and baffling the Wicked Designs formed against
her Honour, marrying her Lovelace, and that on her own terms—
educating properly and instructing her Children—What however
useful, however pleasing the Lesson, I had done more than I had
done in *Pamela*? [*Letters*, 93]

By distinguishing *Clarissa* from two similar works (*The Fair Penitent* and *Pamela*), Richardson assumes the position of a judicious
moralist and artist who is intent on communicating particular ideas
to the readers of *Clarissa*. Richardson defines these ideas, with an
almost disappointing clarity, in one of his early letters to Aaron Hill.

It is one of my principal views, to admonish parents against forc-
ing their children's inclinations, in an Article so essential to their
happiness, as marriage. . . . And then I was willing to explode
that pernicious notion, that a reformed rake makes the best husband. I had further intended to make her so faultless, that a
reader should find no way to account for the calamities she met
with, and to justify moral equity but by looking up to a future
reward; another one of my principal doctrines. [*Letters*, 73;
October 29, 1746]

Warning parents against forced marriages, children against "reformed rakes," and looking to the afterlife for justice—these are
three lessons Richardson hopes to inculcate in his reader. How does
he do it? He arranges the sequence of the action to give each of
these ideas special urgency. Thus, the attempt by Clarissa's family
to foist Solmes on Clarissa is presented as the key factor in pushing
her toward Lovelace. Richardson explains, "I was desirous, that
it should appear to a reader, that had so excellent a creature been
left to her self, well as she might have liked him had he been a moral
man, she would have overcome her liking to him, and despised him."
Further, if Clarissa had been forewarned of the danger of rakes, and
the difficulty of reforming them, she might not have trusted Lovelace. Finally, Richardson makes Clarissa so generally "faultless"
that a search by the reader for a justifiable cause for her fall must
prove largely fruitless. This leads to the reader's revision of the meaning of the ending, so that it tallies with Clarissa's proven virtue; her
death is not a sign of sin and disfavor, but a passage toward an enduring reward in heaven.

In all these ways, Richardson interprets his novel by appealing to
a code or system which Richardson is sure holds sway in "real"

life, that he has woven into the unfolding of his text and which he expects the reader to resort to in interpreting the events of the story: the idea that the events of the world are ultimately shaped into a providential pattern which reflects the rewards and punishments of a just God. In an earlier chapter we have seen that the idea of life as the scene of judgment is never far from Clarissa's consciousness. It is the guiding principle in the shaping of her book. Richardson praises Clarissa for upholding this legal, ethical system.

In a moment when her life seems to take a wrong turn, Clarissa severely blames herself for continuing her correspondence with Lovelace, against paternal prohibition. Richardson explains by quoting the novel: "She charges herself with this Fault, I think very exemplarily in the Woodhouse—when surprised and terrified at finding from behind the Wood, a Man coming towards her, who proved to be Lovelace.—'O thought I, at that Moment, the Sin of a prohibited Correspondence!'" (*Letters*, 199; March 2, 1752). What is the "theme" Richardson communicates in *Clarissa*? Less the three messages described above, though they are important, than the general notion of a providential, rule-governed, judicial system that the reader must assume and utilize in order to read those three messages. God lies at the center of that system as it is assumed to function in the world; but Richardson makes himself the God-like judge and architect who sets that system working in the novel called *Clarissa*. This is why he never questions his own right to award Clarissa a heavenly crown, and Lovelace his final punishment.

But the efficacy of the position of judge depends on the judge's impartiality and disinterestedness—and his separation, in the most decisive fashion, from the struggle his courtroom reenacts. And during the course of Richardson's correspondence with Belfour, interesting evidence comes to light which puts Richardson's impartiality in doubt. To see how this happens we need to note an important way in which the Belfour-Richardson exchange resembles the struggles between Clarissa and Lovelace. Through the course of the protagonists' struggle, Clarissa continually expands the range of her response to Lovelace. Increasingly she imitates Lovelace in using contrived melodrama to participate in the novel's big scenes, and she surpasses him in subtlety of artifice when she writes him the allegorical note about "going to my father's house." Adversaries in struggle—like the two parties in a duel—often offer mirror images of one another. This helps to explain why Belfour's correspondence greatly expands the range of Richardson's comments on his own text; for the first time, we begin to see what Richardson's relationship to the novel's characters might be.

In pushing for a happy ending, Belfour can think of rational arguments to give cogency to her position: Clarissa's virtue should be rewarded, not punished; Lovelace may be reformed in gradual steps; and the violent rape of Clarissa will be an example of evil for the unguarded reader (*Corr.* IV, 179; 196; 201). But Belfour never conceals the level of "dumb assertion" that impels her advocacy of a happy ending. She admits to making Lovelace the "faultless husband" of Clarissa, "up to her own heart's wish" (*Corr.*, IV, 180; see also above, p. 162). She does so because she simply *wants* it that way. And when Richardson professes surprise and concern that Lovelace "should meet with so much favour from the good and virtuous," Belford rejoins, "You may assure yourself the good and virtuous are utter enemies to all his wickedness, and are only pleased with the distant view and hopes of his becoming the good, the virtuous, the tender husband of Clarissa" (*Corr.*, IV, 195). Because of the directness and urgency of her own participation in the fiction, Belfour is disinclined to accept the more elaborate reasons Richardson offers in defense of his ending. Thus, when Richardson sketches out the carefully related intrinsic and extrinsic factors that justify the deaths of Clarissa and Lovelace, Belfour simply responds by accusing him of being sadistic toward Lovelace: "I fancy, Sir, you found yourself remarkably easy as to Lovelace, when you had sent him to destruction, both of body and soul. It seemed to be a favorite point with you" (*Corr.*, IV, 244). This kind of accusation could not fail to provoke a spirited rejoinder from Richardson.

Richardson responds to Belfour's plan for a happy ending with these words:

> And as to reforming and marrying Lovelace, and the Example to be given by it, what but This that follows, would it have been, instead of the amiable one your Good nature and Humanity point out?—here, says another Lovelace, may I pass the Flower and Prime of my Youth, in forming and pursuing the most insidious Enterprises—I may delude and ruin my Miss Betterton, I may form Plots against and destroy my French countess. As many of

the Daughters and Sisters of worthy Families, as I can seduce, may I seduce, Scores perhaps in different Climates—And on their Weakness build my profligate Notions of the whole Sex—I may at last meet with and attempt a Clarissa, a Lady of peerless Virtue. I may try her, vex her, plague and torment her worthy Heart. I may set up all my Batteries against her Virtue. And if I find her Proof against all my Machinations, and myself tired with rambling, I may then reward that Virtue. I may graciously extend my Hand. She may give me hers, and rejoice and thank Heaven for my Condescension in her Favour. [*Letters*, 93]

Richardson offers this parody of Lovelace as part of an apparently reasonable argument. A Lovelace who could marry Clarissa, after his manifold offenses, would offer a bad example to readers. Richardson makes his point by bringing Lovelace back to life at the moment when he has decided to accept the injured Clarissa as his wife.

But the result is hardly a dispassionate presentation of evidence. Richardson is not interested in imagining the possibility of a Lovelace who has been changed by his ordeal with Clarissa; he refuses to join Belfour in envisioning Lovelace as a "good," or "virtuous," or "tender" husband for Clarissa. Instead, Richardson presents a Lovelace who is a caricature of himself—the libertine par excellence. His life has become a catalogue of seductions, and his relationship with Clarissa (and all the mutuality of struggle it involves), a place where it pleases his fancy to come to rest and exercise a "condescension in her favour."

Richardson's parody of Lovelace serves as a reminder that imitation can be a form of revenge—a way of fixing, and anathemizing, an enemy.[10] This parody captures the side of Lovelace which Richardson must have hated: his smug egotism, his sublime self-centeredness, above all, his sense that he could have or do anything he wanted. Thus the whole passage is structured around repetitions of the words "I may." And it is to this comprehensive sense of personal license which Richardson responds with his own will and assertion—his determination that Lovelace *may not* have Clarissa.

After the second installment was out, Richardson wrote Aaron Hill, "I intend another sort of happiness for my heroine, than that

10. On mimesis and revenge, see René Girard, *La Violence et le sacré* (Paris: Grosset, 1972).

which was to depend upon the will and pleasure, and uncertain reformation of a vile libertine to whom I could not think of giving a lady of such excellence—And to rescue her from a rake, and give a triumph to her not only over him but over all her oppressors, and the world besides, in a triumphant death—I thought as noble a view, as it was new" (*Letters*, 87; April 10, 1748). Richardson "rescues" Clarissa from Lovelace by spurning openings toward union and compromise, and going forward with the rape that must estrange these lovers. It is this "outrage"—which is Richardson's as much as Lovelace's—that begins the separation of Clarissa from her antagonist. It is from the vantage point of the rape that Richardson insists on Lovelace's meanness, and Clarissa's incalculably greater value:

> Clarissa has the greatest Triumphs even in this World. The greatest I will venture to say, even *in*, and *after* the Outrage, and *because* of the Outrage that ever Woman had. And wherein would have been her Triumph, had she been so *dishonest* I will call it, to her own Fame and Glory, as to marry the Man, whose Vices and Attempts had made him so infinitely her Inferior, and who was meanly Capable of being Jealous of a Wife's superior Talents, instead of glowing in the Acquisition, and that he could call a Jewel in full and absolute Property his own. [*Letters,* 108]

But who is Richardson to be assessing the true value of Clarissa and Lovelace? What is Richardson's relationship to this story? "Where" is he in relation to this text? We have seen that he pretends to stand outside, surveying its elements and motions with calm interest, so as to see it whole. He even poses as a judge who can stand back, appraise character, award crowns, and deliver stern sentences. But when we see *how* Richardson becomes involved in the struggles of interpretation which open around this text, when we notice the level of sheer assertion in his lowering of Lovelace and his exaltation of Clarissa, we must revise this picture. For in spite of all his judicial poses, Richardson can never really stand outside—he is really always right in the middle—of the struggle between Clarissa and Lovelace which "is" this text. And even when Clarissa and Lovelace descend to the quiet of their graves, their struggle is displaced into a new arena as the interpretive struggle between two kinds of readers: those who glory in Clarissa's triumph and those who admire the departed Lovelace. And Richardson becomes a partisan in this struggle.

Richardson never had any difficulty envisioning the errant reader of his own text; he was always getting letters from them. That is why his parody of Lovelace is delivered, not by Lovelace himself, but by a reader who becomes "another Lovelace" through a conscious imitation of the rake. Richardson is intent on putting every possible obstacle in the way of such a reader. One way is to send Lovelace down to defeat before the superior swordsmanship and bravery of Clarissa's cousin Morden. Another is to present Clarissa as a stark and imposing ideal of virtue. These ambitions for Clarissa make the compromises Belfour urges to win a happy ending most unappealing to Richardson. He asks Belfour, "But let us suppose the Story to end, as you, Madam would have it; what of extraordinary would there be in it? After infinite Trials. . . ." Richardson then ticks off all the "painful circumstances" Clarissa would have to cope with, and asks "What in a Happiness so common, and so private, (The Lady of equal Degree with the Gentleman, and of superior, at least equal Talents, so not preferred by the Marriage for her sufferings) worth troubling the World about?" (*Letters*, 106). The final phrase gives us a key to Richardson's intention: he is determined to "trouble the world" with the story of Clarissa Harlowe. In a letter to a young barrister named David Graham, Richardson explains why his novel meets with such resistance:

> Whoever aims to give the World a good Character either of Man or Woman, provokes a Scrutiny into it; and as every one will take measure of it by their own Standard, no wonder, that with some its very Perfections are made its Faults. It is an invidious Task to set up an Example to those who are resolved not to look out of themselves for one; and whose Errors are wrought into Habit. The best Lessons will be treated by such as Reflections upon their own Conduct and Morals. [*Letters*, 157; May 3, 1750]

One of Richardson's female correspondents, Francis Granger, warns Richardson that his heroine exerts an unpleasant pressure on the reader. The women who accept Clarissa must "own themselves very weak and her very wise, and what lady would choose to do that?" Richardson heartily agrees:

This is the very Reason by which I have taken the Liberty to ac-
acount, elsewhere, for the good Reception the Character of the
weak, the insipid, the Runaway, the Inn-frequenting Sophia has
met with. In that, as in the character of her illegitimate Tom,
there is nothing that very Common Persons may not attain to;
Nothing that will reproach the Conduct or Actions of very ordinary Capacities, and very free Livers; while Clarissa's Character,
as it might appear unattainable by them, might be supposed Pru-
dish, too delicate, and a silent Reproach to themselves. [*Letters,*
143; January 22, 1749/50]

The extraordinary success of *Tom Jones* cast a pall over the reception of the last installment of *Clarissa*, and the enthusiastic reception
given Fielding's novel is part of the context for Richardson's efforts
to defend his heroine. Richardson will not indulge his reader's weak-
nesses; he hopes to teach difficult lessons. He explains one of these
lessons to Belfour, by quoting Clarissa's description of life as "the
greatest disease of all." He adds a statement that shows a bit of
perverseness: "Such are the Lessons I endeavor to inculcate by an
Example in natural Life. And the more irksome these Lessons are to
the Young, the Gay, and the Healthy, the more necessary are they to
be inculcated" (*Letters,* 91).

How does one reconcile Richardson's pose as a judicious moralist
and artist with his partisanship in the Clarissa-Lovelace confrontation, or the pleasure he seems to take in being "irksome" to many of
his readers? The role of judge allows Richardson to exert authority
over his adversaries—whether they be Lovelace or those who read
with Lovelace—*while* he seems to administer laws, and work within
a system of justice that exists apart from and above all the exigencies
of struggle. Intrinsic and extrinsic justifications for his own ending
conceal and disguise the simplest strata of the text: the level of
"dumb" assertion at work in his exaltation of Clarissa, and the defeat of Lovelace. The position of judgment, with its attendant claims
to authority, is simply the subtlest creation of passions, attachments,
and ambitions that are human—all too human.

Richardson's Defense of Clarissa, 2: Taking Sums

By now we can see that Richardson was more than willing to involve himself with the reception *Clarissa* won. When Aaron Hill "misread" *Clarissa*, Richardson spent a year revising the text for publication. When Belfour urged a happy ending to the story, Richardson opened an extensive correspondence designed to explain the reasons for the ending he composed, an ending he was sure would satisfy every attentive reader. But when the completed novel was delivered to the public, and readers *still* persisted in asserting a misguided understanding of the novel, a new tone of irritation entered Richardson's correspondence. At best, these readers are accused of being guilty of flagrant inattention to the novel's design; at worst, an immoral admiration for Lovelace. Richardson met this challenge to his art by carrying out significant changes in the body of *Clarissa*. These modifications came in two waves. In April 1749, six months after releasing the final installment of the first edition, Richardson published a second edition that included footnotes and a long index summary of the novel, placed at the beginning of the text. Over the next two years, serious "errors" of reading continued, so in the spring of 1751 Richardson published a third edition that wove two hundred pages of additional material into the text.

By adding notes and an index to *Clarissa,* Richardson did not feel that he was changing his novel. Rather, he was regulating the reader's experience of the novel. Reflecting on the need for this, Richardson wrote to Aaron Hill, "While the Taste of the Age can be gratified by a Tom Jones . . . I am not to expect that the World will bestow Two Readings, or One indeed, attentive one, on such a grave Story as Clarissa" (*Letters*, 126; July 12, 1749). What does Richardson mean by an "attentive" reading? And how does he guarantee there will be one? *Clarissa* is constructed by piecing together the narratives of Clarissa, who would like to give a full and faithful account of proceedings but lacks the information to do so, and Lovelace, who has the information but prefers to tease his reader by sprinkling his account with half-truths and possibilities (Who is Tomlinson? Is there a respectable woman named Fretchville who will sell her house to Lovelace, so Clarissa may leave Sinclair's?).

Richardson's text requires a reader who can juggle divergent accounts, sift each bit of evidence, be patient enough to entertain many possibilities, and revise old understanding in the light of new information. Mark Kinkead-Weekes describes Richardson as a "dramatic" novelist for his ability to let the meanings and directions of his fiction unfold in subtle movements which involve the reader. Thus when Clarissa is favorably impressed by Lovelace's "respectful behavior" at the woodhouse, an "attentive" reader will remember that Lovelace planned it that way: "By *my* humility will I invite *her* confidence" (I,175–76). When Anna tells Clarissa of Lovelace's generous treatment of Rosebud, the "attentive" reader will not follow Clarissa in thinking well of Lovelace. He will remember that one reason Lovelace offers for his restraint in sparing Rosebud is the possibility that his behavior at this inn will be reported at Harlowe Place. When most of the first readers of the novel failed to bring this skeptical and analytical perspective to bear on Lovelace's actions, Richardson guided them to this kind of reading with a long footnote (I,353).

Richardson expected the reader to become a moral detective who would piece together the evidence of Lovelace's plot against Clarissa and judge the whole proceedings with the appropriate measure of indignation. The notes scattered through the second edition help the reader who has not been up to this strenuous work; they show the part Lovelace's plottings play in many apparently unrelated events in the novel's first two installments. Thus the Harlowe family presses Clarissa to marry Solmes quickly, because Joseph Leman, functioning as a "double agent" for Lovelace, reports that Lovelace is planning to kidnap Clarissa. Every reader discovers this late in the novel, but the "attentive" reader has already been given the clues to deduce this subtle dimension of Lovelace's plottings. Clarissa is shrewd enough to suspect Joseph Leman of double-dealing, but can't be expected to understand all of Lovelace's doings (I,315). This means the attentive reader will sometimes read beyond Clarissa's suspicions. When too many readers fail to do so, Richardson provides a note (I,425).

The long index-summary added to the beginning of the second edition advances the same ends as the supplementary notes, but it also serves a broader function. In an introductory note to the index Richardson tells his reader, "the index will not only point out the principal facts, and show the connection of the whole; but will enable the youthful reader of both sexes to form a judgment as well of the *blameable* as of the laudable conduct of the principal persons." Richardson is being a little circumspect here about *who* is laudable and *who* is blameable in these proceedings.

But once the reader has finished the index, there will be no doubt who is good (Clarissa and her friends) and who is evil (Clarissa's enemies). The reader of the novel can no longer be trusted to begin the novel with an open mind, ready for careful discriminations. By providing a long rehearsal of the action in the index, Richardson will teach the reader to focus his attention correctly, train him to judge—to have prejudged—the combatants, even before the battle begins. Richardson, in a letter to Aaron Hill, is more candid about the other ways he has shaped the reading experience with the index:

> I chose in my second edition to give a little abstract of the story, that it might be clearly seen what [the book] was, and its tendency; and to obviate as I went along, tho' covertly, such objections as I had heard (as I have done by the italicks) altho' I made many persons masters of the story to my detriment as to sale.

Richardson adds that, since some have read the installments at great distance, the index would serve "as a help to [the readers'] recollection, and to their understanding of it, in the way *I chose to have it understood in*" (*Letters*, 126; July 12, 1749; emphasis added). Thus the index does not simply "point out" events and "show the connection of the whole." It "covertly" engages the major objections raised against the novel, so as to anticipate and defuse possible misreadings. But this index does something else even more cunning. Knowing that many of his readers had read the first and second installments twelve and eighteen months before, and further suspecting they would not reread the whole novel, Richardson provides them with a summary of the action which will *make use* of their laziness and failures of memory by shifting and displacing the text toward Richardson's understanding of *Clarissa*. The index will "help" them in their "recollection" and "understanding" of the novel, but only in "the way I [Richardson] chose to have it understood in."

If *we* have understood anything from our reading of this novel, it is the difficulty of rendering an authoritative judgment of Clarissa and Lovelace. Has Richardson been "fair" in his summary presentation of evidence to the reader? We can see it by comparing one entry in the index with the text of the letter it purports to summarize. The letter, written by Clarissa to Anna Howe, comes one-fourth of the way through the first installment, soon after the dismissal of

Hannah, and directly after letters from Clarissa's mother and father (I,121–24). Her parents insist that their daughter obey their command to accept Solmes and accuse her of being undutiful because of a "predisposition" for Lovelace. Here is Richardson's index summary of Clarissa's letter to Anna:

> Is desirous to know the opinion Lord M.'s family have of her. Substance of a letter from Lovelace, resenting the indignities he receives from her relations. She freely acquaints him *that he has nothing to expect from her contrary to her duty.* Insists that his next letter shall be his last. [I,519]

These four sentences have the obstinate simplicity of a list—and a freedom from ambiguity that seems entirely inappropriate to the letter they summarize. To negotiate the contradictory movements of Clarissa's letter, we must make use of the three codes of meaning this text habitually invokes to interpret Clarissa's situation: Clarissa must assert herself against her family's aggressions and Lovelace's encroachments (the code of struggle); Clarissa rejects her family's advice and turns toward Lovelace because of her love for him (the code of love); because of her sense of duty toward her family, and of justice toward Lovelace, Clarissa moves along a precarious boundary-line between dangerous antagonists (the code of the paragon). The multivalence and ambiguity of *Clarissa* arises from the uneasy coexistence of these three very divergent codes of meaning. By carefully reading through Clarissa's letter to Anna, we can watch these codes fade in and out of prominence, sometimes pulling the text in two or more directions simultaneously. After a close reading of the letter, we can return to Richardson's index summary and re-pose the question of its function for this text.

Clarissa's letter begins with the quotation and summary of Lovelace's most recent letter to Clarissa. Lovelace is angry over the treatment she has suffered at Harlowe Place, and indignant enough at the Harlowes' public behavior toward him to act desperately if he has no hope of her favor. He demands that she "engage [her] honour to him, never to have Mr. Solmes." Clarissa expresses amazement at his knowledge of events in her family, and then makes a most dubious request. She asks Anna to use independent sources to find out what opinion Lovelace's relatives have of her, given her rebellious behavior in the last few weeks:

By my lord's signing Mr. Lovelace's former letter; by Mr. Love-lace's assurance of the continued favour of all his relations; and by the report of others; I seem still to stand high in their favour; but, methinks, I should be glad to have this confirmed to me, as from themselves by the lips of an indifferent person; and the rather as they are known to put a value upon their alliance, be-cause of their fortunes and family. [I,122]

There is a very obvious way to interpret this request—by reading with the code of love. Clarissa has a secret (or unconscious) love for Lovelace that expresses itself in seeking the approval of a family which, if she married Lovelace, would become a new and loving family—one to replace the family that has recently directed so much hostility toward her. This request for information has the effect of making us wonder how dutiful Clarissa really is, and whether she isn't quite willing to have Lovelace after all. An intuitive understanding of this "reading" of Clarissa's request leads her to hedge the request by invoking the two alternative codes available for interpreting this behavior.

Before the request, Clarissa appeals to the code of struggle: "It is natural, I believe, for a person to be more desirous of making new friends in proportion as she loses the favour of old ones." This way of putting things effaces two facts: this particular group of "new friends" can only be known as part of an approach to marriage with Lovelace, and the "old ones" whose favor she is losing are her own family. Clarissa seems to be conscious of this embarrassment, so she adds: "yet, I had rather appear amiable in the eyes of my own rela-tions, and in your eyes, than in those of all the world besides." With these words, Clarissa reaffirms her desire to be dutiful just at the moment when her loyalty to her family seems most in question. After her request to Anna, Clarissa explicitly deflects the possibility that she is in love. In effect, she tells Anna, the code of love does not apply to this behavior, because the code of the paragon pre-dominates: "Curiosity at present is all my motive; nor will there ever, I hope, be a stronger, notwithstanding your questionable *throbs*—even were the merits of Mr. Lovelace much greater than they are." By her own account, Clarissa's "curiosity" is held in check by a sense of propriety which recognizes Lovelace's lack of merit. But the words "at present" and "I hope" preserve the ultimate

meaning of Clarissa's behavior for the reader to interpret and subsequent events to determine.

There is a short break in Clarissa's letter while she replies to Lovelace. Then she quotes and paraphrases parts of her letter to Lovelace.
Again uncertainties of meaning proliferate. Clarissa tells Anna: "I
assure him 'that were there not such a man in the world as himself
I would not have Mr. Solmes.'" Now, just two pages before this
letter, Clarissa's mother has told her she shouldn't promise Lovelace
anything with regard to Solmes, because the promise would imply an
intimate relationship between Clarissa and Lovelace: "What have
you to do to oblige him with your refusal of Mr. Solmes? Will not
that refusal be to give *him* hope? And while he has any, can *we* be
easy or free from his insults?" (I,119). Mrs. Harlowe's words give
the reader a context for interpreting Clarissa's promise—it is not
the code of the paragon (Clarissa actively working to avoid a confrontation between her family and Lovelace) but Clarissa disobeying
her mother in making this promise, disobeying her father in writing
at all, and being contentious so as to interact with Lovelace (code
of struggle; code of love).

As the letter proceeds, divergent possible meanings of Clarissa's
behavior continue to abound. Clarissa's reply to Lovelace works to
shape Lovelace's action: "That the moment I hear he visits any of
my friends without their consent, I will make a resolution never to
see him more if I can help it." Because this warning actively inter-
venes where her family has demanded passivity, it is disobedient
(code of struggle); because it threatens a break, it implies a present
relationship with Lovelace (code of love); and because it seeks to
avoid conflict, it works for the collective good (code of paragon).
Next, Clarissa reasserts her choice of a "single life," and implores
Lovelace to make his next letter "the very *last*; and that only to
acquaint me with his acquaintance that it shall be so." Here Clarissa
apparently follows her mother's advice to cut off the correspondence.
But the *way* she puts her request engages the code of love, by which
the woman implores the man to make this his last visit, his last kiss,
his last letter—a request that is generally overcome by the ardor of
the man's love for the woman.

Now, let's look back at Richardson's summary of this letter, and
keep in mind the multitude of different possible meanings we have
found active in it. The only trace of the code of love is the rather

enigmatic opening phrase, "Is desirous to know the opinion Lord M.'s family have of her." The ways in which Clarissa is disobedient (by writing to Lovelace, by promising not to marry Solmes—the whole code of struggle) has been actively effaced. And the code of the paragon is given direct support through a thematic reduction of Clarissa's letter: "She freely acquaints him *that he has nothing to expect from her contrary to her duty.* Insists that his next letter shall be his last." Here Richardson is concealing the way he has used the code of the paragon to read and interpret Clarissa's letter so that a certain message—Clarissa as dutiful daughter, thus a paragon enduring difficult trials—is emitted. Then this interpretation is made to stand in as the summary of a complex, contradictory, striated text. In the text of her letter, Clarissa never speaks of her "duty" to anyone, so this particular summary is surprising. It even seems treacherous. Richardson has engaged in a calculated impoverishment of his own text so this letter may serve, through his summary, as an illustration of one of the main themes of his interpretive struggle with Clarissa's detractors. Many readers accused Clarissa of being undutiful to her parents; this index entry proclaims her intention to be dutiful.

Reading Clarissa's letter in terms of three codes of meaning has this advantage. It shows the way in which reading, in the sense of basic comprehension, and interpreting, in the sense of determining what is going on before us, are profoundly interdependent. These three codes are not extrinsic to the text; they rush in the moment we try to make any sense of the story. And our difficulty in getting Clarissa's letter to have any single clear sense helps to disclose all in this text that resists Richardson's summary.

But what is a summary? The *OED* offers these definitions: "A statement of account, containing or comprising the chief points of sum and substance of a matter"; and more rarely, that which is the "highest; supreme." To get to the "chief points . . . of a matter," the summary operates by dividing the text into "primary" and "secondary" elements, selecting the primary elements of the text, and presenting them in series. These elements are considered primary because they are assumed to be more "essential," or "significant," than the other elements of the text. But essential for what? significant for whom? The concentration of the primary elements of a text in a summary will often make that summary seem more dense and powerful than the text it summarizes. If there is a loss in detail, there is a gain in lucidity.

The special appeal of Richardson's summary derives from the way it apparently allows the reader to know the text without interpreting it. The events in Clarissa's letter are simply listed: her request to Anna, Lovelace's anger, Clarissa's dutiful response. They are listed in such a way that we seem to be able to defer the adjudication of the different possible meanings of this letter. Questions of motive are suspended; the ambiguity of Clarissa's response to her situation has been filtered out. No need to wonder if Clarissa is in love, or if she is acting the way she is because she's engaged in struggle; Clarissa is simply a dutiful daughter.

And this brings us to the characteristic duplicity of Richardson's index summary. For while Richardson pretends the index (like an "index" finger) merely points, it actually offers an interpretation of Clarissa's behavior: it *asserts* Clarissa's identity as a paragon. It asserts an interpretation of the heroine under the guise of a simple summary. And though Richardson's summary is anything but "simple," simple and whole and unified is what Richardson's second edition addenda have tried to make *Clarissa* appear to be. This novel explicitly thematizes the value of purity and importance of simplicity. Little wonder that Richardson protects his heroine against skeptical critics by trying to simplify his text and heroine. Richardson's footnotes link disparate events in the novel to a single element of the text: Lovelace's plot against Clarissa and her family. The index summary offers the reader an advanced simplified version of the action. But the simplicity won is specious. It's merely an optical illusion. The index does not make the text simple; it just attempts to conceal the problematic dimensions of Clarissa's behavior and the contradictory movements of the text. The text has been bordered with a band of footnotes and wrapped with the smooth surfaces of the index summary, but the jagged edges of the striated text beneath are still visible.

The index summary of the second edition attempts to subject the text to the author's control. This is not the first time a summary has served this end in *Clarissa*. When Anna Howe learns, through accident and investigation, that Clarissa is being kept at a "vile House," she writes her friend a long letter. She has discovered Tomlinson is a fraud and suspects there is no such woman as Mrs. Fretchville. In light of these evidences of Lovelace's treachery, Anna subjects Clarissa's whole experience with Lovelace to analysis and interpretation. She concludes that Lovelace harbors the darkest designs against Clarissa's person. This letter is never delivered to Clarissa because she escapes from Sinclair's before it arrives. But Lovelace reads the letter, and it is placed by Richardson at the very end of the second installment (III,1–13).

Like the notes and index subsequently added to the text, this letter guides the reader of the first edition in revising his understanding of Lovelace. But there is a significant difference between these two kinds of summary. Anna's letter is a thoroughly paritsan performance which ends by ascribing Clarissa's preservation to the "native dignity" she has sustained in dealing with Lovelace. Anna feels no need to take full account of the proposal scenes that might have ended in marriage. Anna's letter is part of the novel's ongoing interpretive struggle. Thus, Lovelace puts asterisks in the margins of the letter "to mark the places which call for vengeance upon the vixen writer, or which require animadversion" (III,1).

Anna's summary of Clarissa's life is no more "objective" than Belford's panegyrical description of Clarissa's life as the true "fair penitent" or Lovelace's parodic summary of Clarissa's life as the "pretty little miss" at a country fair (IV,119; III,316–17). Each of these three summaries is but one position of the text, trying to control the whole text by taking its sum, by being its summary. But each only asserts the limited vantage point of an Anna, a Belford, a Lovelace. When Richardson puts a summary index at the very gateway to the text, it is intended to be much more—but it never stops being simply one *more* interpretation of *Clarissa*.

Richardson's Defense of Clarissa, 3: Character, Plot, and Theme

Richardson's index formulates a distinct interpretation of the novel; in a sense, it is the first critical essay written on *Clarissa*. This interpretation serves several related purposes: it presents evidence to strengthen Clarissa's position in the text, deflects the criticism of the novel Richardson received, and lays down the guiding principles for the "restorations" to the text made in the third edition. Richardson's index resembles the summary argument made before the jury at the end of a trial. Like a prosecutor or defense attorney,

Richardson offers a spare reconstruction of events, giving periodic emphasis to a fact whose meaning seems self-evident—that is, evident enough, in itself, to be entered as evidence in a sequence of citations which culminate in an unambiguous climax (guilty! not guilty! hang the fiend! etc.).

Richardson cannot operate on *Clarissa* this way without habitual use of the techniques of simplification we have just examined in the index entry which summarizes Clarissa's letter. There, the most dubious behavior is simplified to become proof of Clarissa's strict adherence to duty. The index reports: "[Clarissa] freely acquaints [Lovelace] *that he has nothing to expect from her contrary to her duty.*" Notice that the index here adopts the manner of quotation, though really offering a paraphrase, which distorts what it represents. To grasp the broader tendency of the index, let us see how it acts upon the first installment of the novel.

The index summary provides an essay in apologetics for the climactic crisis of the first installment—Clarissa's flight with Lovelace. In a sense, the index reopens the interpretive efforts made by Clarissa, throughout the novel, to account for her involvement with Lovelace, her defiance of parental authority, and her fateful departure from Harlowe Place. This has become necessary because many readers were cavalier enough to accuse Clarissa of disobedience in corresponding with Lovelace, excessive pertness in dealing with her family, and a lapse of propriety in promising to meet Lovelace in the garden. These criticisms leave Clarissa all too responsible for the evils which subsequently engulf her, and this threatens to separate the readers from any urgent participation in the heroine's crisis. Richardson responds with an index which carefully defines and limits Clarissa's culpability. How is this managed? Richardson uses the index summary to give special emphasis to certain elements of the text: the character of Clarissa's antagonists; their plots against her; Clarissa's especially treacherous position; and the particular sequence of actions which become a snare for the heroine.

But the index does not just cite elements of the text; it changes their aspect in the most decisive fashion. Near the beginning of the index, the Harlowe family ambitions are alluded to: "*the views of her family in favouring the address of Solmes*" (I,518). Then the pressures brought to bear on Clarissa to advance this plan are periodically described in terms of the character of Clarissa's family members: her father's *"ill-temper,"* her mother's *"passiveness"*; "her sister's envy, unnatural behavior and violence . . . [and] her brother's insolent answer" to Clarissa's letter (I,517,520). Anna Howe commiserates with Clarissa by offering "severe censures of the Harlowe family, for their pride, formality, and other bad qualities" (I,521). One letter of Clarissa's is said to give "further particulars of the persecutions she received from her violent brother" (I,521). Notice that the index here cites moments of violence, with language which asserts the permanent nature of one of the agents: James does not simply act violently, he is Clarissa's "violent brother." This is one of the most common shifts affected by the index. It cites Clarissa's stormy second "interview" with Solmes this way: "of the parts occasionally taken in it by her boisterous uncle, by her brutal brother, by her implacable sister, and by her qualifying aunt. [Clarissa's] perseverance and distress" (I,524).

In describing Clarissa's antagonists, the index carries out a significant inversion. The text presents Clarissa, her family, and Lovelace engaged in a struggle—and allows analysis of characters by characters to emerge from the matrix of that struggle. The reader is left to make up his own mind. In contrast, the index to the text states the character of Clarissa's enemies, so their actions seem to derive from that character. This is particularly obvious in the summary of Lovelace's first letter:

character	Pride, revenge, love, ambition, or a desire of conquest, his avowedly predominant passions. His early vow to ruin as many of the fair sex as he can get into his power. His pretense for it. Breathes revenge against the Harlowe family. [I,519]
anticipated action	

Many of the first readers of the novel were puzzled and charmed by the mixture of pride, honesty, and irony found in Lovelace's opening letters. This summary leaves little doubt as to Lovelace's true nature and the sort of actions which will follow from that nature. But his very next letter shows Lovelace doing things which seem to contradict this version of his character. He spares Rosebud, the innkeeper's daughter, his most comprehensive attentions, and gallantly grants her a small dowry so she may marry her loved one. Richardson, in the index entry, is at pains to make sure we don't get the wrong idea: "[Lovelace] resolves to spare [Rosebud]. *Pride and policy his motives, and not principle*" (I,519). The index fixes Lovelace's nature and focuses his will with regard to Clarissa: "If he thought he had no prospect of [Clarissa's] favour, he would *attempt to carry her off*; that, he says, would be a rape worthy of Jupiter" (I,520). But in the letter here summarized, Lovelace is much more tentative about how he might act. He writes that, if he had no hope of "her favour," "[he] should be tempted to carry her off." The index has turned a lover's temptation into a certainty.

Having established the character and intentions of Clarissa's antagonists, and reminded the reader of how she is beset on both sides, the index describes Clarissa's efforts in this "unhappy situation": "All her present wish is *to be able to escape Solmes* on the one hand, and to avoid incurring the *disgrace of refuging with the family of a man at enmity with her own* on the other" (I,524). The index displays Clarissa's actions and character so as to emphasize the just balance and moral rigor of the position she labors to sustain. This helps to answer the various criticisms leveled at her. To the charge that Clarissa has merely fallen in love and absconded with a dissolute rake, the index reminds us that Clarissa gives explicit reasons *"for not giving way to a passion for Lovelace,"* and even offers *"to give up all thoughts of Lovelace if she may be freed from Solmes address"* (I,518). To deflect the charge that Clarissa shows too much coldness toward her suitor, we are reminded that Lovelace himself clears her of "intentional pride, scorn, haughtiness, or want of sensibility" (I,519). Special emphasis is given to those moments when she is solicitous about his bad health, acknowledges "tenderness and regard for him" because of his generosity toward Rosebud, and even confesses to Anna that "were [Lovelace] *now* a moral man, she would *prefer* him to all the men she ever saw" (I,522–23, 523, 520). Finally, to the charge that Clarissa is undutiful, we are told that Clarissa warns Lovelace "he has *nothing to expect from her contrary to her duty.*" (That phrase again!) We are also given evidence of this: Clarissa defends her family against Anna's harsh criticism; she expostulates with Lovelace when he threatens to use force against her family; and she is "impartial" in responding to Anna's satirical sketch of Lovelace, Solmes, and James (I,522, 524, 521).

The index goes much further in defining the sources of Clarissa's crisis than these accounts of the pressures directed at Clarissa and the resistance she offers to them. It calls attention to a sequence of events which drive Clarissa toward an elopement she never wants and finally decides against. The sequence begins in the second entry of the index: "[Clarissa's] *mother connives at the private correspondence between her and Lovelace, for the sake of preventing greater evils*" (I,517). (This is a flagrant distortion of the text it summarizes, but we'll let this offense against fair play pass.) Then the index periodically indicates the pressures directed at Clarissa by her family and Lovelace (I,518–23). The special circumstances which lead to Clarissa's acceptance of Lovelace's plan for escape are then carefully described:

> Overhears her brother and sister exulting in the success of their schemes, and undertaking *the one to keep his father up to his resentment* on occasion of Lovelace's menaces, *the other her mother*. Exasperated at this, and at what her Aunt Hervey tells her, she writes to Lovelace, *that she will meet him the following Monday,* and throw herself into the protection of the ladies of his family. [I,525]

There follow references to Clarissa's "frightful dream," the way Clarissa "repents of her appointment," and the long list of special conditions she lays down for Lovelace to observe in carrying through her escape. She holds out the distinct possibility that she may cancel her plans to flee with him, and if she does, "*she will take the first opportunity to see him and acquaint him with her reasons.*" Clarissa's regrets mount, she confers with Anna by letter, and finally "determines NOT to *withdraw with Lovelace*" (I,525). She writes Lovelace "revoking her appointment. Thinks herself obliged as well by promise as in order to *prevent mischief,* to meet him, and to give him her reasons for revoking" (I,526).

It does not take very much astuteness to surmise what message Richardson is communicating about his heroine in the index summary of the first installment. Clarissa is virtuous in the extreme, though she is humbled by the events which overtake her; she's profoundly innocent, yet an object lesson to others. Most of the responsibility for Clarissa's departure with Lovelace has been displaced by the index into the character and ambitions of the Harlowe family, the chararacter and plottings of Lovelace, and the peculiar intersection of persons and events that take her to the garden gate to meet Lovelace. Clarissa's character is distinguished, in the index, by all that should *separate* her from her fall: her dutiful behavior to her family, her sense of justice, her impartiality. On only one matter is her culpability readily conceded; by a single slender thread is Clarissa tied to her fateful departure with Lovelace. The index summarizes Clarissa's reflections of her predicament this way: "[Clarissa] lays all to the fault of corresponding with [Lovelace] at first *against paternal prohibition*" (I,526).

We are now ready to comprehend the broader importance of Richardson's index repetition of the text. This re-presentation of evidence uses certain categories and takes a peculiar form—one that offers a precursor of the dominant modes of interpreting the novel, from the eighteenth century to the present: the index replays *Clarissa* as a coherent system, where "characters" of fixed identity interact to trace a "plot," which expresses a certain "theme." How is this done? The agents, who in the unfolding of the text seemed capable, at any given moment, of acting in many different ways— these agents are endowed with a "character" or nature which makes their behavior predictable and their actions "characteristic." The events of the fiction no longer open onto many futures. They are linked by the index and restorations with two determining factors: the "character" of the characters, and the plots against Clarissa devised by the Harlowes and Lovelace. These events look all the more inevitable because the index presents them as a finished chain of events, related as causes and effects, so as to form a well-made "plot."

From this convergence of character and plot emerge lessons or "themes" which Richardson freely states. We can see all this in the index treatment of the second installment, where Lovelace and Clarissa are living at St. Albans and Sinclair's. Lovelace is characterized as cruelly manipulative, the Harlowes as vindictive, and Clarissa as wisely cautious in her relations with Lovelace. Almost all control over the direction of events rests with Lovelace; the proposal scenes are almost entirely effaced. Pains are taken to demonstrate that Lovelace would have violated any woman with a less guarded delicacy. From this version of "character" and "plot," Richardson finds a "theme" which answers those who, like Belfour, wish Clarissa had let her guard down long enough to say yes to Lovelace: "THE WOMAN . . . WHO RESENTS NOT INITIATORY FREEDOMS, MUST BE LOST" (II,538).

In adding "restorations" to the text in the third edition, we catch Richardson doing something that must make any fair-minded judge and reader of this story wince. If the index advances an interpretation of *Clarissa* organized around the categories of "character," "plot," and "theme," then with his "restorations" Richardson *plants evidence* for this interpretation. A cursory glance at major addenda to the text shows how this is done. Two additions help to give new definition to Clarissa's character. One scene is added to show Clarissa unusually meek, hopeful, and compliant in a long exchange with her sister Bella (I,221–28). Clarissa's meditation at Sinclair's presents the protagonist making a careful analysis of the faults of her own character (II,377–79).

But Richardson's efforts to fix Lovelace's character are much more subtle and extensive than additions directed at perfecting Clarissa. Richardson shapes Lovelace into a type, so every reader might say what Clarissa says of him: "Lord bless me, thought I, what a character is that of a libertine" (II,89). Thus, the scene from which this line comes is added to show him as a hopelessly theatrical penitent (II,88–89). Other addenda stress Lovelace's desire to cut a fine "figure . . . in rakish annals" by "act[ing] in character"; his penchant for making generalizations about the fair sex; and his determination to win revenge on the Harlowe family (II,250–51; III,401; II,190). It is entirely appropriate that the addenda should greatly expand Lovelace's description of himself, by a familiar Hobbesean analogy, as a rakish predator who takes pleasure in hunting and capturing the creatures he chooses to make his victims (II,246–47, 426).

Some addenda are contrived to imbue the events of the story with an aura of necessity. This helps them cohere as the "plot" of the novel. The first step is to magnify Lovelace's obsession with plots and stratagems: Richardson adds Lovelace's ingenious plan to abduct Anna and Mrs. Howe; also, his plan to seduce Mrs. Moore, Miss Rawlins, and Mrs. Bevis is lengthened (II,418–25; III,215–16). Then Lovelace's apparent control over events is extended: he gives instructions to Belford on how each of their rakish brotherhood must act when he meets Clarissa; Lovelace exchanges letters with Joseph Leman, discussing his earlier affair with Miss Betterton and telling

Joseph additional ways to manipulate James Harlowe; and Lovelace explains his motives for leaving Clarissa for only one day (II,215–17, 143–47, 209). All of these addenda deepen Lovelace's responsibility for the final catastrophe, and make that catastrophe appear all the more inevitable. Richardson further advances this end by filling out the cause-effect continuum that lies behind the events of this story. Thus, segments of text are added to present causes for Mr. Harlowe's forbidding harshness and Clarissa's extraordinary virtue; Clarissa explains why she cannot return to her family; and Lovelace ascribes his renewed assaults on Clarissa, after the rape, to the "women" at Sinclair's (I,132–33; IV,564; II,63; II,432; III,275–76).

Richardson is not content to rigidify agents into predictable characters, or stiffen a sequence of events and actions into a plot. He must tally character and plot to deduce the theme of this text. The theme is finally Clarissa—put before the reader as an example of virtue, worthy of imitation (author's preface, I,xiv; postscript, IV, 564). When some readers go astray in comprehending Clarissa, Richardson adds material which protects this theme. Some thought the story encouraged children to disobey their parents in matters of love. Richardson adds an exchange of letters, between Mrs. Howe and Anna's suitor Hickman, to help distinguish Clarissa's revulsion for Solmes from Anna's capricious resistance to Hickman. This affirms Clarissa's right to oppose her parents over marrying Solmes, and also Mrs. Howe's right to countermand Anna's trivial objections to Hickman (I,335–38). Several additions communicate the limits which Clarissa rightfully imposes on her love for the hero, and another greatly lengthens Anna's panegyrical "character" of Clarissa so Richardson may give practical advice on everything from female learning and art to household economy and the proper style of handwriting for a young lady (II,104–05; II,438; III,155–57; IV,491–510).

Richardson's Defense of Clarissa, *4: Taming Time with Corrective Surgery*

Richardson offers the notes and index to the second edition of *Clarissa* as marginal supplements to the text. They are "marginal" because they are placed on the edges of the text (at its beginning, and at the bottom of its pages): they are "supplements" because they help to complete a text which is already whole. When readers fail to be guided by these additions to the novel, Richardson initiates a much more drastic intervention in the text. He adds "restorations from the original manuscripts" of *Clarissa* to the third edition (1751). He considers them so important that he has them published separately, for the use of readers of the first edition. In the eighteenth century a "restorer" could be an original artist. But here, as in more general usage, a "restoration" is designed to improve an art-object by bringing it closer to an original, anterior condition. But, as with the policy of aggressive restoration of early masterpieces adopted by the National Gallery in London, one must often be suspicious that the restoring hand uses its overt desire to reappropriate a lost original, to serve its *own* idea of an artwork's form and meaning. This is certainly the case with Richardson's "restoration" of *Clarissa*. In 1959 Kinkead-Weekes demonstrated that most of these "restorations" were composed expressly for the third edition, to deflect criticism of the novel.[11] Even the few passages which probably belonged to the long early drafts of the novel, like the added scene between Clarissa and Bella, Lovelace's instructions to his rakish friends, or Lovelace's scheme to abduct the Howes, were selected from the large quantity of discarded material so as to advance Richardson's interpretive debate with his readers (I,222–28; II,215–18; II,418–25).

We have seen the ways in which the "restorations," like the index and notes, help put forward a character-plot-theme interpretation of the novel. But the "restorations" have another complementary mission. They also carry out corrective surgery, so as to efface the most unstable moments of the text. This is managed by making additions which will help control what we might call the "temporality of the text." In the first edition of *Clarissa,* events and actions sloppily blend accident and intention so as to advance with a random-looking successiveness. The story happens from moment to moment, and each moment is partially disjunct from the next. At any particular moment, divergent possibilities open before the characters and reader: at one instant Lovelace can have Clarissa, at another Clarissa can accept Lovelace, at another the story almost ends in

11. See "Clarissa 'Restored'?" *RES,* n.s. 10 (1959): 169. A recent study of the third edition addenda by Shirley Van Master argues that Richardson was not affected by criticism of the novel in shaping most of these restorations. My own analysis of the addenda in this section supports Kinkead-Weekes on this question. Almost all the addenda have a direct, if sometime subtle, bearing on the struggles of interpretation.

marriage. With his "restorations," Richardson corrals these contingent, suspenseful moments of the story by interpolating interpretive perspectives actually developed later in the story—by Clarissa, after the rape, by Richardson, during the struggles of interpretation which followed publication of the first edition.

One set of additions to the text blocks a future outcome that many characters and readers wanted, by indicating how "it would have been" for Clarissa and Lovelace if they had married. Richardson has Clarissa reflect on the guilt she would feel if Lovelace became a good husband but she were still estranged from her family:

> Even her pleasures, were the man to prove *better* than she expects, coming to her with an abatement, like that which persons who are in possession of ill-gotten wealth must then most poignantly experience . . . when, all their wishes answered . . . they sit down in hopes to *enjoy* what they have unjustly obtained, and find their own reflections their greatest torment. [II,207]

Richardson is very skeptical about the kind of husband Lovelace would be, so he scatters evidence that will discourage any unwonted optimism. Early in the second installment, he has Anna comment that "handsome husbands" must often make "a wife's heart ache." Anna predicts that, when a lover's "ardour" turns to a husband's "indifference," Lovelace's pride will "expect homage [rather] than pay it" (II,105).

But Richardson is not satisfied with the estimates of others as to Lovelace's behavior. After meeting Clarissa, Belford earnestly importunes Lovelace to marry the lady. Lovelace deals a blow to this idea by explicitly stating, in a "restoration" to the text, that he is not ready to keep the marriage vows (II,250–51). And even after the rape, Clarissa's escape, and Lovelace's numerous avowals of his sincere desire to marry Clarissa, Lovelace confesses to Belford, in one of Richardson's most incriminating interpolations, that he has had "retrograde motions," and is quite sure that if he and Clarissa marry, "*Recurrings* there will be; hankerings that will, on every but remotely favourable incident . . . pop out" (III,474).

Richardson finds a way to go to still more vivid lengths to block the marriage option. He has Lovelace describe scenarios for the proposal scenes that might occur after Clarissa has been physically subdued. In the first, Clarissa is so meek and quiescent that when Lovelace announces his intention to marry her, she overflows with gratitude. As Lovelace writes, "all the studies of her future life . . . vowed and devoted (when she can speak) to acknowledge and return the perpetuated obligation!" (II,252) In the second scene Lovelace takes sadistic pleasure in Clarissa's attempt to bring up the question of marriage:

> She will be about it, and about it, several times; but I will not understand her: at last, after half a dozen hem-ings, she will be obliged to speak out: *I think Mr. Lovelace—I think, sir—I think you were saying some days ago*—Still I will be all silence—her eyes fixed upon my shoe-buckles, as I sit over against her. Ladies, when put to it thus, always admire a man's shoe-buckles, or perhaps some particular beauties in the carpet. *I think you said that Mrs. Fretchville*—then a crystal tear trickles down each crimson cheek, vexed to have her virgin pride so little assisted. [II,314]

Lovelace makes the motives for these anticipated manipulations very clear: "But, come, my meaning dear, cry I to myself, remember what I have suffered *for* thee, and what I have suffered *by* thee!" (II,314–15) These two fanciful scenes, invented by Richardson to discredit Lovelace, must have discouraged even the most determined advocates of a happy ending.

Now all these speculations of what "would have been" if Clarissa had accepted Lovelace are based on a rigid, malevolent view of Lovelace's character. By contrast, the first edition shows us a Lovelace who is open to a wide spectrum of emotions, and many different configurations for the future. When Clarissa exults that a reconciliation with her family may be at hand, Lovelace can't restrain unexpected sobs of sympathy (II,461,466). At another moment, after two "happy days" with Clarissa, Lovelace wonders why he continues his plottings. He even seems to *enjoy* the prospect of eventually marrying Clarissa:

> Why cannot I make every day equally happy? It looks *as if it were in my power to do so*. Strange, I should thus delight in teasing a woman I so dearly love! I must, I doubt, have something in my temper like Miss Howe, who loves to plague the man who puts himself in her power. But I could not do thus by such

an angel as this, did I not believe that, after her probation time
shall be expired, and, if she be not brought to *cohabitation* (my
darling view), I shall reward her as she wishes. [II,342]

Both Richardson and Clarissa seem to be alert to these more auspi-
cious potentials of Lovelace's character. Clarissa is several times
allowed to ruminate how happy she "could have been" with Lovelace. Richardson uses several "restorations" to put new emphasis on
this stratum of the text. After a good day with Lovelace at church,
Clarissa reflects that Lovelace is "at bottom . . . a good natured
man." Then she goes on to confess, "I think I could prefer him to all
the men I ever knew, were he but to be always what he has been
this day" (II,225). At another point, Clarissa takes positive "pleasure" in Lovelace's tears of compassion—"these beautiful proofs of a
feeling heart " Then, in a short addendum, Clarissa communicates
her willingness to marry Lovelace by expecting Anna's "kind con-
gratulations" for the "agreeable prospects" opening before her (II,
466–67).

Richardson contrives these additions to the text as the best possible answer to those who found Clarissa too cold and delicate in her
dealings with Lovelace. Richardson even adds a short addendum in
which Lovelace attributes her diffidence to his own "teasings."
When he stops them, he "doubt[s] not to find [her] all silk and
silver at bottom, all soft, bright, and charming" (II,393). At first
glance it may seem curious that Richardson plants some additions
to the text which aver that Clarissa would have been desperately
unhappy married to Lovelace, and others which encourage hopes
for marriage by showing her quite willing to accept him. Indeed,
these addenda *are* partially contradictory. But both blacken Lovelace, for both shift responsibility for the catastrophe onto his shoulders.

What is Richardson doing in contriving these addenda to his novel?
In large degree, arguments against marrying advanced by Clarissa
late in the novel, and arguments advanced by Richardson to justify
his ending, are simply "read back" into the earlier action. Sometimes
this is done in a sloppy and rather unlikely fashion. When Lovelace
presses Clarissa to marry him "tomorrow," or name a day near at
hand, Clarissa firmly urges delay. Richardson adds three short polemical passages to Clarissa's narrative of this scene. Each shifts the

culpability for delaying their marriage onto Lovelace: "To leave it to me, to choose whether the speedy day he ought to have urged with earnestness, should be delayed or suspended!"; "Had he given me *time* to answer . . . but, *in the same breath* he went on"; "Is it not plain, my dear, that he designs to vex and tease me? . . . Why, why will he take pains to make a heart wrap itself up in reserve?" (II,311–12)

These "restorations" nearly upset the tautness and drama of this scene, because they exaggerate the importance of questions of behavior which only become pivotal or urgent *after* Clarissa's rape. It is true that these addenda help condemn Lovelace, clear Clarissa, and justify the final form of Richardson's novel. But the revisions also have important consequences for the "time" in the text. For through these addenda, the past is redefined in terms of its future; the past is scattered with evidence, reasons, and causes for subsequent events; and gradually, an aura of necessity, a melancholy but ultimately reassuring fatality, overtakes the reader's sense of the relationship between the text's past and its subsequent future. With the pressure of these changes, Richardson tries to attenuate the volatility of certain earlier dramatic moments—where the sheer force of agents contending seemed capable of transforming (in any one of several ways) the novel's entire social configuration.

No moments are more critical, for the "futures" of this text, than the three genuine proposal scenes. This is why Richardson performs his most subtle corrective surgery at the moments of genuine proposal; the elaborateness of these efforts is the surest evidence of the immense generative potential of these moments. Our earlier analysis of the proposal scenes indicates why. We found three scenes where Lovelace proposes to Clarissa with complete earnestness: in the long melodramatic encounter which almost ends in linking the lovers (II,135–43); when Clarissa falls ill after learning of her father's curse (II,175–76, 182–84); and after Lovelace returns to St. Albans after an absence of only one day (II,209–10). Several factors help make these moments that can go either way—toward marriage or death: a spirit of fair play, which leads Lovelace to enter the ebb and flow of struggle willing to marry Clarissa should she win the "game" he has set going; an opening toward comedy and love that counterbalances the current of suffering and fatality in the text; and finally, those important moments when

Lovelace creates in imagination a Clarissa with so much beauty that he loses the power to resist her (see above, chapters 2 and 4).

For all these reasons, the proposal scenes are, in the most literal sense, the moments of "crisis" in this text: they are "turning points," as in the progress of a disease, the motion of the stars, or any course of action which has "decisive importance for the issue of the event" (life/death, success/failure, etc.). It is in the proposal scenes that the density of the text's potential futures reaches its apogee; it is this scene, in its various forms, which becomes a critical, or interpretive, crux for the many readers of Clarissa's situation both inside and outside the book. If one remembers the etymological affiliations between *crisis, critical,* and *critic,* it will seem appropriate that the "critic" or interpreter of this story bring his judgment and discernment to bear here. Little wonder that, when an interpreter like Belfour sets out to change the shape of the fiction, she directs her compositional invention at precisely this point in the text. Belfour finds an ingenious way to satisfy her own desire, and make the text her own, even after the rape. In her proposed ending, she reenacts the proposal scene on Lovelace's deathbed, changing Clarissa's book-long negative to a "yes" (see above, pp. 162–66). But because the desires of different interpreters keep converging on this scene, it becomes difficult for any one "critic" to convincingly control this moment of "crisis" for very long.

How does Richardson labor to overcome the disequilibrium which the proposal scenes engender? He adds a long new proposal scene, very early in the Clarissa-Lovelace transactions (II,75–84, 98–100). In some ways, this scene is very similar to the three proposal scenes in the first edition—scenes that come later in the story, and which we have already examined. But in certain subtle ways this scene is decisively different. And these differences embody important evidence of the way Richardson works to modify his own text. The "proposal" comes rather unexpectedly, while Lovelace and Clarissa are arguing about whether she should assume control of her grandfather's estate (Lovelace argues yes, Clarissa no). Clarissa's narrative of this scene communicates her skepticism about the very frail methods of Lovelace's proposal:

> he urged me to make a demand of my estate. He knew it, I told him, to be my resolution not to litigate with my father.

Nor would he put me upon it, he replied, but as the *last* thing. But if my spirit would not permit me to be *obliged,* as I called it, to anybody, and yet if my relations would refuse me my own, he knew not how I could keep at that spirit without being put to inconveniences which would give him infinite concern—unless— unless, he said hesitating, as if afraid to speak out—unless I would take the only method I *could* to obtain the possession of my own. What is *that,* sir?

Sure the man saw by my looks, when he came with his creeping *unlesses,* that I guessed what he meant. Ah, madam! can you be at a loss to know what that method is? They will not dispute with a *man,* that right which they would contest with *you.*

Why said he with a *man,* instead of with *him*? Yet he looked as if he wanted to be encouraged to say more. So, sir you would have me employ a lawyer, would you, notwithstanding what I have ever declared as to litigating with my papa?

No, I would not, my dearest creature, snatching my hand, and pressing it with his lips—except you would make *me* the lawyer.

I blushed. The man pursued not the subject so ardently, but that it was more easy as well as more natural to avoid it than to fall into it. Would to Heaven he might, without offending! But I *so* overawed him! (*Overawed* him—*your* notion my dear [Anna]) And so the overawed, bashful man went off from the subject, repeating his proposal that I would demand my own estate, or empower some man of the law to demand it; if I *would not* (he put in) empower a happier man to demand it. [II,75–76]

As before, Clarissa is nettled by Lovelace's way of bringing up marriage, so she suggests he leave her presence immediately so she may be reconciled with her family. Her motive: "I was willing to try whether he had the regard to *all* my previous declarations which he pretended to have to some of them." Thus, the chess game goes forward: Lovelace uses his early promise not to mention marriage as a way of embarrassing Clarissa; Clarissa uses his vow to leave her presence as a way to upset Lovelace. Other similarities are apparent: in this scene, the protagonists have evidently drifted into the topic of marriage almost accidentally; Clarissa begins feeling some embarrassment but ends quite angry; Lovelace begins in control but then drifts into a state of rapture, where he offers himself to Clarissa unequivocally; finally, both of the protagonists' narratives are hostile to the opening toward marriage their accounts disclose.

But even before considering Lovelace's account of this scene, certain significant differences between this proposal scene and the others are evident. Throughout this scene, Clarissa never loses her air of detachment and control. She is in the early stages of her relationship with Lovelace, so she displays none of the emotional entanglement which disturbs her assurance later. Also, her situation has not yet taken on the aspect of an urgent personal crisis. She still has not heard about her father's curse. This is one reason Clarissa never loses control in this scene. Lovelace's allusion to marriage only provokes a single blush. She is never hushed with thought or paralyzed with indecision, so there does not seem to be any genuine potential for a sudden reorganization of this independent woman into Lovelace's bride.

Richardson's new proposal scene works a complementary change in Lovelace. His opening allusion to marriage is exceedingly circumspect, and when he finally does feel unequivocal rapture before Clarissa, he never actually mentions marriage. But more significantly, Lovelace's rapture has taken on a completely different tone and value. In other moments of proposal, Clarissa's dramatic art intersects with Lovelace's penchant for adorning the object of his desire, and, at this moment, Clarissa is experienced as someone of overpowering beauty, capable of reconciling opposites effortlessly. This experience induces Lovelace's awe, stillness, and passivity. He suddenly wants to assimilate himself to Clarissa. This leads to a heartfelt proposal. But in this scene, Clarissa's gestures and statements trigger a physical desire to possess, and even swallow, the heroine. When Lovelace reproaches Clarissa for having nothing but "kind thoughts" for her family, while she judges Lovelace very strictly, Clarissa responds, "Excuse me, *good* Mr. Lovelace (waving my hand and bowing), that I am willing to think the best of my father. Charming creature! said he, with what a bewitching air is that said!—And with a vehemence in his manner, would have snatched my hand" (II,78). Clarissa reports that, a bit later, "snatching my hand . . . his behavior was so strangely wild and fervent that I was perfectly frighted. I thought he would have devoured my hand" (II,80–81). At these moments, Lovelace's rapture is neither still nor silent. He becomes a ranter, who uses all the overinflated language of the heroic drama to proclaim Clarissa's powers and offer himself to her:

> Darkness, light; light darkness; by my soul!—just as you please to have it. O charmer of my heart! Snatching my hand, and pressing it between both his, to his lips, in a strange wild way, take me, take me to yourself; mould me as you please; I am wax in your hands; give me your own impression, and seal me for ever yours. We were born for each other!—you to make me happy, and save a soul—I am all error, all crime. [II,80]

With the "restoration" of this fantastic language to the text, Richardson does his best to show his readers that Lovelace is not the man to make a suitable husband for a nice girl like Clarissa.

The turbulent course of this scene also invites the reader to wonder about Lovelace's actual disposition toward Clarissa. At the end of her letter to Anna, Clarissa guides the reader in formulating suspicions:

> Yet you see he but touches upon the edges of matrimony neither. And that at a time, generally, when he has either excited one's passions or apprehensions; so that one cannot at once descend. But surely this cannot be his design. And yet such seemed to be his behavior to my sister, when he provoked her to refuse him, and so tamely submitted, as he did, to her refusal. But he dare not—. [II,81]

Suspicions of Lovelace's behavior are deepened by Clarissa's next letter, which is part of the same third edition "restoration." There Clarissa informs Anna that Lovelace is suddenly polite, pliant, and willing to follow all her orders. He presents Clarissa with kind letters from his relatives. After quoting his speeches Clarissa pointedly asks Anna, "What think you, Miss Howe? Do you believe he can have any view in this?" (II,83) The reader of this "restored" proposal scene may still be in doubt as to Lovelace's motives. But Lovelace's narrative of this scene, in a "restored" letter to Belford, gives a precise explanation of the events of the proposal scene, and some ominous answers to Clarissa's questions (II,98–100).

Lovelace's tempestuous enthusiasm for Clarissa is not a momentary passion—it is attributed to a relentless desire for the lady, which must be satisfied. When Clarissa defends her father with a charming gesture, Lovelace writes, "I could hardly forbear taking her into my

arms on it . . . So much wit, so much beauty, such a lively manner . . . O Belford! she must be nobody's but mine." Lovelace compares himself with the most determined and desperate lovers of the
past: "I can now account for and justify Herod's command to
destroy his Mariamne, if he returned not alive from his interview
with Caesar"; Clarissa's panic is like that of "Semele . . . when the
Thunderer . . . was about to scorch her to a cinder." The magnitude
of this passion almost drives Lovelace to a rape: "had I not, just in
time, recollected that she was not so much in my power but that she
might abandon me at her pleasure, having more friends in that house
than I had, I should at that moment . . . have decided all" (II,98).

Through the subtle art of Richardson's "restorations," the proposal is no longer a moment that opens the participants to new futures. Instead, Lovelace is a confirmed libertine and schemer who is
determined to achieve Clarissa's seduction. A series of remarks,
made while Lovelace is describing the scene, demonstrates how he
is pushing the present toward an apparently inevitable catastrophe:

He makes a wish: "Lord send us once happily to London!"

He makes a prediction: "I saw she was frightened; and she would
have had reason had the scene been London, and that place in London which I have in view." (He'll have his way at Sinclair's.)

He analyzes the consequences of Clarissa's caution: "But, O Belford! had she had but the least patience with me; had she but made
me think that she would forgive this initiatory ardour; surely she
will not always be thus guarded." (Thus, if she relents at all, he'll
get her.)

He reflects on his own loss of control: "It is exceedingly difficult,
thou seest, for an honest man to act in disguises; as the poet says,
Thrust Nature back with a pitchfork, it will return." (This makes
Lovelace's love for Clarissa a "drive" which must eventually express itself.)

He feels a surge of anger and revenge: "Curse upon her perverse tyranny! How she makes me wait for an humble audience. . . . A
prince begging for her upon his knees should not prevail upon me
to spare her if I can get her to London—Oons! Jack, I believe I
have bit my lip through for vexation! But one day *hers* shall smart
for it."

He may decree her fate: "Nor . . . would the presence of her Norton, or of her aunt, or even of her mother, have saved the dear creature had I decreed her fall."

After his outburst, his plan takes another turn: he acts kind and conciliatory. Since he has "stepped out of the *gentle,* the *polite* part I had so newly engaged to act, I thought a ready obedience was the best atonement. . . . I was resolved to sacrifice a leg or an arm to make up all again, before she had time to determine upon any new measures."

This whole scene, and these passages from Lovelace's letter, involve Richardson in a massive intervention in the text of Clarissa. By attributing this kind of language to Lovelace, Richardson tries to make all that subsequently happens seem preordained.

Why does Richardson interpolate this long new proposal scene into the text? It is not a genuine proposal scene; it is counterfeit. It is not a moment of crisis or play. It could not invent or disclose a new future for the protagonists. This counterfeit proposal scene bears the same relationship to the genuine ones following it that a simulation bears to a space shot. It is designed to turn an open-ended event into a repeatable, predictable, comprehensible process, where Lovelace's designing ways and malevolent passions interact with Clarissa's entirely justifiable "delicacy" to create the impasse that leads to disaster. With this simulated proposal scene, Richardson gives the reader a (false) guide to reading and interpreting the proposal scenes which follow. To compose this counterfeit proposal, Richardson has had to parody elements of his own text. He does this for much the same reason that Lovelace parodies Clarissa (or we parody Clarissa or Richardson): he hopes to diminish the force, the authority, and the disruptive potential of the original proposal scenes.

There is another way to state what Richardson is doing here. All of his addenda work to replace one kind of time with another. There is a "time" in the text of *Clarissa* which is the result of the collision of the opposing interpretive positions sustained by the protagonists in struggle. This "time" is discontinuous from one moment to the next; it is essentially unpredictable; it is able to accommodate either member of a simple stark alternative—like the choices between marriage and death, or "yes" and "no" which organize the proposal scenes. This kind of "time" is contingent, suspenseful, and uncertain. It is what Heidegger calls "authentic temporality." But as Richardson begins to (try to) close down the struggles of interpretation, and as he offers his own interpretation of this text, we find him advocating a very different notion of time. Now time is modeled upon the apparent presence of the present moment. Temporality becomes something stable, and stablizing—a continuous sequence of present-past, present-present, and present-future which unfold into one another. Time becomes what Heidegger calls a "pure sequence of nows." This "time" is the time of a process, or the development of knowable subjects. As with Richardson's "restorations" to the text of *Clarissa*, this second kind of time belongs to a single authoritative act of retrospective interpretation. It holds few surprises because it is an adjunct to the act of explanation. From this standpoint, the different possibilities active in the time of the past just fade into a sequence of fateful-looking events. This is a conception of "time" which is fully compatible with organization of this text into "character," "plot," and "theme."[12]

Where does the interpretation of the novel into character, plot, and theme come from? Sometimes the index reads like a grotesque reduction of the novel's action; the "restorations" often look like fanciful extrapolations from the norms of behavior operative in the first edition of the novel. Though Richardson's increasing temporal distance from the production of this text makes some of his addenda seem "senile," neither the index nor the "restorations" are the crude contrivances of one intent on enforcing an eccentric reading of *Clarissa*. In their fundamental logic, Richardson's index and restorations extend and develop Clarissa's interpretation of the novel's action. This is why the reader of this critical text should have a sense of déjà vu on reading about the compositional aims of Richardson's index. They repeat, in displaced form, the composi-

12. In order to work out the relationship between temporality and interpretation in *Clarissa*, I have been aided by William Spanos's article, in the Heidegger issue of *boundary 2*, entitled "Heidegger, Kierkegaard, and the Hermeneutic Circle: Towards a Postmodern Theory of Interpretation as Disclosure." The whole of Division Two of *Being and Time* is valuable here, especially chapter 3, sections 61–66, "Dasein's Authentic Potentiality-For-Being-A-Whole, and Temporality as the Ontological Meaning of Care." Inauthentic temporality as a "pure sequence of 'nows'" is discussed on p. 377 of *Being and Time*, trans. S. Robinson (New York: Harper & Row, 1962). Jacques Derrida seems indebted to Heidegger's discussion when Derrida turns to the same question: see *Of Grammatology*, trans. Gayatri Chakravorty Spivak (Baltimore: The Johns Hopkins Press, 1976), pp. 66–67. Questions of temporality, authority, and interpretation, and a whole theoretical perspective on this study of *Clarissa* are developed in my article for the winter 1978 issue of *boundary 2*.

tional labors of Clarissa: first in her narrative, then in the private meditations and melodramatic scenes, and finally in the construction of her book. In each case, Clarissa hypostatizes agents into characters, links events into the causal sequences of a plot, and carries out a thematic exegesis of her own history. In our analysis, we have placed these interpretive activities of Clarissa in the context of her struggle with others, and her efforts to find a secure form for the subject. But Richardson takes the categories embedded in Clarissa's discourse (character, plot, theme) and gives them a specious objectivity by using them as tools to carry out an apparently neutral act of description.

With the addenda, Richardson finally plays his hand—in fact he overplays his hand—and shows us something that's been there all along: an active alliance between Clarissa and Richardson, which makes itself felt in every phase of the text's operation. Clarissa has always been the surrogate, in the text, for Richardson's compositional efforts (so that all her writing concerns are also his); and conversely, Richardson, as an editor defending the book, makes himself a functionary of Clarissa: he protects and extends her accomplishments according to methods and prescriptions she has laid down. We can get a fuller understanding of these affiliated acts of interpretation by taking a close look at the text of one letter—Clarissa's explanation of her reasons for refusing to marry Lovelace.

After his return to England, Clarissa's Cousin Morden satisfies himself that Lovelace is willing to marry Clarissa. Morden then writes to Clarissa, urging her to accept Lovelace and effect a general reconciliation. Clarissa acknowledges her confidence in Lovelace's sincerity, but then counters with a vivid explanation of why she is determined to reject him:

> Nor think me, my dear cousin, blamable for refusing him. I had given Mr. Lovelace no reason to think me a weak creature. If I *had*, a man of his character might have thought himself warranted to endeavour to take ungenerous advantage of the weakness he had been able to inspire. The consciousness of *my own* weakness (in that case) might have brought me to a composition with *his* wickedness.
>
> I can indeed forgive him. But that is because I think his crimes have set me above him. Can I be above the man, sir, to whom I shall give my hand and my vows, and with them a sanction to

the most premeditated baseness? No, sir, let me say that your Cousin Clarissa, were she likely to live many years, and *that* (if she married not this man) in penury or want, despised and forsaken by all her friends, puts not so high a value upon the conveniences of life, nor upon life itself, as to seek to re-obtain the one, or to preserve the other, by giving *such* a sanction which (*were she to perform her duty*) would reward the violator.

Nor is it so much from pride, as from principle, that I say this. What, sir! when virtue, when chastity, is the crown of a woman, and particularly of a wife, shall your cousin stoop to marry the man who could not form an attempt upon *hers* but upon a presumption that she was capable of receiving his offered hand, when he had found himself mistaken in the vile opinion he had conceived of her? Hitherto he has not had reason to think me weak. Nor will I give him an instance so flagrant, that weak I am in a point in which it would be criminal to be *found* weak.

One day, sir, you will perhaps know all my story. But, whenever it is known, I beg that the author of my calamities may not be vindictively sought after. He could not have been the author of them but for a strange concurrence of unhappy causes. [IV,250–51]

If there is one passage central to our understanding of Clarissa's interpretation of her life, this is it. Notice that three paragraphs of assertion and argument (against marrying Lovelace) are followed by Clarissa's inviting allusion to "all my story." This is appropriate, because Clarissa's assertions and her story are reciprocally dependent. Her story, and the book constructed to convey that story, will offer the evidence which justifies Clarissa's assertions; and these assertions about Lovelace, herself, her past, and her future set up the conditions (of death, of absence) which make Clarissa's history urgent reading. But what is the content of these assertions?

Clarissa offers a highly compressed version of her situation. The very simplicity of this formulation enhances its power. Lovelace is an agent of fixed "character" who plots Clarissa's destruction. Clarissa is defined by her resistance to his depravity. If character is simple, plot is a direct extension of character. In the recent past Clarissa has been tempted to a "weakness" which would draw her into "composition" with his "wickedness." For the future, she is determined not to undermine their separateness through marriage.

In this way, Clarissa asserts her adherence to the principles of "chastity" and "virtue." These principles and the triumph they bring become the theme or meaning of the story. Through the ineluctable "logic" of Clarissa's presentation, Cousin Morden's question—will Clarissa marry Lovelace or not?—has been defined out of existence: "his crimes have set me above him. Can I be above the man, sir, to whom I shall give my hand and my vows, and with them a sanction to the most premeditated baseness?" In Clarissa's formulation, Lovelace (with an abject nature) and marriage (with the strict duty it would entail for Clarissa) appear as incompatible ideas.

A closer look at the rhetorical forms of this passage will take us deeper into the design of Clarissa's position. Clarissa makes an assertion about the past and a vow about the future. She twice asserts her fundamental innocence by insisting on her separateness from Lovelace and the violence he does her: "I had given Mr. Lovelace no reason to think me a weak creature," and "hitherto he has not had reason to think me weak." In reply to these assertions, skeptical observers of Clarissa's behavior can point to three actions which have linked her to Lovelace: her willingness to write him, her willingness (at one point in the action) to leave Harlowe Place with him, and her willingness to meet him in the garden alone. But beyond these three occasional links with him, Clarissa feels an emotional and physical attraction to Lovelace which becomes more and more apparent in the second installment (remember their ride in the country and the ipecacuanha plot, II,430–39). If allowed to develop without violence, this love would have ended in marriage and sexual union. But Clarissa is tied to Lovelace in another way— through the intensity of the struggle she carried on with him. This struggle reaches one of its natural possible culminations in the rape.

Clarissa is keenly aware of all the ways in which skeptics link her with Lovelace. But rather than confirm Lovelace's victory over her through marriage, she enhances the authority of her assertions about the past by vowing, in the most extravagant terms, never to have the depraved man. The first vow develops a sentimental strain (you can hear the violins of suffering building in this prose): "no, sir, let me say that your Cousin Clarissa, were she likely to live many years, and that . . . in penury or want, despised or forsaken by all her friends, puts not so high a value upon the conveniences of life, nor upon life itself . . . etc." The second vow glories in advancing strenuous ideals of feminine virtue: "What sir! when virtue, when chastity, is the crown of a woman, and particularly of a wife, shall your cousin stoop to marry the man who could form an attempt upon *hers.* . . ."

But Clarissa goes beyond these assertions and vows, and shows real daring and imagination in articulating her relationship with Lovelace. She does not name or describe the rape, but she weaves the language of desire and seduction into her passage, so that the rape, as the crucial fact of Clarissa's history, will never be far from the reader's mind. These suggestive phrases are scattered throughout the letter: "weak creature," "to take ungenerous advantage," "form an attempt," "crimes," "vile opinion," "violator," and "chastity." By writing her text in the margins of the rape scene, Clarissa concedes to Lovelace a physical dominance which ensures her moral superiority; she summons their moment of greatest intimacy to give credence to the idea of their essential separateness; she acknowledges the body's penetration as a way of asserting the self's inviolable integrity. With her story inscribed into the rape scene, Clarissa gives plausibility to her presentation of Lovelace as the "violator," herself as the "violated," and their mutual transactions as an elaborated one-sided plot against her innocence. The rape will be the unspeakable deed which Clarissa's whole life and story will speak over and over again. The proximity of the rape, understood as a heinous crime, also justifies the inflated rhetoric of this passage, and the manichean oppositions it articulates ("baseness"/"chastity," "weakness"/"virtue," etc.).

In this context, each of Clarissa's statements about her disposition toward Lovelace is strangely reversible. Thus she writes, "I can forgive him," but the reasons she gives for doing so—"his crimes have set me above him"—show that she has not relented, or let their contentions pass into memory. To "forgive" just reopens the struggle on a new and higher plane. Clarissa also writes that it is not "pride but principle" which leads her to reject Lovelace. But her assertions of superiority always seem to leave pride and principle hopelessly entangled: she will not "stoop" to marry a man who could hold a "vile opinion" of her; rather, she will glory in her "chastity." Finally, though Clarissa hopes Cousin Morden won't "vindictively" seek after Lovelace, she still refers to Lovelace as "the author of my calamities," and Morden (and every reader of this text) has little difficulty reading the covert messages of the letter—that the struggle goes on, Clarissa's pride is bruised but now broken, she will not forgive Lovelace, she must be revenged. By novel's end, Morden has obliged his cousin.

The rape scene has yet another function for Clarissa in this passage. All through the text "time" has been a horizon of uncertainty, the boundary along which Clarissa has had to confront play, doubt, and chance. When Lovelace suddenly proposes in earnest, when Cousin Morden writes pressing her to marry Lovelace—at these moments new futures open and the unexpected becomes possible. When Belfour sketches a happy ending for the novel, or skeptics question the purity of Clarissa's motives, Richardson must respond to proposals which *play,* in disturbing ways, with his design. At each of these points, time enters the text, and the text opens onto time, because a countervailing interpretation suddenly confronts Clarissa and Richardson as a hostile force which threatens to disrupt the interpretive figures of life and text that Clarissa and Richardson have labored to fix. Clarissa's answer to Cousin Morden is analogous to Richardson's revision of the proposal scenes. It should be understood as a response to the incursion of "time." Morden's letter reintroduces Clarissa to the active "time" of the genuine proposal—the moment of multiple futures and critical choices. Clarissa answers from the standpoint of another scene, the rape, and another whole version of the Clarissa-Lovelace relationship: one where there is evidently only one role (the virtuous victim), one future (death), and no apparent choice.

Clarissa writes her answer in such a way that the rape appears as a single still point, a vivid moment of clarity from which she can overcome time. By writing of her life and situation from within the rape scene, Clarissa can make her life seem to stand still. She situates herself within an "interpretive present" where she can characterize herself and Lovelace, plot past present and future, and thematize their story. The subtle evocation of one compelling melodramatic image (Clarissa being raped) has made a character-plot-theme interpretation of the story plausible; and this interpretation attempts to swallow "time," to put "time" and its uncertainties out of play. Little wonder that, several pages after Clarissa's letter to Morden, Belford reports to Lovelace that Clarissa has chosen to adorn her casket with the device of "a crowned serpent, with its tail in its mouth, forming a ring, the emblem of eternity" (IV,257)

Since beginning our lengthy treatment of "character," "plot," and "theme," we have demonstrated how Richardson used these categories in writing notes and an index summary to extend interpretive control over the text. When "restorations" were added in the third edition, they too bolstered the plausibility of a repetition of the text in terms of the notions of "character," "plot," and "theme"; they also helped to control the destabilizing moments and interpretations in the text. Finally, we have found this interpretive reduction of the story operative in Clarissa's presentation of her situation in an important letter to her Cousin Morden. By discovering the central importance of "time" to the design of Clarissa's position, we can now see *why* this triad of categories held special appeal for Richardson and Clarissa. By stopping "time" in one moment (the rape), and the text in one pattern (a repetition of the action in the form of character, plot, and theme), they try to seal the text off from any subsequent acts of interpretation, any unwelcome bounty from the text's life in future time.

There are several reasons why the character-plot-theme interpretation Clarissa and Richardson elaborate has an immense appeal to many later readers of this text. (In the next chapter I shall describe these readers as "humanist.") These readers like the way Clarissa and Richardson have helped to fix the meaning of the text. But they are especially comfortable with the figure of man and his life to which this interpretation helps to give authority. With the notion of "character," a benign, humane, knowable version of man enters the novel. This man is not an enigma, an actor, or a trickster—he is a known quantity, an identity, a nature. A "character" is an agent embalmed; it is an agent divested of genuine choices, or any unconscious. If the author teases the reader for a moment by giving his character an "inner nature" (such as Clarissa's "pride," or her love for Lovelace), this is only a passing puzzle. It is speedily resolved to the satisfaction of author, reader, and character. There must be nothing disturbing or unnamable in this "character"— nothing that would interrupt its functioning as a reliable mechanism that always does the thing which is utterly "characteristic." In this schema, time holds no surprises. Time only exists to allow the being and nature of the character to emerge. When man becomes a "character," he loses all wonder and anxiety about himself.

"Plot" is the form in which a character will want to know his past, present, and future. To see why, we must keep in mind the varied etymological resources of this little word. "Plot" begins by meaning a patch of ground, then the plan or map of that ground, or a structure on that ground. Sometimes a "plot" is a scheme or design for accomplishing some purpose. The term is also applied to literary works, with special emphasis given to the sequence of events in a play or a novel (see *OED*). None of these meanings of the word *plot* ever entirely loses its original connection with the idea of an articulated space. In chapter 4, above, we have seen that Clarissa plots her story with two related moves: (1) a decision to die which marks out a plausible beginning and ending for her story, and converts a linear "series" into a circular "whole"; and (2) she imbues the events of her own past with a subjectlike intentionality, so that the past becomes organized into a cause-and-effect chain with a discernible telos and meaning. Richardson extends these two operations: (1) by speeding up, through the index summary, his presentation of the "whole" arch of the novel's action, and (2) by multiplying the causal connection between events with his corrective surgery. In their compositional activity, Clarissa and Richardson accurately repeat the logic (and illogic) of Aristotle's description of "the proper construction" of a plot in the seventh chapter of the *Poetics*:

> Having thus distinguished the parts, let us now consider the proper construction of the Fable or Plot, as that is at once the first and the most important thing in Tragedy. We have laid it down that a tragedy is an imitation of an action that is complete in itself, as a whole of some magnitude; for a whole may be of no magnitude to speak of. Now a whole is that which has beginning, middle, and end. A beginning is that which is not itself necessarily after anything else, which has *naturally* something else after it; an end is that which is *naturally* after something itself, either as its necessary or usual consequent, and with nothing else after it; and a middle, that which is *by nature* after one thing and has also another after it. A well-constructed Plot, therefore, cannot either begin or end at any point one likes; beginning and end in it must be of the forms just described. Again: to be beautiful, *a living creature*, and every whole made up of parts, must not only present a certain order in its arrangement of parts, but also be of a certain definite magnitude. . . . Just in the same way, then,

as a beautiful whole made up of parts, or *a beautiful living creature,* must be of some size, but a size to be taken in by the eye,
so a story or Plot must be of some length, but of a length to be
taken in by the memory. . . . [My emphasis]

In this passage, Aristotle apparently simply instructs the artist how
to achieve the "order" and "magnitude" a "plot" will need to be
"beautiful." For the plot to imitate an action which is "complete
in itself" and "whole," the artist must do what Clarissa and Richardson do: weave the events of the story together so that they follow "necessarily" from each other. But this depends on a very
arbitrary separation of the action within the plot from what comes
before and after it. For once one has accepted the necessity of a
cause-and-effect interpretation of events, how is it really possible
to find a true "beginning" or "end" to an action like Clarissa's life?—
either an origin "which is not itself necessarily after anything else"
or something (like an end) that has "nothing else after it."

Why does Aristotle insist that a plot have such severely articulated
limits? The answer is indicated by his use of the modifiers "naturally . . . naturally . . . by nature . . ." and becomes explicit in the
words with which Aristotle turns to consider the proper "magnitude"'
of the plot. He writes: "Again: to be beautiful, a living creature and
every whole made up of parts, must. . . ." Aristotle's conception of
the artwork, and the character of wholeness a "plot" must attain,
is commanded by a metaphorical substitution: to be "beautiful"
an artwork must be (like) a "living creature." This metaphorical
substitution (and the mimetic assumptions that enable this substitution) authorize Aristotle to invoke the regulating category of "nature," establish the formal properties of "nature," the proper forms
of the "natural." So wholeness and unity of parts become the
crucial formal means by which an artist may get an arbitrary construction (an artwork) to take on the natural beauty of a "living
creature": and in the same movement, an object with form and
presence, a cunningly constructed plot, will be allowed to stand in
for a succession of contingent moments.

R. S. Crane and the Chicago school of critics refine and extend Aristotle's concept of plot. By incorporating "character" and "thought"
into an enlarged conception of "plot," and taking account of the
reader's expectations and desires as he negotiates the story, R. S.

Crane goes beyond a notion of plot as "mere mechanism" and insists that the "form of the plot" is its "distinctive 'working or power'" on a reader. And its quality will depend upon "the power of its particular synthesis of character, action, and thought . . . to move our feelings powerfully." In this way the plot becomes the "first principle" of the artwork and the surest touchstone to its nature and value. Although this introduces energy into the concept of plot, the appeal and strategic usefulness of the word *plot* (for Aristotle, Clarissa, Richardson, and the Chicago school of critics), connected as it always is with the word *form,* derives from the way "plot," as an articulated space, becomes a privileged means, in Western art, to represent something much more unstable—temporality.[13] When a work of art represents events in time in form of a "plot," it takes events that were diachronic, often discontinuous with one another, and always open to happening in many ways, and arranges them into a pattern which is synchronic, mutually dependent, and connected in such a way that every event seems to happen at once, in one interpretive instant. In other words, "plot" works to spatialize time. This maneuver helps to obscure what we noticed in our analysis of the proposal scenes in chapter 4 and 6: the events of the past are reported, after the fact, by self-interested parties in the form of a necessary sequence of actions, ascribed to definable characters. But if the event has happened in another way—if Clarissa and Lovelace had said "yes" to one another, or Belfour had won Richardson to her cause—then reporters with different interests would have plotted a very different sequence of actions, carried through by very different-looking "characters."

It is not difficult to see how "character," "plot," and "theme" work together to enhance the legitimacy of one another as tools of representation. The idea of "character" turns man into a reliable vector whose actions are largely predictable. Several vectors interact to shape an action or plot whose form now appears inevitable. This plot, which is the history of the characters, recoils back on their

13. *The Basic Works of Aristotle* (New York: Random House, 1941), trans. Richard McKeon, pp. 1462–63. For R. S. Crane's discussion of plot, see "The Concept of Plot and the Plot of 'Tom Jones,'" in *Critics and Criticism* (Chicago: University of Chicago Press, 1952), pp. 62–93. Wayne Booth further develops the relationship between plot and reader expectations in *The Rhetoric of Fiction* (Chicago: University of Chicago Press, 1961). See also the citation under "plot" in W. F. Thrall and A. Hibbard, *A Handbook to Literature,* revised and enlarged by C. Hugh Holman (New York: Odyssey Press, 1960), pp. 356–58.

lives so as to endow them with a tone and fatality, which ratify the character of the characters. With characters defined and plot given form, it is easy to exhume some lesson, or portable piece of knowledge, from the story. Rescuing a "theme" from the story will vindicate the effort of the interpreter; the whole operation has enabled the text to *speak* to the interpreter. Along the way, this reader-interpreter has, by using this valuable triad of categories, eluded certain discomfiting experiences: "character" elides man's separateness from himself and others; "plot" overcomes his doubts about the past and anxiety over the future; "theme" converts inchoate experience into an intelligible message.

But when we cease to consider "character," "plot," and "theme" as innocent descriptive terms, and inscribe them into the interpretive struggle which animates this text, each of these terms shifts toward the less benign meanings their etymologies disclose. While "character" can be a "distinctive feature" or "essential nature," its derivation from an engraved mark or character used in writing opens its other important meaning—a part assumed by an actor on a stage. A "plot" can be a diagram, but it also is a scheme or wicked design contrived to dupe others. "Theme" is the subject or central message of a discourse, but it is thought to derive from a legal term meaning "a proposition to be debated."[14] Now, while Clarissa and Richardson emphasize the upright, truth-oriented meanings of these terms, each also opens on to its Lovelacean aspect: where Clarissa's "character" becomes her "act," her life-sequence becomes a "plot" to gull her readers, and her "theme" (virtue) becomes, not the message or meaning of this text, but the proposition that opens our debate.

Clarissa and Richardson have labored to arrest time—to take the "time" in the heroine's life and the "time" in the author's text and still it, cage it—characterize, plot, and thematize it. But because recalcitrant readers, like Lovelace, never stop drawing *their* figures in the text, time goes on, time escapes and then returns, bringing new things, new perspectives, new interpretations. Time returns as history, and places even the efforts to escape time back in time, as one moment in an unending and ongoing struggle of interpretation.

14. Skeat, *A Concise Etymological Dictionary* (Oxford: Oxford Press, 1882.)

7: The Humanist Sublime: *Clarissa* as the Agent of a Humanist Ideology

The cause of the origin of a thing and its eventual utility, its actual employment and place in a system of purposes, lie worlds apart; whatever exists, having somehow come into being, is again and again reinterpreted to new ends, taken over, transformed, and redirected by some power superior to it; all events in the organic world are a subduing, a becoming master, and all subduing and becoming master involves a fresh interpretation, a structuring through which any previous 'meaning' and 'purpose' are necessarily obscured or even obliterated.

Nietzsche, The Genealogy of Morals

In disposing of Clarissa's body and personal effects, Belford is determined to follow her will to the letter. Lovelace has other ideas: "Although her will may in some respects cross mine, yet I expect to be observed. I will be the interpreter of hers." [IV,377]

Clarissa is miraculously free. . . . She is both grasped; and mysterious, self-existent, unpredictable. She is created both by the most remorseless analysis, and by letting the subconscious go in the dramatist's projection. She is both subject to the full conditioning of her and her creator's society; and yet her reality is quite beyond the representative.[1]

This passage is not a casual or random effusion. This is merely the last in a long line of testimonials to Clarissa that have their own peculiar natural history and archeology. And when we have placed its author, Mark Kinkead-Weekes, in this history, we shall discover that each of the things he says about Clarissa, and each of the ways he says them, has an unexpected coherence and intelligibility. As early as the eighteenth century, *Clarissa* came under the influence of what I have chosen to call the "humanist" interpretation of the novel. Since that day, this interpretation has been advanced by a group of unwitting collaborators who share a secular, non-Christian, moral interest in man. And though to be a humanist may sound affirmative and civic-minded, we shall find that these critics are no less

---

1. Mark Kinkead-Weekes, *Samuel Richardson: Dramatic Novelist* (Ithaca: Cornell University Press, 1973), pp. 501–02. Hereafter cited as *SR:DN.*

willful and self-interested than the other participants in the struggles of interpretation.

Humanist critics make themselves the caretakers of an institution that is designed to use literature in general, and *Clarissa* in particular, to enforce a particular conception of man, and to uplift and "humanize" the reader. It will be the work of this chapter to investigate the sources and the logic of this way of reading *Clarissa*—the most important force in shaping *Clarissa*'s reception in modern times. And though we cannot explore the matter here, many of the insights we shall develop by reading these humanist critics are of general use in understanding the dominant interpretations of many of the English novels of the last two centuries.

Who are these humanist readers of *Clarissa*? They are Joseph Spence, Sara Fielding, Henry Fielding, and Dennis Diderot in the eighteenth century; and William Sale, Ian Watt, Mark Kinkead-Weekes, and others in this century. The humanist critics are not hostile to the interests and categories Clarissa and Richardson bring to bear on the text. In fact, these humanist readers affiliate their interpretations of the text with Clarissa's and Richardson's by describing the text in terms of "character," "plot," and "theme." The humanist critic is anxious to efface the contingency of events; he also wants a sturdy, reliable image of man. Thus, humanist criticism is replete with tributes to Richardson's "power" of characterization, and Kinkead-Weekes even evinces enthusiasm for Clarissa's gradual growth toward wisdom and spiritual strength.

Finally, however, the humanist critic is simply more secular than Richardson, less concerned with the scene of judgment than Clarissa. He is not nearly so anxious, as either author or heroine, to establish Clarissa as an exemplar of virtue. Instead, the humanist critic labors to cement an interpretive alliance with the text so that he may carry on two activities: he reads *Clarissa* as a novel which plumbs the depths of the human psyche, and he orchestrates a reader experience of *Clarissa* that he hopes will "humanize" the reader, making the reader more sympathetic, more humble, and more full of admiration for the good in others. We must look closely at these critics' reading to learn what these two tasks might mean. But it is not premature to note one result of their activity: in attempting to achieve these tasks, the humanist critics displace the text away from many of the concerns and ideals of Richardson and Clarissa.

Taking the Torch to the Back of the Cave

In his *Life of Johnson*, Boswell quotes Johnson as distinguishing between Fielding's "characters of manners" and the "characters of nature" Richardson creates:

> Characters of manners are very entertaining; but they are to be understood by a more superficial observer than characters of nature, where a man must dive into the recesses of the human heart.[2]

The figurative comparison of Richardson and Fielding that Johnson used to elucidate his point leaves little doubt as to where his own sympathies lay: "there was as great a difference between them as between a man who knew how a watch was made, and a man who could tell the hour by looking on the dial-plate." To "dive into the recesses of the human heart"—this is the adventure the humanist critic urges us to embark upon in reading Richardson. And this journey is charged with significance, because the humanist critic makes man's interiority—his heart, mind, or consciousness—the locus of human value. In humanist criticism the heart becomes an object of delicious mystery, a source of pleasure, and the touchstone to man's nature. Richardson's novel is said to meet the needs of this heart and to teach the reader the secrets that lie buried there. The humanist critic sees himself as the handmaiden who will help deliver these truths and experiences from the book to the reader.

No one has done more to advance the reading of Richardson as an artist of the psychological than Ian Watt. For in his (hi-)story of "the rise of the novel," Richardson occupies the place of honor precisely because of the "subjective and inward direction" Richardson is said to give his fiction. Richardson plays a significant part in the great shifts in world views described by Watt: "the transition from the objective, social, and public orientation of the classical world to the subjective, individualist and private orientation of the life and literature of the last two hundred years."[3] Why does Richardson play this part? It is not just his Protestantism, nor simply the fact that he was remarkably in tune with the needs and ideals of a large, new

---

2. *Life of Johnson*, ed. R. W. Chapman (London: Oxford University Press, 1953), p. 389.
3. Ian Watt, *The Rise of the Novel* (Berkeley: University of California Press, 1957), p. 176.

middle-class readership. More than anything else, it is his use of the "letter form" which "offered Richardson a short-cut, as it were, to the heart." In Ian Watt's account, Richardson's protracted investigation of the human heart, through the use of the letter form, put readers and later novelists in touch with what man, in his complex interiority, "really" is:

> It is this minute-to-minute content of consciousness which constitutes what the individual personality really is, and dictates his relationship to others: it is only by contact with this consciousness that a reader can participate fully in the life of a fictional character.[4]

Given this understanding of Richardson's art, it is not surprising that Watt structures his reading of *Clarissa* around a succession of more and more probing descriptions of Clarissa's psychology. At the highpoint of analysis, Watt approvingly quotes a passage from Diderot's "Eulogy for Richardson":

> It is Richardson who carries his torch to the back of the cave; and it is he who teaches you to discern the subtle and dishonorable motives concealing themselves from view behind other motives which are honorable, and that hasten to show themselves first. He breathes on the noble phantom that presents itself at the mouth of the cave; it vanishes, and the hideous Moor it masked appears.[5]

This is the single most famous tribute to Richardson as a psychologist. It is cast in terms that make a movement into the mind of man and the adjudication between the specious surface and the lurking evil an exciting, even a melodramatic, process.

The claims which Johnson, Ian Watt, and Diderot make for Richardson's art raise another question: *how* does Richardson succeed in taking the reader into the mysterious regions of the heart to uncover hidden truth? Of all Richardson's critics, none posed this question more forcefully, or pursued this question with more cogency, than Diderot. His eulogy for Richardson is charged with admiration for Richardson's art and regret at his death. But Diderot is also fascinated

---

4. Ibid., p. 192.
5. All quotations from Diderot are my translations from Dennis Diderot, *Oeuvres Esthétique* (Paris: Editions Garnier Frères, 1965), pp. 32ff. Hereafter *OE*.

with the new possibilities this art opens for the novel as a genre. Like many of his contemporaries, Diderot found himself strangely involved in the fate of Richardson's fictional characters. But when a married woman of his acquaintance abandoned a dangerous correspondence of long standing after reading *Clarissa*, Diderot was decisively impressed. He wrote to Sophia Volland, "Look at the good effect of this book! Imagine if this work were spread over the surface of the world—in this way Richardson would be the author of a hundred good deeds each day!"[6]

Diderot's eulogy becomes a polemical essay on behalf of the ethical potentials of this new kind of art. Diderot also probes the processes of this kind of art to discover how it reshapes the reader's heart in terms of virtue—how it can even make the reader *desire* virtue. Diderot attributes these unusual powers to two tendencies of the novels: the Richardson novel gives the reader an intimate knowledge of the human heart; and it impels the reader into a rapturous identification with the main characters. Diderot explores these two ideas, and their consequences, in the five sections of his eulogy. The first section names the special powers of Richardson's art; the second describes the techniques of this art; the third section characterizes the reader's experience of the novels; the fourth shows how the novels become the catalyst for forming a new social community; and the last section offers a final, humble farewell to Richardson.[7]

Three passages from the eulogy describe how Richardson teaches the reader to read man's heart. The first passage comes after Diderot's warning about the "artful and temperate tone" that the passions often "affect." Richardson helps the reader see around the most cunning disguises:

> In Richardson men of all ranks and conditions, and in all the various circumstances of life, converse in the style, that we recognize to be natural to them. If some secret sentiment lurk at the bottom of the heart of a character he introduces, listen attentively, and you will hear some discordant tone betray it. Richardson knew that falsehood could never perfectly resemble truth;

6. The editor describes this episode and quotes Diderot's letter in his introduction to the eulogy; see *OE*, pp. 24–25.

7. These five sections correspond to the following pages of the above edition: I:29–33; II:34–36; III:36–41; IV:41–47; V:47–48. All subsequent citations from the eulogy will be given in the text.

for the latter will always remain truth, and the former must still
be falsehood. [*Eulogy*, 32]

Diderot begins by assuring the reader that man's appearances in Richardson's text correspond most exactly with his appearances in our
experience. But with one change. Since Richardson knows that
"falsehood will never perfectly resemble truth," if there is any
"secret sentiment" lurking in the heart, he places "some discordant
tone" in their speech so that the attentive reader will be able to discern this sentiment. In this way, art has been faithful to nature by
making sure that a diacritical mark, added by the author, makes the
distinction between truth and falsehood visible.

In the second passage, Diderot compares our way of knowing
nature's changing aspect with our way of understanding a man's
changing countenance:

A hundred times you have seen the setting of the sun, and the
rising of the stars; you have heard the fields resound with the
song of birds: but which of you has perceived, that it was the
noise of the day that rendered the silence of the night more delightful? It is the same with moral phenomena as it is with physical: the voice of the passions has often struck your ears, but you
have been far from penetrating the secret of their tones and expressions. There is not any passion that does not have its facial
expression; and all these facial expressions occur in their turns on
one countenance, without that person ceasing to be the same;
and the art of the great poet, and the painter, is to exhibit to you
a fugitive detail, that would have escaped your eye. [*Eulogy*, 35]

Now we can see how Diderot understands the teaching power of
Richardson's text. Just as the distinction between truth and falsehood was present in appearance but absent to the eye, so the "noise
of the day" was present, secretly, in our experience of "delight" in
the "silence of the night"—but it takes art to show us this. In an
analogous fashion, we are in ignorance as to "the secret" of the
"tones and expressions" of the human passion. Since a succession
of facial expressions are common to all men, but each looks slightly
different on different faces, it takes a "great poet" or "painter" to
show us that "fugitive detail" which will alow us to read a man
correctly.

But what is the "secret" we are trying to read? It is not here named by Diderot. What does this "fugitive detail" allow us to know? The third passage devoted to reading characters gives us an answer. Diderot has been praising the amplitude of Richardson's creation and the sheer numbers of his distinguishable characters:

> But what is most astonishing, each of these [characters] has his particular ideas, expressions, and manners; and these ideas, these manners, these expressions, vary according to the circumstances, interests, or feelings of the moment, as we see different passions succeed each other on the same countenance. No man of taste will take a letter of Mrs. Norton for a letter of one of Clarissa's aunts, the letter of one aunt for that of another [*sic*], or of Mrs. Harlowe, or a note of Mrs. Howe for one from Mrs. Harlowe, though these persons are in the same situation, and have the same opinions with respect to the same subject. In this immortal work, as in nature at springtime, one does not find two leaves of the same green. What an immense variety of nuances! [*Eulogy*, 39]

When paired with the first two passages, two somewhat contradictory ideas emerge from this passage. We might call the first idea the miracle of the completely realized character. Diderot is in awe of Richardson for having used his art, and subtle scattering of "fugitive details," to create characters each of whom has a "particular," distinct nature. And this is especially remarkable when one considers the materials he had to use (which are paradoxically also the obstacles that stand in Richardson's way); for these very characters are composed of "ideas, expressions, and manners" which shift with "the circumstances, interests, or feelings of the moment" and *are shared* with all other men, just as all men share the catalogue of "passions" and "facial expressions" that "succeed each other on one countenance."

Diderot's analysis makes one thing clear. Not only is the individual character a complex amalgam of ideas, expressions, and manners changing through time, but the artistic process which articulates this individual is also complex. Out of this dialectic of similarity and difference Richardson rescues perfected individual characters. The example Diderot offers does not explain this mystery. It simply insists that the reader is able to distinguish the letters of a chain of characters "in the same situation," and having "the same opinions with respect to the same subject" (in this case, probably Clarissa's elopement).

There are two possible explanations for this creation of individual characters. One is merely to ascribe godlike powers of creation to Richardson. In this spirit, Diderot tacitly compares Richardson to God by insisting that the range and nuance of his work of art rivals nature's at springtime. Richardson is simply able, as a genius, to add the nuance, the shade, the "fugitive detail" that designates the "secret" distinguishing mark of a character's nature. But if we place emphasis on another side of Diderot's explanation, we note that the language of the passions and social behavior is held in common by all men, and the reader's sense (or illusion) of the identity of any one individual comes from the way Richardson arrays these common elements in relationship to one another. Thus, in terms of the example Diderot provides, the very similarity of opinion on Clarissa's elopement, as shared by Mrs. Howe, Mrs. Harlowe, Mrs. Norton, and Clarissa's aunt, offers a context for Richardson in which to illustrate their distinct modes of response. In this way, the reader is given an intuition of the distinct characters of each.

In the first explanation of Richardson's characterization, the artist's genius is like God's finger touching Adam's in Michelangelo's Sistine Chapel ceiling—it places a divine spark of individuality at the center of each human heart. The second assumes a public language of the passions and a general psychology of man. We get further support for the second idea by watching how Diderot describes the new powers that Richardson's text has given him:

> I form to myself an idea of the persons whom the author brings on the stage: their faces are familiar to me: I recognize them in the streets, in public places, in society: they inspire me with attachment or aversion . . . some portion of [Richardson's] picture is incessantly before my eye. I seldom find six persons together, without associating with them the idea of some of his characters. . . . [Richardson] has taught me to know [men] by fine and ready marks. [*Eulogy,* 38–39]

Here Diderot is less interested in the radical uniqueness of Richardson's characters than in the way these characters become types that allow Diderot to read the men he meets in his daily experience. And this leads to another intuition. In Diderot's discussion of how Richardson teaches the reader to know men, the notion of the rich particularity of the individual functions as a screen for another, equally important idea: the essential similarity of all men. Diderot says as much in the paragraph of his eulogy which follows the third passage devoted to Richardson's characterization.

Echoing an argument from Aristotle's *Poetics*, Diderot values Richardson's novelistic art over history. History records "a few individuals" in "a portion of time" on "a point on the surface of the globe." Richardson "paints the human species." "All times, all places are embraced in his works. The human heart, which was, is, and always will be the same, is the model which you have copied" (*Eulogy*, 39–40). Notice Diderot uses the singular—it is "*the* human heart" which "was, is, always will be the same." This single object serves as the ground of truth and knowledge about man upon which Richardson creates characters who are not simply unique, but also somehow speak a general, universal truth about man.

At this point in our analysis we confront a contradiction. Diderot praises Richardson for offering the reader characters who have the rich, complex particularity that he associates with real humans; but this artistic process and novelistic psychology imply and depend upon a unified general conception of Man. We cannot overcome this contradiction, but we can watch it function for Diderot when he turns to discuss the second crucial power ascribed to Richardson's novels: their ability to win the reader's identification with its characters.

> If it be of importance to men to be persuaded, that, setting aside every consideration beyond the present life, nothing is so conducive to happiness as virtue, how great is the service Richardson has rendered the human species! He has not demonstrated the truth, but he has made us feel it: at every line we are compelled to prefer the lot of suffering virtue to that of triumphant vice. Who would be Lovelace, with all his advantages? Who would not be Clarissa, in spite of her misfortunes? Often, in reading him, have I said: "To resemble her I would willingly sacrifice my life; I would rather die, than be that man." [*Eulogy*, 32]

In this passage Diderot shows us how Richardson's text wins the reader to virtue. Early in the eulogy Diderot asks, "What is virtue?"

and answers, "It is a sacrifice of one's self" (*Eulogy*, 31). Now, the text impels the reader to self-sacrifice *not* by "demonstrating" the truth of a proposition ("nothing is so conducive to happiness as virtue"), but by making us "feel" this truth by being a text that makes the reader simply want to "be a Clarissa, in spite of her misfortunes." By identifying with Clarissa, by seeking to "resemble" her, we "sacrifice" ourselves and our own interests. This indicates one reason for characters that appear as complex and unique as God's creations. Only such characters could be substantial and interesting enough, and thus "real" enough, to win the reader's identification.

But Diderot does not just let this identification take place. He guides and enforces the reader's identification with Clarissa by using rhetorical techniques that habitually recur in the humanist readings of *Clarissa*. First he bullies his reader into proper sympathies through two rhetorical questions: "Who would be Lovelace, with all his advantages? Who would not be Clarissa?" Diderot's reader must sense that anyone who dares answer in the affirmative will be declared less than human. And then Diderot uses the gentle and more insidious technique of the personal testimonial to guide his reader into conformation with his own response to the text: "Often, in reading him, have I said: 'To resemble her I would willingly sacrifice my life.'" Now we can see why Diderot must assert a general psychology of "the heart of man." If the reader of *Clarissa* is going to respond to Lovelace and Clarissa with any uniformity, if he is to obey the imperatives set up by Diderot's hortatory description of *his* response to *Clarissa*, if the reader is going to be virtuous through identification with the heroine, then the union of these minds in one mind, the dissolution of all these readers in the consciousness of a Clarissa as conceived by Diderot, necessitates an acceptance by all these readers of the general psychology of man that Diderot invokes.

Before seeing how Diderot works to achieve this consensus, we must pause to consider the logic of the moral ideal Diderot conceives for the reader. Once the reader has sacrificed himself, he "no longer exalt[s] the trifling qualities that are useful to [him]" (*Eulogy*, 32). Diderot claims this kind of moral breakthrough for himself:

Owing to Richardson . . . I feel more love for my fellow-creatures, more inclination for my duties; for the wicked only pity, for the unfortunate more compassion, for the good more respect; more circumspection in the enjoyment of the present, more indifference to the future. [*Eulogy*, 38]

Here Diderot seems to have succeeded in dissolving his ego, so that he can survey all the world with a wise and sublime disinterestedness. The mood does not last long, for he is soon venting his anger at the cruelty of the Harlowes, his contempt for Prévost's abridgments, and his scorn for modern readers of "frivolous taste" who don't have time to read Richardson.

But Diderot does not simply draw his reader to his idea of virtue with glowing descriptions. He, like other humanist critics, has a much more subtle technique. Diderot tempts his reader with a strange bargain: he asks that the reader detach himself from his self, his interests, and his rich individuality, and be governed by his bond with the suffering Clarissa. In return the reader receives assurances that all men have the rich individuality he experiences, vicariously, through the character embodied in the text. Crudely stated, if the reader will relinquish his will, interests, and particular perspective, he will receive in return a guarantee that he has these things through Clarissa. But, as we shall see, this bargain, if accepted by the reader, exposes him to special forms of manipulation by the humanist critic.

Diderot knows that the most powerful way to guarantee the consensus he seeks is to establish a community of readers. He issues a call for membership, and promises his readers very special pleasures:

Come, and learn of him to reconcile yourselves to the evils of life: Come, we will weep together over the unhappy of Richardson's fictions, and say: "If misfortune overwhelms us, at least the good will lament over us also." [*Eulogy*, 33]

In this program, Richardson's book becomes the catalyst which forms a sympathetic community of readers. Now, if life should involve misfortune, there will be this compensation: their own misfortunes will become, like Clarissa's, a sentimental fiction for others to enjoy. In his eulogy Diderot takes certain steps to forge this community of readers. First he defines criteria for membership in this community, casting out readers not worthy of consideration by making this comparison: Diderot tells us there is a dissipated group of readers of frivolous taste who are distracted by life and engulfed in the noisy preoccupations of a trivial world. This group does not possess fit readers of *Clarissa*. But one can also find "the man of solitude and tranquility . . . [who] prefers the shades of retirement, and to cultivate the tender feelings of the heart" (*Eulogy,* 34). Diderot's community of readers will be formed of individuals like this.

Members of this community become so absorbed in the illusion of the fiction that they will not acknowledge any secure boundary between the fictional and the "real." For them, there will be no significant difference between characters of the novels and real people. They will carry on debates and conversations which become so "interesting" and "animated," they will discuss "the most important points of morals and taste," and "Pamela, Clarissa, Grandison [will be] praised and blamed as if they had been persons living, of our own acquaintance" (*Eulogy,* 37). To someone dropping into the room at this moment, Diderot points out, the discourse will seem to be about real people. And this is one of the purposes of the humanist critic's casual and familiar way of referring to the characters of a novel. If a character seems like a personal acquaintance of the critic, he must be real, and the critic must "know" this character very well.

Since these novels encompass so much of life and morality, the reader can use them as a "touchstone" to judge the morals and sensibility of the readers he meets. There are some responses so perverse that they lead Diderot to cast certain individuals out of his community of readers. Thus Diderot quotes the letter of a woman correspondent and fellow admirer of Richardson. This woman has another friend, also a woman, who has had the temerity severely to criticize Clarissa. Her criticisms are quoted, then refuted, in a letter to Diderot which he includes in the eulogy:

> *She laughs, when she sees this child in despair at the curse of a father.* She is a mother, and she laughs at it! Such a woman can never be a friend of mine: I blush, that I ever thought her so. Do you think the curse that appears already accomplished in several important points, must have been terrible to a daughter of her disposition? And who shall say, that God will not ratify hereafter the curse pronounced by a parent here? [*Eulogy,* 43]

What does this strange passage accomplish? It quotes and discards a response—Clarissa ridiculed as a "child" for worrying about her father's curse—which is unacceptable to the community of sympathetic readers Diderot seeks for Richardson's art. Diderot's friend not only defends Clarissa by outlining the logic of Clarissa's behavior (her pious "disposition," a curse already "accomplished in several points"); she also casts this false reader out of the human community. Thus Diderot's friend insists that "such a woman can never be a friend of mine," and the writer wonders that she could be "a mother," questioning whether she *should* be a mother. Later this supposed critic of Clarissa declares that Clarissa is a complete fraud. Diderot's friend, and true reader, is scandalized, and writes: "Surely to think and feel thus, is a great curse: so great, that I would rather my own daughter should expire this moment in my arms, than know it to be entailed on her."

The "P.S." of this letter to Diderot suggests reading the account of Clarissa's funeral and last will to this false reader. (They were not included in the Prévost translation.) Diderot's friend presumes that this false reader's "laughter" would "accompany Clarissa to her last home." Thus, by a strange twist, and the ground rules peculiar to this community of readers, this acquaintance of Diderot's correspondent is led to assault Clarissa directly, somehow adding to Clarissa's final suffering (*Eulogy*, 43–44).

What is the purpose of all this? Readers are being tested and divided by the way they respond to *Clarissa*. Diderot and his lady friend define a certain band of acceptable responses to the text: unquestioned faith in Clarissa's sincerity, deep sympathy for her in her suffering, etc. Another set of reader responses is anathematized: skepticism about Clarissa's motives, laughter at her extreme sensibility, etc. This rather severe regulation of the reader's activity establishes norms of response which are less descriptions of actual responses than an articulation of the way man should be: humane, sympathetic, optimistic. The pity that Diderot's friend directs at her correspondent is an appropriately "humane" response for a member of a self-confident little community of readers to direct at a false reader and wayward human being. Perhaps Diderot surmises that his friend's letter has been a little harsh with this false reader, and thus puts in question his own claim to be an "enlightened" critic of "liberal" principles. So, after quoting his friend's letter, he makes this amusing confession: "Thus we see, in matters of taste, as in religion, there is a kind of intolerance, which I condemn; but from which I cannot free myself without an exertion of my reason" (*Eulogy*, 44). In this eulogy, Diderot does not exert himself very much.

After the boundaries of the reader community have been guaranteed, Diderot moves into a more pleasant strain. He gives instances, in his best testimonial style, of the great effect *Clarissa* has had on its readers. Then Diderot remarks, in tones of pleasure, surprise, and admiration, on some of his favorite passages in the novel (*Eulogy*, 44–47). This kind of discourse, which resembles the mail of a fan club, is often used by humanist critics to stoke collective enthusiasm for the book or author the group admires. At the end of Sara Fielding's *Remarks on Clarissa*, after the "conversations" which deflect the "incorrect" responses to the novel, Miss Gibson and Bellario exchange letters which bind their community of readers together. The goal of this kind of community is the unhampered communion between the true readers and the text, in the presence of the author (a meeting of the Browning Society, with Browning in attendance). Thus Diderot's eulogy begins by affirming his sense of communion with Richardson—he calls him a "dear friend"—and Kinkead-Weekes describes the final satisfaction this kind of relationship could bring: where the "author, at his most imaginative, and the ideal reader at his most perceptive . . . [meet] at their fullest extension beyond the relativities, absolutely and objectively."[8]

Humanist critics like Diderot and Kinkead-Weekes are reluctant to acknowledge the political implications of their criticism. But if they did, I doubt they would favor an unruly struggle of interpretations. Instead, they would be most comfortable with a benign dictatorship where the author would sit enthroned like a king at the center of a dominion of loyal readers, to guarantee a continuity of response to his book. Diderot never raises the question of Richardson's conscious intentions. But in his eulogy he makes use of Richardson's death and absence to invent a new Richardson who will offer guidance to the well-regulated community of readers which Diderot labors to institute.

8. Kinkead-Weekes is here describing the way the reader should strive to know Richardson. See *SR:DN*, p. 455.

The Navel of the Text

It is a well-known fact that critics are wont to disagree—with the authors they read and with each other. But there is one idea that all the humanist critics of *Clarissa* seem to embrace with equal fervor: the notion that *Clarissa* is a book that constitutes a "unified whole." Ian Watt has *Clarissa* play a decisive part in "the rise of the novel," because, as he writes, "in *Clarissa*, even more completely than *Pamela*, Richardson resolved the main formal problems which still confronted the novel by creating a literary structure in which narrative mode, plot, characters, and moral theme were organized into a unified whole."[9]   But it is Sara Fielding, in *Remarks on Clarissa*,[10] not Ian Watt, who is the first critic to embrace this idea. If we attend to her language, we shall discover that there is much more to this critical commonplace than first appears. One of her characters praises *Clarissa* by quoting a French critic:

> An indifferent Wit may form a vast Design in his Imagination; but it must be an Extraordinary Genius that can work his Design, and fashion it according to Justness and Proportion: For 'tis necessary that the same Spirit *reign throughout*; that all contribute to the same End; and that all the *Parts* bear a secret relation to each other; all depends on this Relation and Alliance. . . . [Bellario himself finds that in *Clarissa* the] Author had all Nature before him, and he has beautifully made use of every labyrinth, in the several minds of his characters, to lead him to his proposed End.[11]

Over two hundred years later, a modern critic of Russian Formalist persuasion, Irving Gopnik, concludes his study of the style of *Clarissa* by asserting the same idea in somewhat different language:

> The [foregoing] analysis reveals the esthetic integrity of an extremely complex but masterfully ordered ironic manipulation of language of which the major structural elements are subtle but pervasive networks of verbal motifs. An understanding and

9. Watt, *Rise of the Novel*, p. 208.
10. A pamphlet written by Henry Fielding's sister to counter adverse criticism of *Clarissa*.
11. *Remarks on Clarissa* (London, 1749), p. 36. Hereafter cited in the text as *Remarks*.

appreciation of this verbal art leads . . . to an admiration of the esthetic excellence of its intrinsic structure.[12]

Taken together, these two passages communicate a distinct idea of the book.

These passages define the text as a coordination of parts having a "secret" relationship with one another, so that a whole is formed which is mysteriously more than the sum of its parts. The breakthrough for the artwork comes from the way "complexity" has been mastered but also sustained (kept complex) by the structure the artist creates. Thus Gopnik praises Richardson's "structure" as "extremely complex but masterfully ordered." In *Remarks on Clarissa*, Sara Fielding communicates this idea by using a stage or architectural metaphor to describe the author's treatment of the various characters: "all [the characters] are essentially different, and rising in due proportion one after another, till all the vast building centers in the pointed view of the author's design" (*Remarks*, 41). This notion of structure leads to several related forms of response by humanist critics.

First, Gopnik expresses "admiration" for the "esthetic excellence" of the work, and Fielding says Richardson has executed his art "beautifully." The artwork looks so charged with reserves of harmoniously related energies that it seems to come alive. Fielding says "the same spirit reign[s] throughout" the text, and she attributes this to the "extraordinary genius" of the author. The affiliated meanings of "spirit" and "genius" add credibility to each claim. Gopnik's language does not indulge in the metaphorical or the animistic, but he comes as close as he can to this when he attributes the harmonizing unity of the text, not to a "reigning spirit" but to "subtle but pervasive networks" of language.

But the text is not just said to be alive, it is also aligned by these critics with its heroine, Clarissa. We should be alerted to this by Gopnik's pronouncement of the text's "aesthetic integrity." The word *integrity* is used in the novel, and throughout humanist criticism of the novel, to denote Clarissa's moral stand against Lovelace. Gopnik's use of the word follows an unwritten law of the humanist criticism: all that is said of Clarissa as a character is true of the text

12. *A Theory of Style and Richardson's Clarissa* (The Hague: Mouton, 1970), p. 117.

that bears her name, and all that is said of the text also applies to Clarissa as a character. Thus, the most important "complexity" the artwork's "structure" has caged belongs to Clarissa, for her mind is the most intricate "labyrinth" in "the several minds of the characters." And it is this act of capturing or embodying which allows art to master nature, so that Sara Fielding can say that Richardson has "all nature before him."

The idea of a text as a "unified whole" assumes a radical demarcation between the inside of the text, and that which lies outside (recall that Gopnik describes the text's structure as "intrinsic"). This means that the text, like the virgin Clarissa, should not be touched; it is "inviolable." As Sara Fielding writes, "The Web is wove so strongly, every part so much depending on and assisting each other, that to divide any of them, would be to destroy the whole" (*Remarks*, 50). Little wonder that Richardson follows the lead of Sara Fielding and Joseph Spence, and uses the idea of the necessary relationship of the parts to the whole, in order to defend *Clarissa* from critics who would shorten or modify the text. And, in fact, Gopnik and Fielding recapitulate other elements of the whole complex of ideas present in Spence's little Allegory of Art and Nature described in the previous chapter: (1) the book as a gloriously alive totality; (2) a general valorization of nature over art; and (3) Clarissa as a figure of surpassing beauty, which attracts the solicitude and erotic interest of the true critics. This leads to an intuition. Perhaps the idea of the text as a unified whole is grounded in an eccentric erotic relationship between the humanist critic and *Clarissa*. We can explore this possibility by examining how three humanist critics defend the text against abridgment or alterations.

Just as Spence condemns the carping critics who would shorten *Clarissa*, so Diderot finds several ways to attack Prévost's abridgment of *Clarissa*. We can easily agree with Diderot's opposition to the abridgment while we probe, more skeptically, the grounds of that opposition. He links these abridgments to the "frivolous taste" of the modern French audience; he describes the touching scenes that readers of Prévost's translation have missed; and he adumbrates a delicious fantasy:

An idea has sometimes suggested itself to me . . . that I had purchased some old mansion; that rummaging some day its apartments, I had perceived in a corner a chest, which had long stood there neglected; and that, on breaking it open, I had found the letters of Clarissa and Pamela lying in it mingled together. After reading a few, how eagerly should I have ranged them in the order of their dates! How should I have been grieved were there any deficiences in them! Can it be supposed, that I would have suffered any rash, I had durst said sacrilegious, hand to blot out a single line of them? [*Eulogy, 36*]

The fantasy is reminiscent of the pleasures Belford promises himself in reading Clarissa's personal correspondence after her death; it allows Diderot to adopt the role of the pious editor, which the text of *Clarissa* perfects in the figure of Belford. From this perspective, abridgment (any gap in the letters) is experienced as an unbearable intervention in the highly charged intimacy between a reader (Diderot, Belford) and a character (Clarissa) who has undergone apotheosis into an object of worship.

It is easy enough to dismiss (as Diderot does) the wayward reader or editor who would tamper with the text as the author designed it; for we have seen that the humanist critic is deeply respectful of authority, and has nothing but contempt for those who are not. Such readers/abridgers can simply be dismissed as "outsiders," hostile to the author's true intentions. It becomes a much trickier matter for them to contravene Richardson's authority. But when Richardson does things, in the second and third editions of the novel, which threaten their concourse with the text, humanist critics find ingenious ways to abridge and circumvent Richardson's authority. Nothing disturbed these humanist critics more than one footnote, added in the second edition (1749), clarifying Clarissa's role as an "example" of virtue to the reader (II,313–14). The footnote comes over halfway through the second installment, during a scene where it seems possible that Clarissa can "name the day" of her marriage to Lovelace. The editor breaks into the story with apparent reluctance:

[1] We cannot forbear observing in this place that the lady has been censured by some of her own sex, as *over-nice* in her part of the above conversations. But surely this must be owing to want of attention to the *circumstances* she was in, and to her *character*, as well as the *character of the man she had to deal*

with: for although she could not be supposed to know so much of his designs as the reader does by means of his letters to Belford, yet she was but too well convinced of his faulty morals. . . .

By this time the reader will see that she had still *greater* reason for her jealousy and vigilance. And Lovelace will tell the sex . . . *Nothing but the highest act of love can satisfy an* indulged Love.

But the reader perhaps is too apt to form a judgment of Clarissa's conduct in critical cases by *Lovelace's complaints of her coldness*: not considering his views upon her; and that she is proposed as an *example*; and therefore in her trials and distresses must not be allowed to dispense with those rules which perhaps some others of her sex, in her delicate situation, would not have themselves so strictly bound to observe; although, if she had *not* observed them, a *Lovelace* would have carried all his points.

[II,313–14]

For most of the footnote Richardson defends his heroine on the basis of the "circumstances" of her situation, her own "character," and Lovelace's "character."

All this affirms the existence of an independent fictional world which follows the rules of the "real" world. But when, in the third paragraph, Richardson reproaches the reader for judging Clarissa's conduct by "Lovelace's complaints of her coldness," Richardson can't resist adding another kind of reason for Clarissa's delicacy: the fact that she is "proposed as an example." Suddenly Clarissa is not just a character with the nature of a "real" person, but a trope—an element in the rhetorical functioning of a work of art. The passive construction of the clause somewhat conceals this sudden turn in logic: no author stands forth to "propose" Clarissa as an example, she is merely "proposed" as one. Richardson seems to realize he has just crossed an imaginary line; for, in the final clause of the footnote, he shifts back to the logic which governs the rest of the text. He insists that if Clarissa had not observed rules of delicacy, "Lovelace would have carried all his points."

This footnote precipitates a small crisis for Irving Gopnik and Mark Kinkead-Weekes, because in it Richardson deals a blow to the humanist idea of the text as a "unified whole." Thus Gopnik criticizes the footnote in these words:

Here the explanation and justification of [Clarissa's] conduct is removed completely from the context of the work itself and related to the explicitly didactic goals of the author. It makes of Clarissa merely an allegorical model for a particular doctrine of virtue instead of the richly complex character which emerges from the novel. This intrusion is all the more surprising when we take into account Richardson's own statements about the character of Clarissa: "I designedly drew Clarissa with some Defects of Judgment. . . ." This editorial intrusion looks all the more like merely an unfortunate and isolated lapse in "point of view" when we find that none of the other footnotes which have an apparently didactic purpose make any such appeal to authorial standards outside of the work itself.

For the humanist critic, even an apparently rationalistic one like Gopnik, the sweetest harvest of *Clarissa* is the "richly complex character" who "emerges" from the novel—Clarissa. Gopnik here reproaches Richardson for replacing this precious object of interest with a wooden, impoverished version of mankind, "an allegorical model for a particular doctrine of virtue." How has this happened? Richardson, by introducing "authorial standards outside of the work," has violated the "aesthetic integrity" of the unified structure which represents man's "richly complex" character in art. Gopnik makes himself Clarissa's protector by tacitly accusing Richardson of violating his own text. Thus Richardson's footnote is described as an "intrusion," "an unfortunate and isolated lapse," whose damage Gopnik tries to minimize by describing the footnote as an anomaly whose presence we must try to overlook.

Gopnik and Kinkead-Weekes treat the "example" footnote as a breach in the text which threatens to split the unified body. But Richardson did not imagine that this one footnote was incompatible with the broader tendencies of his art. It is perhaps most accurate to see the "example" footnote as the navel of the text. A man's navel reminds him that he came from somewhere; it is the trace of his original attachment to someone else. In the light of any extravagant claims to autonomy or seamless unity, a navel will be experienced as a flaw. And this footnote/navel does not just announce the novel's connection with Richardson as its author. It also links the text to all those compromising struggles of interpretation: hopes and schemes of wayward readers, and the vulgar counterassertions of a Richardson who is all too intent on having his own way, by naming his intentions with indelicate explicitness (see above, chapter 4). This little linguistic navel—the "example" footnote—becomes an intrusion of human will and art into the center of a text which these humanist critics long to know as a seamless body—virgin, whole, and self-complete.

Kinkead-Weekes abhors this footnote as much as Gopnik, but he has a solution. He advocates producing a new modern edition of *Clarissa,* shorn of those addenda that violate the best tendencies of Richardson's art. There is a fascinating ambiguity in this proposed move. It allows Kinkead-Weekes to return the text to its original chasteness and virtue, *by undressing it.*[13] To see how he arrives at this daring position, we must backtrack a bit to get a grasp of his understanding of Richardson's art.

Kinkead-Weekes subtitles his study of Richardson "Dramatic Novelist," because he attributes Richardson's achievement to an open-ended exploratory form he calls "dramatic." As he explains, Richardson's use of the epistolary form creates "to the moment dramatic monologues, attempts to catch living voices in the dramatic present." Kinkead-Weekes feels that this form enables the characters, the author, and the reader to participate in a subtle textual process which has the power "to explore, to challenge, and to transcend the attitude from which the fiction begins."[14] When Richardson adds explanatory notes and addenda to the text, Kinkead-Weekes accuses him of betraying the subtlety and drama of his own achievement. Of the "example" footnote he writes:

> [Richardson] begins with a reasonable reminder of her character and circumstances, and the need to keep Lovelace at a distance— though the argument hardly covers [Clarissa's] contrived distance

13. Kinkead-Weekes calls for a new edition of *Clarissa,* based on the first edition, in his essay "Clarissa Restored?" in *Review of English Studies* (1959), pp. 156–71. It is a tacit argument of my whole study that any future edition of *Clarissa* must give up the attempt to be an exact embodiment of Richardson's will (third edition) or our conception of his true artistic "integrity" (first edition, but modified). Instead we should have a striated text that allows itself to be marked and stained by the struggles of interpretation "within" and about this text.

14. *SR:DN,* p. 2. Kinkead-Weekes seems to follow F. R. Leavis in emphasizing a novel's capacity to engage in a moral enactment which transcends its own intellectual premises. See R. P. Bilan, "The Basic Concepts and Criteria of F. R. Leavis' Novel Criticism," *Novel: A Forum on Fiction* 9, no. 3 (spring 1976): 197–216.

lately. Then he tries to justify her in terms of the reader's new knowledge of Lovelace, which is quite beside the point. Most unfortunate of all, he insists heavily that she 'is proposed as an *Example*,' and so cannot be dispensed from 'Rules' as others might be, 'altho' if she had *not* observed them, a *Lovelace* would have carried all his points.' In its dogmatic and prudential emphasis this is Mr. Richardson at his worst, but even that is more forgivable than the falsification of his art. [*SR:DN,* 204]

Kinkead-Weekes goes on to argue that this footnote distorts Richardson's story by simplifying Clarissa's character (he finds her concealing some "moral absolutism," prudery, and personal timidity behind her claims of delicacy), and by distorting her situation (he reminds the reader that there are moments in the action when less strict adherence to the rules of delicacy might have ended in Clarissa's marrying Lovelace, as Pamela married Mr. B.). But Kinkead-Weekes's anger seems disproportionate to Richardson's transgression; he finds it un-"forgivable" that Richardson has "falsified" his own art. Kinkead-Weekes uses this passionate language because this footnote threatens to deface an object that seems to this humanist critic to be beautifully subtle and involving—namely, "female." Kinkead-Weekes's more general description and argument against Richardson's addenda help to demonstrate this:

In the second and third editions [Richardson] tinkered with the book to drive its morality home in terms which the crudest of readers . . . could understand. In irritable footnotes, in the proliferation of italics directed at the reader and breaking the subtle indirection of the epistolary form, in the further directing of response through the index, and in many insertions in the text, he hardened the outlines of his achievement into a cruder black and white . . . and in order to enforce this he was driven on several occasions to blur or even subvert his original achievement. [*SR:DN,* 195]

Kinkead-Weekes's study celebrates the female virtues of Richardson's art: its lightness of touch, its soft lines, its "subtle indirection," and all the art that allows this novel to stand in for nature. It is part of his mission as a critic to return readers of this century to an appreciation of these virtues, so evident in the first edition. This means he must rescue *Clarissa* from the editor of the second and third editions. So Kinkead-Weekes condemns Richardson's "heavy" didacticism, and the "crudeness" he would give his own text or pander to in his reader. He accuses Richardson of making "insertions" in the text which would "harden" the "outlines" of the subtle "achievement" he so admires. Kinkead-Weekes's critical art has the effect of reconstituting the fine feminine lines of *Clarissa*. To see what else he and other humanist critics choose to do with her, we must turn to the climactic moments of their readings.

Toward the Humanist Sublime

The humanist reading of Clarissa reaches its culmination when the critic modulates into what I call the "humanist sublime." The humanist sublime is a useful rhetorical weapon for giving a logical appearance to a very illogical activity: the glorification of man. It responds to the contradictory ideas and imperatives we have found compelling to the humanist critic: (1) to know a character in his or her uniqueness, and still assert a general psychology of Man; (2) to regulate reader response by founding a community of readers; and (3) to describe the text as a "unified whole," at the same time that everywhere in the formulation of the "humanist sublime" there is evidence that the critic knows the text, and is constantly inviting other readers to know the text, as an object of erotic interest in a way that would divide the text. What role, postures, narratives—in short, what kind of rhetorical position—emerges from these imperatives? Here are four different moments of the rhetorical position I am calling the humanist sublime.

1. *The art that goes beyond art.* At the high point of his act of reading, the humanist critic finds the artwork elevated high above himself, purified by its separateness, and capable of containing everything of consequence within itself. The artwork is no longer merely the function of a technique; it has become all-powerful. Diderot's astonishing description of *Clarissa* will serve as an example of this moment of reading:

> The interest and charm of the work conceals the art of Richardson from those who are best equipped to perceive it. Often have I begun to read Clarissa as a study, and as often have I forgotten my purpose before I had read twenty pages. I have only been struck, like other readers, with the genius that could suppose a

young lady of the greatest goodness and prudence not taking
a single step but was wrong, yet without our being able to blame
her, because she has inhuman parents and an abominable lover;
that, without offending in the least against probability, could
give this young prude a lively, madcap friend, who says and does
nothing but what is consonant to right reason; and this friend, a
worthy man for a lover; yet, with all his worth, dull and ridicu-
lous, and laughed at by his mistress, notwithstanding the countenance and appropriation of her mother: that could unite in
Lovelace the noblest and most detestable qualities, meanness and
generosity, seriousness and levity, violence and coolness, good
sense and folly; and make of him a villain, that we hate, love,
admire, and despise; who astonishes us in whatever form he appears, and never remains for an instant the same. [*Eulogy*, 40–
41]

In many ways, this description of *Clarissa* (the text) repeats Lovelace's desciption of Clarissa (the character) at those moments when
he experiences her as an object of overpowering beauty (see above,
chapter 2). Diderot presents *Clarissa* as a chain of antithetically
related elements which builds momentum and energy as the number
of these elements mounts. Thus Clarissa's "greatest goodness" conflicts with "wrong steps" she takes, which exist in paradoxical
tension with our inability to blame her; and Clarissa as a totality is
daringly combined with "a lively, madcap friend who says and does
nothing but what is consonant with right reason."

Diderot's account makes the text an object that magically reconciles contraries, and, for this reason, the text is experienced as possessing surpassing power and beauty. As with Lovelace before Clarissa,
this is a moment when the admirer is "done in" by the object he
admires. For the critic who usually knows by judging is suddenly
assimilated to the artwork and becomes its enraptured functionary.
Thus, Diderot says he starts out eager to "study" Richardson's
"art" but invariably ends entangled in its "charm." The text's very
power has imposed a limit on the critic/reader's ability to explain
the text's operation; so Diderot protects these mysteries by declaring
he is simply "struck" with Richardson's "genius." And it is this
"genius" which is the subject and force that "supposes" a Clarissa,
and "gives" her an apt but unlikely friend, and "unites" the most

diverse qualities in a Lovelace. Having situated all power in the art-work, and "genius" in the author, the critic's own position must necessarily be somewhat lowly. This brings us to the second moment of the humanist sublime.

2. *The humility of the critic.* Since, by any normative standard, the text has been *overvalued* by the humanist critic, it is appropriate that he feels so poor and powerless that he *undervalues* himself. And, in fact, in all his writings there is a vague sense that he has erred in some way. Diderot closes his eulogy on a note of failure and apology; for some reason, he is anxious to efface his own presence before his reader. To Richardson he writes:

> I knelt at once at the feet of your statue, and worshipped you, seeking in the bottom of my heart expressions adequate to the admiration I felt, but could find none. You who read these lines, which I have traced without connection, without design, and without order, just as they were inspired by my tumultuous feel-ings, if you have received from Heaven a heart of greater sensi-bility than mine, blot them out. The genius of Richardson has stifled what I had. His phantoms wander continually through my imagination. If I would write, I hear the plainings of Clementine, the shade of Clarissa rises to my view, Grandison stalks before me, Lovelace agitates me, and the pen drops from my hand. And you, more gentle shades, Emily, Charlotte, Pamela, and dear Miss Howe, while I converse with you, the years adapted to labor and the season of gathering laurels pass away, and I ap-proach my end, without having attempted anything that would also recommend me to posterity.

Here Diderot adopts the confessional tone of a contrite sinner before his God. And like the sinner taking communion, he seems to repeat an aesthetic equivalent of the words of *The Book of Common Prayer*: "We are not worthy so much as to gather up crumbs under Thy table."

But what is the critic's sin? The critic is dimly aware that he has interceded in the life of the artwork; Diderot regrets that he dared to speak in the presence of its truth. And this points to a difficulty that always bedevils the humanist critic. Since all authority resides in the artwork, Diderot has no authentic way to justify his own effusions.

So Diderot, like many a humanist critic since, ends his own text (1) by pointing to *Clarissa,* (2) by invoking the memorable presences of Richardson's art (Clarissa, Grandison, et al.), and (3) finally by willing his own silence. (The pen drops from his hand; his genius has been "stifled" by Richardson's.) But all these modes of self-abasement serve a dual purpose: they protect the critic's limited but extensive intervention in the text's reception, *while* they assert his humility.

Diderot enhances the persuasive power of his criticism by finding ways to make his responses look sincere. (Sincerity is always a crucial concomitant of the testimonial mode the humanist critics use.) Diderot does this by telling his reader that the composition was uncalculated ("without connection, without design, and without order") and merely emerged "as . . . inspired by my tumultuous feelings." But, someone might ask, are these effusions actually sincere, or are they simply ways to manipulate the reader? My answer is "both." Man is a variable, flexible, crafty creature. The humanist critic may suddenly find himself experiencing the artwork as elevated, pure, and all-powerful; and at that moment the humility of the humanist critic is probably quite genuine. But when he represents this experience to himself, he finds that it can be put to use: to regulate the reader's response by orchestrating a similar experience for him. In a similar way, late in the novel when Clarissa is dying, Lovelace finds that his accounts of his earlier rapturous subordination to Clarissa can be used to "prove" his willingness to marry her. And though I have represented this as a sequence which occurs—first, authentic experience of awe and humility, then, calculated representation of awe and humility—actually, the experience and the representation of the experience are probably hopelessly entangled and help to motivate one another. Though these activities are somewhat contradictory, they may be reconciled in the pleasure the critics experience in both. For it is as pleasing to feel one's own awe and humility before a text as it is to manipulate another's experience of it.

3. *The descent into the mind, and the experience of the heroine as pathetic.* All the while that the humanist critic praises text and author, and in spite of his avowals of humility, he is busy giving *his* account of the text. These stories interpret *Clarissa* by purporting to articulate the essence of the novel's action. For Ian Watt, *Clarissa*

takes the reader on a descent into the mind, which he praises and testifies to with all the eloquence he can command:

> This is Richardson's triumph. Even the most apparently implausible, didactic or period aspects of the plot and the characters, even the rape, and Clarissa's unconscionable time a-dying, are brought into a larger dramatic pattern of infinite formal and psychological complexity. It is this capacity for a continuous enrichment and complication of a simple situation which makes Richardson the great novelist he is; and it shows, too, that the novel has attained . . . formal resources capable . . . of leading [Richardson] away from the flat didacticism of his critical preoccupations into so profound a penetration of his characters that their experience partakes of the terrifying ambiguity of human life itself.[15]

With these words, Ian Watt ends his reading of *Clarissa*. This passage is a fine example of the humanist sublime; for, while it apparently simply talks about a book, it dignifies the very idea of Man. For Watt, *Clarissa* is a work of art which goes beyond art because it penetrates its characters so completely that their "experience partakes of the terrifying ambiguity of human life itself." The little word *itself* means that, according to Watt, Richardson has broken through to the life you and I and Ian Watt apparently share. And here Ian Watt's analysis of *Clarissa* coincides with Gopnik's and Kinkead-Weekes's.

The representation of lifelike human "complexity" is said to depend on the "complexity" of the artwork's "form." But how does Watt demonstrate the "psychological complexity" of the characters and the "continuous enrichment and complication" of their situation? How does he prove that Richardson's "profound penetration" of these characters can stand in for the "terrifying ambiguity" of *our* lives? He presents a sequence of analytical passes with which he acts out Richardson's (purported) penetration of Clarissa's mind.

First, Watt takes elements of the text, such as Clarissa's position as an example of virtue, and gives them psychological importance. Thus, as Watt writes, "if the need arise, Richardson the novelist can silence Richardson the writer of conduct books. . . . [So Clarissa's] error of judgment [in meeting Lovelace] was itself the result of

15. Watt, *Rise of the Novel,* p. 238.

Clarissa's very excellences: 'So desirous,' she taunts herself, 'to be considered an example!'"[16] And after his long, careful description of the conflicts in the story, Watt begins again: "if this were all, the conflict in *Clarissa* would still, perhaps, be too simple for a work of such length. Actually, however, the situation is more complex and problematic."[17] Watt proceeds to quote Freud and Samuel Johnson to show how Clarissa acts out the "unconscious duplicities" of her culture by refusing to admit her early love for the protagonist.

After another pause in his analysis, Ian Watt takes us still deeper into the mysteries of human psychology. Thus he begins with this flourish: "But Richardson's explorations of the unconscious forms taken by the sexual impulse also took him much further . . . [to what] may be regarded as the ultimate and no doubt pathological expression of the dichotomisation of sexual roles in the realm of the unconscious."[18] Watt then analyzes the imagery of the protagonists' letters to expose the "sadism" of Lovelace's "masculine role," and the "masochistic role" and "masochistic fantasy," that Clarissa "unconsciously" "courts," first in her sexual violation, and then in her own death.[19] It is entirely appropriate that, at this point in his reading, Watt quotes Diderot on "carrying the torch to the back of the cave" to expose the "hideous Moor" who hides there. The emergence of these dark and unexpected passions helps to justify Watt's claim that Richardson has exposed "the terrifying ambiguity of human life itself."

Note that each "turn" in Watt's analysis helps to create a sense of increased complexity—a movement toward a new, deeper, and more unconscious truth. But while this kind of narrative helps to justify Watt's characterization of Clarissa as complex, what begins as the analysis of one unique individual (Clarissa Harlowe), proceeds to successively more generic terms; so the analysis of concealed female love is said to be part of a general social duplicity, and the protagonists' sadomasochism is described in archetypal terms. Thus, as we journey deeper and deeper into Clarissa's mind, we find a psychic landscape which applies with equal force to all men, and paradoxically, as Watt/Richardson teaches us more and more about the unconscious,

16. Ibid., p. 219.
17. Ibid., p. 228.
18. Ibid., pp. 230–31.
19. Ibid., pp. 232–33.

we are forced to accept the essential "ambiguity" of human life. And *both* the generality and the mystery of this psychology help to make Watt's analysis more authoritative and attractive to us; for the typical quality of Clarissa's mind makes her crisis our crisis, and we all like to think of our life as protected from probing eyes, by mystery.

Watt's way of "knowing" Clarissa is psychological and analytical, and though his identification with Clarissa is compatible with his analysis, it only becomes visible in his final tribute to Richardson's art. But Sara Fielding, Henry Fielding, and Mark Kinkead-Weekes are much more explicit about participating in the pathos of the heroine's crisis. Thus they climax their readings with a treatment of one scene of the novel: Clarissa's suffering and frenzy following the rape. Sara Fielding writes:

> [Clarissa's] madness equals, (I had almost said exceeds) any thing of the kind that ever was written: That hitherto so peculiar beauty in King Lear, of preserving the character even in madness, appears strongly in Clarissa: the same self-accusing spirit, the same humble heart, the same pious mind breathes in her scattered scraps of paper in the midst of her frenzy. . . . Her letter to Lovelace, where, even in madness, *galling* reproach drops not from her pen, and which contains only supplications that she may not be farther persecuted, speaks the very soul of Clarissa, and by the author of her story could have been wrote for no one but herself. Whoever can read her earnest request to Lovelace, that she may not be exposed in a public mad-house, on the consideration that it might injure *him*, without being overwhelmed in tears, I am certain has not in himself the concord of sweet sounds, and must, as Shakespeare says, be fit for treasons, stratagems, and spoils.
>
> [*Remarks*, 42]

How can we account for this act of identification with the novel's heroine? Here the humanist critic uses the "humanist sublime" to assert a delicious personal intimacy between the reader and the heroine. And this is done at the point in the text closest to Clarissa's sexual violation. The humanist critic seems to want to eavesdrop on her at precisely this moment. Perhaps the very extravagance of the critic's praise betrays a secret shame for participating, vicariously, through eager acts of reading and writing, in Clarissa's violation. She compensates for this transgression by turning her own language into a tribute to the noble and suffering Clarissa. And, at this moment, the humanist critic finds herself feeling that she knows Clarissa in her essence. Thus Clarissa's letter to Lovelace is said to "speak the very soul of Clarissa."

But if we ask what this means—what "character" Clarissa has preserved in her "madness," we get a surprising answer. We find that she has shown the "same self-accusing spirit, the same humble heart, the same pious mind" she had demonstrated earlier. But being "humble," "pious," and "self-accusing" is the duty of every Christian and the apparent achievement of many. These words only function as a character sketch because the word *same* makes them work as an index, or pointer, to an identity the reader *already* knows. The humanist critic and his reader recognize the "same" qualities during Clarissa's madness which they have seen earlier, so Clarissa's way of behaving seems "right," because it seems so like Clarissa. And it is precisely this resort to tautology that protects Clarissa from being reduced to a critic's insipid summary.

Henry Fielding writes with a comparably calculated vagueness in his testimonial to the effects of Clarissa's crisis. In his famous letter to Richardson he writes:

> Can I tell you what I think of the latter part of your volume? Let the overflowing of a heart which you have filled speak for me.
>
> When Clarissa returns to her lodgings at St. Clairs the Alarm begins, and here my heart begins its narrative. I am shocked. . . . The circumstances of the fragments is great and terrible; but her letter to Lovelace is beyond any thing I have ever read. God forbid that the man who reads this with dry eyes should be alone with my daughter when she hath no assistance within call. Here my terror ends and my grief begins which the cause of all my tumultuous passions soon changes into raptures of admiration and astonishment by a behavior the most elevated I can possibly conceive, and what is at the same time the most gentle and the most natural.[20]

Henry Fielding does not try to describe the heroine or her behavior. He simply says her letter to Lovelace is "beyond any thing I have

---

20. See E. L. McAdam, Jr., "A New Letter from Fielding," *Yale Review* 38 (1948): 300–10.

ever read," and insists that her behavior is "the most elevated I can possibly conceive." This limitation of the critic's activity puts "the very soul" of Clarissa before the reader to know, insists on the exemplary force of her "elevated behavior," but at the same time sustains a sense of mystery and "beyond" about the heroine. And Sara Fielding further enhances the authority of *Clarissa* (as a masterpiece and a work of genius) by comparing it with *King Lear,* and using Shakespeare's definition of the human ("the concord of sweet sounds") to insist that Clarissa's suffering is a touchstone to test the humanity of the reader.

Both these humanist critics bully their readers into accepting their regulation of the reader's response. Thus, Sara Fielding demands that the reader be "overwhelmed with tears" (or else be "fit for treasons, stratagems, and spoils"); and Henry Fielding writes, "God forbid that the man who reads this with dry eyes should be alone with my daughter." Sara Fielding depends upon the urgent personal tone of her language to earn her reader's trust; but Henry Fielding uses two ingenious devices to communicate the sincerity of his sentiments. First he uses the fiction that his "heart" has narrated the account of his response; and then he graciously ends the letter by insisting that he could not "flatter" one the world supposes him to "hate," because both are "rivals for that coy Mrs. Fame."

4. *The emergence of a theme* (integrity). There is no way to adjudicate between the rival claims, found throughout the humanist criticism of *Clarissa,* that, on the one hand, Clarissa is a perfectly realized individual, but that, on the other hand, her story communicates a general psychology of man. Clarissa's individuality is declared by fiat. Her story is said to imply a general psychology because it carries certain verities of a universal human situation, and it induces (or should induce) a uniform response in all readers. The concurrent assertion of *both* of these ideas allows for the emergence, within a moment of the "humanist sublime," of a "theme": the universal fact of man's uniqueness. In a recent review in *Eighteenth Century Studies,* Chester Chapin reports an unusual consensus as to the theme of *Clarissa* within the institution of English studies. Chapin is reviewing Brophy's study of Richardson's aesthetics, *The Triumph of Craft:*

As Brophy says, Clarissa's sexual battle with Lovelace is significant of a 'larger theme—the integrity of the individual' (Brophy,

p. 97). And that, of course, as critics are now increasingly beginning to realize, is what the great novel is all about. This theme
gives the book its universal and timeless quality, for in *Clarissa*
Richardson succeeds in dramatizing a perennial source of human
tragedy and waste—the use of other human beings as objects of
egotistic gratification. Clarissa refuses to be so used; for our time
as for her own she is, as Richardson intended her to be, 'exemplary.'[21]

There are two surprising things about this pronouncement. First, one
wonders why Chapin insists that there is something novel about this
version of *Clarissa's* theme: "Critics are *now* increasingly *beginning*
to realize." After all, a long time ago Christopher Hill noted Clarissa's economic independence, and William Sale achieves an early
instance of the humanist sublime in declaring, "The stultifying atmosphere of Harlowe Place is so pervasive that even the kindly in-
stincts of some of the clan prove abortive. Clarissa alone is a free
spirit, struggling desperately to preserve her integrity and her independence of mind and soul."[22]

But still more surprisingly, why does Chapin announce this theme
with such certitude? He names the theme and adds, "And that of
course . . . is what the great novel is all about." After putting the
theme in his own terms (Clarissa refuses to be "used"), he insists
that "for our time as for her own she is, as Richardson intended her
to be, 'exemplary.'" Chapin's domineering manner will not surprise
us if we remember what a "theme" is for the humanist critic. A
theme does not just demand the reader's respect and adherence because it is the meaning the text carries or the message the author
intends for his text (though it is both of these). It is also a precious
fragment of moral and spiritual truth written by a great man (the
genius, the author), and put into his masterpiece for the benefit of
all men. And though this "truth" is often delivered in the guise of
one reader's humble testimonial, it is assumed to rise above the
contingencies of history, and to be true for all time. Little wonder
that the humanist critic often declares the "theme" of the artwork
with the patience, rigidity, and complacency one usually associates
with a missionary.

21. *Eighteenth Century Studies* (1977), p. 456.
22. "From Pamela to Clarissa," *The Age of Johnson* (New Haven: Yale University Press,
1949).

Mark Kinkead-Weekes is the most thoughtful and probing reader of *Clarissa* in this century. And of all the humanist critics, it is he who has read *Clarissa* with the most loving care. He brings the humanist sublime to perfection. By reading him in terms of the four moments of this rhetorical position, we can finally see how this way of reading *Clarissa* comes to serve a general idea of man (and thus a humanist ideology). We have seen that Kinkead-Weekes argues strenuously for a return to the first edition, so as to restore the text to its pure, whole, and unified condition. His long study of Richardson uses a detailed sequential treatment of each novel, which he calls "reading to the moment," so that the reader may be guided in a faithful apprehension of the Richardson text.

Kinkead-Weekes begins to move toward the climax of his reading when he informs us that Clarissa's rape "enables [Richardson] to expose her innermost nature" and answer "the most basic of all questions: the Psalmist's 'What *is* Man?'—or Woman?" (*SR:DN*, 231). Kinkead-Weekes discusses the ten torn papers as unmediated glimpses into Clarissa's self. Here she is groping toward an emotional acceptance of her situation and her loss. There are "childlike" addresses to her father and her friend Anna, self-reproaches for her error and pride, and a stinging renunciation of her own love for Lovelace. Kinkead-Weekes reminds the reader of Clarissa's poignant wish, articulated in her letter to Lovelace, to be put away in a private madhouse. Then he adds, "But at the heart of the letter is a moment of sheer self-revelation, of what it *feels* like to know that she has been raped, and there is no moment like it in the eighteenth century novel." He then quotes Clarissa's letter: "But when all my doors are fast . . . to be where you are, in a manner without opening any of them—O wretched, wretched Clarissa Harlowe! For I never will be Lovelace. . . ." At this point Kinkead-Weekes reminds the reader what a shock the rape must have been to someone of Clarissa's upbringing and character ("taught . . . to think of her body as a fortress locked against attack"). Then he is finally ready to give expression to the novel's theme, through reference to the "heart" of Clarissa's letter, which tells us "what it feels like to know she has been raped":

The experience of the rape is the agony of knowing that the opening in her body, in spite of the fact that her senses and her intellect have been wholly unmoved, has enabled Lovelace . . .

to be always part of her inner consciousness, having touched her most private being. There is a deep psychological truth here; and not for a hundred and fifty years could the English novel begin to approach again a 'new way of writing' which could probe its characters as deeply as this. . . . Richardson has moved behind sex, behind 'character,' behind morality. His imagination told him here that what was really at issue in the situation he had created was the sacredness of a human being's innermost self. . . . What is really unforgiveable about Lovelace . . . is that he cannot conceive or respect the essential private inner core of personality that each individual has a right to dispose of as only he or she may wish. He has not treated her as a human being but as a mere object, a function of his ego, and this she will never accept. We can now see that this . . . is what the whole novel has been about. . . . To prove the existence of that inner core Richardson has had to challenge himself to disintegrate his heroine, to break her down to the last possible distillation before her personality disappears into the mechanism of madness . . . and one is bound to respect the integrity that drives him so far. [*SR:DN*, 241–42]

In this climactic moment, Kinkead-Weekes enunciates his theme: the existence in man of an inner core or center, to which Kinkead-Weekes's analysis has penetrated, that discloses something "sacred"— the "core of personality" that *is* each individual in his or her essence. Now, though this center cannot be named by language—for there is nothing in language unique enough to embody this uniqueness—it may be asserted to be there. Kinkead-Weekes "feels" Clarissa's essential self emerge as an adjunct to a pathetic and moving series of events, and he makes his reading a witness to the existence of this "person," Clarissa, who is as real as art can make her. Paradoxically, a personal testimonial to this experience of Clarissa's uniqueness by Kinkead-Weekes, and his enunciation of a general theme, stand in for the psychological truth (the deep, complex, articulated self) which must remain hidden *in order* to seem real.

At the very beginning of this chapter I quoted Kinkead-Weekes's apostrophe to Clarissa. I am now ready to place that passage in a context that will make its form and content intelligible. Here is the fourth and final subsection of the last chapter of Kinkead-Weekes's study. It is his heartfelt valedictory to his subject, Samuel Richardson:

> . . . Only by the form, the pattern,
> Can words or music reach
> The stillness, as a Chinese jar still
> Moves perpetually in its stillness.

The paradox is that it is a response to Richardson's strengths that causes the reductiveness. It is because, of all the eighteenth-century novelists, his History is the most concerned with verisimilitude, and his Drama the most concerned with consciousness, that his critics have tended to fasten on one element or another, inattentive to the nature of the shaping spirit of imagination that creates and orders the whole. To try to grasp those great still books—taking "great" as a term of quantity!—is a long, difficult, and often tedious process as I fear I have abundantly shown. Perhaps the 'stillness' of which Eliot speaks is the response we make only to the really great work, when we are overcome with a sense of completion, harmony, wholeness, and communication so intense that another word would wreck it. Perhaps the frenzied conflict, the endless exploration, as well as the other Richardsonian faults, are a sign of his inability to reach the 'claritas' of the Chinese jar; as well as of his determination to try. I am certain this is true of my study. Yet just once—at the moment when one imagines one understands the meaning of the rape of Clarissa, and of the challenge Richardson's form has enabled him to pose, and meet in Clarissa's deranged papers—one may feel the stillness, and be moved. I think it is the courage of the imagination, the risks it is prepared to run; and also one's sense that, though the full History pressures of character, society, and the unconscious have been taken, yet Clarissa is miraculously free; that produce the single touch of awe one feels in reading eighteenth-century fiction. She is both grasped; and mysterious, self-existent, unpredictable. She is created both by the most remorseless analysis; and by letting the subconscious go in the dramatist's projection. She is both subject to the full conditioning of her and her creator's society; and yet her 'reality' is quite beyond the representative, as every sensitive contemporary felt, including Richardson's greatest rival and formal opposite. And the final treatment of Lovelace the inveterate actor, is uniquely right too. I do not find it surprising that the warmest tributes to Richardson have tended to come from other writers and from actors. It is also encouraging to find that among one's students, he has always found fit audience, though few. But only by the form. . . .

[*SR:DN*, 501–02]

The citation from T. S. Eliot's "Burnt Norton" that begins this section announces a "poetic" or contemplative stance on the part of the critic. The reader is invited to be thoughtful so he can engage with the critic in a closing nostalgic moment of reverie. The word *only* helps to mark the limits of humanist analysis. Not through his own analysis or description (or his own noisy words) does the humanist critic or reader reach the truth of the text. Rather, the reader must experience the "form" and "pattern" of the artwork, accept its mute opaqueness, sustain a hushed awe, and allow himself to "be moved" by the text. By situating the text outside time and above the reader, Kinkead-Weekes begins his final orchestration of the reader's intercourse with *Clarissa.*

First, he hopes to correct errors. He invokes the idea of the "whole" text to overcome the "reductiveness" of some critics. Richardson's concern with "verisimilitude" and "consciousness" has led critics to "fasten on one element or another"—not very becoming behavior! Kinkead-Weekes's corrective is to insist on a more inclusive "shaping spirit of imagination that creates and orders the whole." Then he describes how this text should be known. He starts with a warning. To "grasp those great still books" is a "long, difficult, and often tedious process." When Kinkead-Weekes confesses to having added to this tedium, we see an example of the kind of humility this critic enjoins every reader to show. This humility is a result of the "sense of completion, harmony, [and] wholeness" we feel in the presence of the text. Since the reader is superfluous, he will want to be humble, "still," and silent before the "really great work." The "frenzied conflict" and effort, on the part of both Richardson and Kinkead-Weekes, are directed at reaching "the 'claritas' of the Chinese jar."

This effort is apparently doomed to failure, but the similarity of *claritas* (light) to "Clarissa" and *clarus* (clear)—the Latin word

Clarissa is named for—points to the locus of achievement and per-fection that Kinkead-Weekes discovers in Richardson's text. For there is a sudden turn away from apparent failure, "yet just once—at the moment when one imagines one understands . . . one may feel the stillness and be moved." This refers to the moment, de-scribed above, when Kinkead-Weekes analyzes the papers written during Clarissa's madness, penetrates to her innermost being, and wins a certain theme (the sacredness of man's "private personal-ity"). Notice that the critic hedges this moment of sublime apprehen-sion with several qualifiers: "when one *imagines* one understands . . . one *may* feel the stillness." Thus, this moment is not epistemologi-cally secure, or for universal consumption. He says it is for "fit audience, though few." With these qualifications Kinkead-Weekes protects as well as disseminates this moment of intimate "communi-cation" with Clarissa.

This definition of the proper way to read *Clarissa* prepares for Kinkead-Weekes's climactic apostrophe to her ("Clarissa is miracu-lously free . . ."). What does this apostrophe do to and for her? The form of this tribute echoes Lovelace's tributes to Clarissa, and Dide-rot's admiration for *Clarissa*: the paradoxical fusion of contraries that takes the object before us beyond logical comprehension and makes it an object of desire. Kinkead-Weekes is testifying to his "love" for Clarissa (as book and character, creation and person). The balanced antitheses and use of hyperbole help to assert and act out (1) Clarissa's freedom: she frees herself from simple physi-cal and social constraints; she is "free" because she is unique, and thus not defined by any other thing; she is "free" to choose how to be and what to do—and she can do so in accord with ethical and spiritual imperatives that are extramundane. (2) Clarissa produces "awe" in the reader: "awe" before her struggle and "awe" before the sense of "beyond" she engenders. (3) There is something "mysteri-ous" and "miraculous" about Clarissa, for though she has a context in (a fictive) history, and a context in an actual work of art (and thus is "grasped" by language and "remorseless analysis"), Clarissa some-how escapes these constraints to become "self-existent" and "un-predictable." In this way she attains a "reality" quite beyond the "representative" or ordinary.

This "escape" can only be felt by the sensitive reader. But if it is felt, then Clarissa will become a vivid "incarnation" in art of what, for Kinkead-Weekes, is quintessentially human. Now all that man hopes for himself—the meaning of his life, the stability of his values, is won for him by this art. The humanist critic's *Clarissa* celebrates Man, in his enthralling mystery, in the labyrinths of humanness, as he is incarnated in great Art. Now, *Clarissa* seems to glow with the human, the humane—with all this is most truly human. But Kinkead-Weekes is a good critic. He knows that the further we get from the text, the more frail this idea of man will seem. So he points us back to the work of art by repeating the first phrase of his citation from Eliot ("But only by the form . . . "). In this way we can preserve our sense of the work's chasteness and wholeness; and Kinkead-Weekes can make it seem that he has not intervened in our concourse with *Clarissa* for so many of his own pages, that he has not taught us how to read and see *Clarissa.* He does not want to let us see the duplicity of the little word *only.* For it is not "only" the "form" or "pattern" of Richardson's text but an eager band of humanist critics who have taught us to see *Clarissa,* and man, and man in *Clarissa,* in this (very) particular way.

Through most of this chapter, I have argued as though the humanist reading of *Clarissa* could simply be denied. But it is not easy to move outside the system of knowing and feeling and valuing called humanism. With its roots in the sentimental movement of the eighteenth century, and the democratic revolutions late in that century, humanism is one of the most powerful ideologies of modern times. It is affiliated with central precepts of Christianity (charity, the soul, the community of believers), and its ways of experiencing are repeated for us daily in nearly every situation comedy and melodrama. In spit of this, a fundamental shift in sensibility seems to be in the making. A subversive critique of humanism comes to us in the work of figures like de Sade and Nietzsche. But it is the assumption of this study that even texts which seem to invite a humanist reading, like *Clarissa,* carry their own protest and antidote against that ideology—in the form of a Lovelace, or the artistic processes Richardson must engage to produce his text.

Whatever its claims on us, *this* reader must finally refuse the humanist's way of reading *Clarissa.* To begin with, cherished humanist themes (like Clarissa's heroic integrity) can only emerge through an exchange with other terms in the text (like Clarissa's self-conscious compositional decisions or her struggle with her adversaries) which the humanist reading seeks to suppress. Further, the humanist reader has no way to account for his own activity, because his notion of the work of art's transcendent value makes the reader and his reading irrelevant. This leads to a humility which is specious, in the literal sense of "showy"; because, though apparently adhering to liberal ideals about the value of debate and freedom of opinion, his own reading is rhetorically shaped to coerce other readers into obeying it while concealing his own acts of coercion. Because of a desire to be a useful social engineer and teacher and certain authoritarian proclivities, the humanist cannot resist a thematic mode, and even if his insistence on man's uniqueness is bedevilled by certain contradictions, he continues to roll the whole text into (this) one meaning and exhibit that meaning before other readers as an improverished substitute for the text. All this is a way of saying that the humanist critic, and his reader, are (and have always been) part of the struggles of interpretation, but that this fact *embarrasses* him.

Something very strange happens if one keeps in mind the whole spectacle of these humanist critics earnestly reading *Clarissa* and *then* reads the few passages on *Clarissa* written by the Marquis de Sade. His comments come in a general discussion of the novel in his "Idées sur les romans." De Sade sees the novelist's task as a "profound study of the heart of man, that veritable labyrinth of nature." This cause is best advanced by engaging the reader's heart in the complex turns of passion found in the characters. Here de Sade seems very close to Diderot. Then de Sade adds that man's interest is engaged *not* through the simple victory of virtue; but "if after the hardest trials we finally see virtue crushed by vice, our souls are necessarily torn, and the weak, having greatly moved us (having, as Diderot said, *stained our hearts with blood at the defeat*), must without doubt create interest, which alone assures laurels." *Clarissa* is introduced as an example of this truth. De Sade doubts that the novel would have won the "delicious tears" of the reader if Lovelace had been virtuously converted and willingly married Clarissa. Then he reiterates the purpose of the novel:

It is, then, nature one must capture in working this genre, it is the heart of man, the strangest of its products, and not at all virtue, because virtue, however beautiful and necessary it may be, is still only one of the modes of this amazing heart, the profound study of which is so necessary to the novelist and which the novel, faithful mirror of this heart, must necessarily map out in all its windings.[23]

The novel's real mission is not some programmatic statement about virtue, as Richardson would have said. It is a "mapping out," thus both an acting out and a representation, of what the human heart "is" and can be. But notice, though this description makes the heart seem like some knowable object the novel may "mirror," this project is put into question when the heart is said to be "nature's strangest product," a "veritable labyrinth." It is not surprising, given de Sade's own practice in *Clarissa*-like works such as *Justine,* that he provides a critique of the humanist readers of *Clarissa.* De Sade is finally not interested in securing some sort of knowledge about man, considered individually or collectively. He does not care to enforce any stable ethical position. Instead he reads *Clarissa* for its pleasures—the pleasure of following the windings of the human heart, the pleasure of seeing virtue crushed so our hearts are "stained with blood at the defeat." But this is not just a critique of humanist prescriptions for the novel (and here is the surprise). It is also a *description* of their practice. For the humanist critics have insisted on Clarissa's unique character, and have then *enjoyed* pursuing this fugitive essence through all the windings of their own analyses; and they have savored the pathos of Clarissa's rape and death, while they insisted on a symbolic victory for the virtue she embodies.

There are several reasons to be skeptical about the messages of these humanist critics. There is what can quickly become the tedious repetitiveness of terms and gestures that work to enforce the humanist ideology—talk of man's "integrity," "depth," "richness," "complexity," etc. There is the pious authoritarianism that attempts to control and improve the community of readers by using a subtle manipulative rhetoric. But what is perhaps finally most dishonest of all is the humanists' timid disinclination to acknowledge the pleasures they've enjoyed in interpreting *Clarissa.*

---

23. *Idées sur les romans,* ed. Octave Uzanne (Geneva: Slatkine Reprints, 1967), pp. 25–26. The translation is mine.

And the Lord God said unto the woman, what is this thou has done? And the woman said, The serpent beguiled me, and I did eat. —Genesis 3:13

Against the value of that which remains eternally the same . . . the values of the briefest and most transient, the seductive flash of gold on the belly of the serpent, *vita*—Nietzsche, *WP*, 577.

Clarissa on marriage: "What, sir! when virtue, when chastity is the crown of woman, shall your cousin stoop to marry [this] man?" (IV,250)

Clarissa on Lovelace: "the *true* bravery of spirit is to be above doing a vile action. . . . How low, how sordid are the submissions which elaborate baseness compels. Yet am I glad this violent spirit *can* thus creep; that, like the poisonous serpent, he *can* thus coil himself, and hide his head in his own narrow circlets; because this stooping, this abasement, gives me hope no further mischief will ensue." (IV,276)

Clarissa on the benefits of using Lovelace's letters for her book: "to which I appeal with the same truth and fervour as he did, who says: *O that one would hear me! and that mine adversary had written a book! Surely I would take it upon my shoulders, and bind it to me as a crown!*" (IV,61)

A Tail-Piece:
THE LADY, THE SERPENT, and THE CROWN

A childhood friend of the Richardson daughters describes a visit to the Richardson household: "After breakfast we younger ones read to [Mrs. Richardson] in turns the Psalms. We were then permitted . . . to walk in the garden, which I was allowed to do at pleasure: for, when my mother hesitated . . . for fear I should help myself to the fruit, Mrs. Richardson said, 'No! . . . I am certain that she will not touch so much as a gooseberry.'"

The principal device on Clarissa's coffin: "neatly etched on a plate of white metal, is a crowned serpent, with its tail in its mouth, forming a ring, the emblem of eternity." (IV,257)

In a pamphlet criticizing Richardson's art: "Thus you act the part of the serpent, and not only throw out to men the tempting suggestions of lust and pleasure, but likewise instruct the weak head and the corrupt heart in the methods how to proceed to their gratification. . . . You tempt them to swallow the forbidden fruit of the tree which they were commanded not to eat."—*Critical Remarks on Sir Charles Grandison, Pamela, and Clarissa*

After the Fall of Man, God punishes Eve and the Serpent: "And the Lord God said unto the serpent: I will put enmity between thy seed and her seed; it shall bruise thy head, and they shall bruise his heel." Genesis 3:14-15

Richardson of Lovelace and Clarissa: "Have you not seen from infancy . . . the one in a manner calling out for punishment, —The other for a heavenly Crown?" (*Lett.* 94)

We have met a host of interpreters at work in the interpretive field set up by the text of *Clarissa*. Clarissa and Lovelace compete to determine the shape of their story; Joseph Spence, Aaron Hill, and "Belfour" intervene to affect the course of the fiction while it is being published; and Richardson uses the role of editor to enforce his own interpretation of the story. Finally, a reception for *Clarissa* is organized by a group of "humanist" readers in the eighteenth and twentieth centuries so the text will serve their idea of man. Of course, I have also indulged in interpretation. And I have intentionally set my own reading of *Clarissa* against a history of all these earlier incidents of interpretation so as to raise general questions and perspectives on the act of interpretation.

What do these interpreters have in common? They are all writers, who emit representations to account for what happens between Clarissa and Lovelace. Sometimes our sense of what "happens" begins to fade beneath the conflicting representations of what "happens." But in spite of conflict as to the facts, these interpretations are marked by a startling convergence of concerns, compulsions, and conceptual metaphors. How can we represent and interpret these acts of interpretation? Two scenes are repeatedly invoked in this text, and by the interpreters of the text: Eve's seduction by the serpent in the Garden of Eden, and Lovelace's rape of Clarissa (the most important instances may be found on the title-page of this chapter). By conflating these two scenes, we can formulate a single scene which represents the story of Clarissa and Lovelace, *while* it allegorizes the matrix of interpretation—the reader's relationship to this text:

> The Lady is the text; the Serpent is the reader. The virgin body of the Lady stands opposite the Serpent. Each is charged with potentiality. The Lady's body shines with beauty, completeness, and integrity. It can make the Serpent seem like a vulgar creeping thing. The Serpent is coiled with the strength to hurl itself at the white nakedness of the Lady; it can level the Lady in an instant.

This scene discloses a series of different possible transactions. In its simplest and most naïve form, the Serpent and Lady are conceived as standing opposite one another as two independent antithetical principles. Their transaction is described as the Serpent's violent intrusion into the virgin body of the Lady. Clarissa, in her most self-righteous moments, sometimes represents her life in this way. She invokes the image of herself as radically innocent, decisively separated from the family turmoils and rakish machinations that victimize her. From this vantage point, Clarissa can say with Eve, "The serpent beguiled me, and I did eat."

Of course, we share the Lord's skepticism. Since Clarissa is capable of playing a wide-eyed Eve, there is little wonder that she actually describes Lovelace as a "poisonous serpent," who can "coil" and "creep," and "hide his head in his own circlets" (IV,276). This simplified version of Clarissa's story implies a relationship between the reader and the text that situates all authority with the text. Thus, when readers "misinterpret" the text, Richardson sometimes claims the position of the innocent and injured Lady for his text. The wayward reader is a Serpent who endangers the Lady with strange notions of Clarissa's culpability and Lovelace's attractiveness. For those who read *Clarissa* in these simple ways, the meaning of the action is expected to be clear before it is even completed. Richardson asks Belfour if she has "not seen from Infancy in [Clarissa] . . . the early Saint? . . . in a manner calling out . . . for a heavenly Crown?" (*Letters*, 94). In a similar spirit, Belford, Joseph Spence, and all the "true" critics of the text, make the text into a beautiful and inviolable Lady they must protect from the "false" critics who threaten to play the Serpent (those who would alter Clarissa's Will; the pert little figure "Art," who trims the dress "Nature" wears; etc.).

But from the beginning, the convergence of the Lady and the Serpent carried more complicated possibilities. The first representation of this scene sees the Lady as simply wronged by the Serpent; a second represents Lady and Serpent as locked in an ambivalent struggle, where each works in complicity with its opponent, to create the other. Thus the virgin purity of the Lady makes the Serpent's role as violator plausible; the Serpent's attack makes the Lady seem chaste. Here the rape is not a moment of violence to be forgotten or overcome. It is a dramatic high point of the action which prepares for a whole series of subsequent (and often conflicting) significations. This helps to explain why Clarissa keeps the rape—as an unspeakable possibility or an unspoken disgrace—constantly in view in the book she constructs. The rape is not just a slash-mark to separate opposites;

it is also a bond which links elements that are reciprocally related.

In addition, we have seen that the Serpent does not just "strike" to gain control of the Lady's body. He takes pleasure in being attracted, seduced, and overcome. And his desire magnifies the value of the Lady, just as his act of "violation" helps to make her appear as a "unified whole" which is complete, autonomous, and virgin. In these ways Lovelace helps to "create" Clarissa, just as Richardson, Spence, Diderot, and Kinkead-Weekes help to create the unified textual body they subsequently desire. But to do so they must secretly encourage, and cite at length, the "false" criticism they claim to abhor.

We are not simply insisting on the indebtedness of the first term in this problematic (the Lady, the text, the author, Clarissa) to the second term (the Serpent, the reader, Lovelace). These terms are still more entangled than this. In order for Clarissa to carry through her final interpretation of her story, she must also *play the Serpent*. How can this happen? The Lady is assumed to be passive; her energy inheres in simply *being* herself. The Serpent is an active creature. He must release his energy in an attack that modifies the Lady's structure by displacing her away from what she "is."

In Clarissa's allegorical letter to Lovelace about "returning to her father's house," she turns the tables on Lovelace by telling the little lie that will deceive the deceiver (but artfully, in such a way that Lovelace seems self-deceived). In acting this way Clarissa is actually following advice Lovelace had given earlier in the action. When Clarissa does not tell her story to Moore and Bevis, and instead depends "upon that security which innocence gives," Lovelace points out that the heart's "goodness . . . cannot be seen into," and that "the whole world is governed by appearance" (III,64). Consequently, Lovelace weaves elaborate and entertaining stories that win Moore and Bevis to his cause, and he tells Belford that Clarissa's innocence "had better have in it a greater mixture of the Serpent with the dove" (III,64). Clarissa puts this advice into practice when she writes the allegorical letter to Lovelace. But in a deeper sense, her narrative letters and the construction of her book have worked all along to control and penetrate, and thus displace, in serpentine fashion, the world she represents.

Richardson discovers that the practice of his art sometimes involves him, in compromising ways, with his apparent opposite. Thus

Richardson as a moral artist claims the position of the Lady, but to involve the reader he must sometimes become complicitous with the rakish ways he condemns. In a critical pamphlet, the "Lover of Virtue" detects this fact and writes that Richardson, in *Clarissa*, "act[s] the part of the serpent, and not only throw[s] out to men the tempting suggestions of lust and pleasure, but likewise instruct[s] the weak head and corrupt heart in the methods how to proceed to their gratification."

This second version of the Lady's encounter with the Serpent represents their struggle as unstable and destabilizing. This is because the struggle of ambivalent and reciprocally related terms cannot guarantee the hierarchies the first version appeared to secure. If Clarissa depends upon Lovelace to "be" the Lady, and she even "plays" the Serpent, why is she any better than Lovelace? If Richardson's aesthetic incites young imaginations to immoral acts, how has he improved on the very romances he disdains? Clarissa tries to cut through these ambiguities by taking the Serpent and bending it into an emblem of her triumph as the *ouroboros* she etches on her coffin. If her triumph over time and death must be left to God, her triumph over the time she has shared with Lovelace comes through the narrative which Coleridge connects with the *ouroboros,* because of the way a narrative weaves linear successiveness into a meaningful pattern—the circle (see above, chapter 4).

The serpent on Clarissa's coffin is not just "ringed," it is also "crowned." Clarissa embraces this symbolic language, and becomes still more explicit about her triumph by taking Lovelace's letters and "bind[ing them] to me as a crown" (IV,61). Clarissa has always been attracted by the quiet mastery promised by a crown. At one point she calls "chastity" the "crown of woman," and we have seen that Richardson judges Clarissa worthy of a "heavenly crown." By using Lovelace's own language in her book, Clarissa acts the Lady by unbending the lethal coiled Serpent and shaping him into the Ringed Serpent that becomes a visible proof and shining crown to symbolize her triumph over the Serpent.

Clarissa's domestication of the dangerous Serpent is attempted through the incorporation of a volatile past (the struggles with the Serpent) into a form (the Book). And the character-plot-theme interpretation of the book elaborated by Clarissa and Richardson is a way of insisting on its existence as a capacious form. In this way, they

hope to divest the Serpent of its autonomy. It will become the ornament or crown of the greater person, the Lady. But for some reason,
these efforts to make a particular interpretation be authoritative,
and hold over time, don't work. The Lady never seems able to control the Serpent for use *as* her crown. Why? There is something about
these attempts to close down interpretation which invites reinterpretation. What makes each act of interpretation unstable? What allows
the Serpent always to come alive and strike the Lady once again with
a new interpretation? This is the question which our text opens up.
This is the enigma posed by the succession of contending interpretations we have recounted. Our "answers" can only be partial and
speculative.

One answer comes from our understanding of what interpretation
is: "an arbitrary imposition of will and meaning that attempts to
pass itself off as inevitable, natural—a simple statement of fact." We
can take the first "genuine" proposal scene as an example. Clarissa
and Lovelace each gives flawed, contradictory accounts that repress
the openings toward marriage that disturb both. Belfour exploits
these romantic possibilities by staging an extraordinary new proposal
scene on Lovelace's deathbed. And Richardson responds with a
counterfeit proposal scene designed to conceal the openness and
possibilities in the text. In each instance, an interpreter is ready to
alter some preexisting situation so as to determine the future of these
lovers in accord with his own will and desire.

Now we can see one reason why interpretation of *Clarissa* never
comes to rest. Authority for interpretation comes from the authors,
institutional contexts, customs, and rules of the game that control
the language written to "read" the text. In the interpretive field of
Clarissa, these "authors" are Clarissa, Lovelace, the editor, Richardson's correspondents, Richardson as reviser, the humanist critics, the
writer of this text. Neither Clarissa nor Richardson can establish
decisive control over the interpretive field of *Clarissa* (i.e., they
cannot crown the Lady and keep her crowned). For though the first
text may remain the "same," the rules for reading steadily change;
the pen that writes the readings of the text passes from reader to
reader and generation to generation. And this pen will inevitably be
guided by the will and desire of the one who holds it.

There is a personal meaning to each reader's reinterpretation of
Clarissa that keeps interpretation going. It is as if the Lady's violation

by the Serpent is a "primal scene" for each of the interpreters of this text—a moment of violence they are compelled to repeat in their own act of reading. And this is their (and our) "primal scene" because it is here that the parents of each reader (Clarissa and Lovelace, Richardson and his readers, the Lady and the Serpent) are seen and imagined to be engaged in an act which is fascinating because it conceals the mystery of our origin as reader; disturbing because of its mute violence; pleasurable because it acts out our desire to penetrate the Lady; and dangerous because this desire is forbidden. And because this scene is so faint in its outlines—always a remote and dangerous memory—we must elaborate its form and meaning "après coup," not through a dream but through an interpretation of the text, an appropriation of the Lady which serves the same purpose as a dream: it tames unconscious material by repeating it in a form that expresses and contains repressed drives, fantasies, and longings.

But more than this, a perverse human urge is gratified when a reader glides toward his text, or the Serpent approaches the Lady. This urge is both social, in that it engenders transactions with others, and aggressive, in that it takes pleasure from mastering others. For why is the Serpent drawn to the Lady? It is her completeness and independence, her very look of serene detachment which invites the creeping subduer. And the very effort to enforce closure, by insisting on the virgin purity of the Lady, invites suspicion and interrogation: what has been hidden away to create this image of completion and purity? Where are the stress-lines holding this spectacle together so it seems to mean simply one thing? What very human desires, what vulgar human passions have been satisfied in the construction of this unearthy symmetry and beauty? With these questions the interpreter mounts the wall of the garden and begins a tour to determine the vulnerable points of the Lady's habitation. And when he has formed his plan, he hurls his coiled strength into an act of interpretation (he strikes).

But in the moment after the strike, the Serpent may be surprised by yearnings as respectable and constructive as the Lady's. He may wish to turn his moment of truth into a lasting habitation where his subject might dwell. At this point he does something to enforce a closure of interpretation that provokes new interpretations. He shapes his interpretation in such a way as to arrest subsequent acts of interpretation, by presenting previous acts of interpretation so that the range of all possible acts of interpretation seems to have been exhausted by his text. We have seen that Clarissa and Richardson are masters at this; and the text you are reading also tempts its reader and author with this delusion of mastery. And there may be a moment when this builder of an interpretation will believe that he is the triumphant Lady who has tamed the Serpent. He will be the one man to have evaded the consequences of God's curse against the Serpent and Man: "Upon thy belly shalt thou go, and dust shall thou eat all the days of thy life; And I will put enmity between thee and the woman, and between thy seed and her seed; it shall bruise thy head, and thou shalt bruise his heel" (Genesis 3:14–15).

Thus the reader imagines he has evaded the sloppy and incessant joust of interpretations by overcoming all previous interpretive positions. And he imagines that he has done this by building himself into a whole secure system and body of interpretation. And though he relishes (the memory of) his life as a Serpent (his moment of liberating motion), those who come after will see him as hopelessly tethered to the texts he reads, condemned to repeat its gestures, an ally of the very Lady he (thought he) had subdued. And finally the interpreter, because he secretly envied the Lady, imitates her so well that, through a strange irony, he who once was the daring Serpent has *become* the crowned Lady on the throne—another Lady, another text, with an aura of completeness and authority that invites the forked tongue of still another Serpent.

Critical Bibliographies

Chapter 1: Clarissa and the Art of the Natural

Two contemporary critics make "conflict," "struggle," and the assertion of will central aspects of their readings of *Clarissa*: Margaret Doody in *A Natural Passion: A Study of the Novels of Samuel Richardson* (London: Oxford University Press, 1974), and Morris Golden in *Richardson's Characters* (Ann Arbor: University of Michigan Press, 1963). Doody follow McKillop's early remarks about Richardson's debt to the heroic drama, and she writes vividly on the "dialectic of will and desire" which characterizes the transactions between Clarissa and Lovelace. By Doody's account, Clarissa rises above these struggles, because while in Lovelace "will" and "love are at odds," Clarissa's "passion, the love of God, allows her to grow in harmony, to achieve a greater identity which does not demand the satisfaction of power over others to realize itself as free" (p. 104). Golden shows a parallelism between the aggressive, manipulative behavior of Richardson's "bold young men," and Richardson's own domineering manner in corresponding with his young lady friends. This opens the interesting (and radical) possibility that Richardson cannot control, or stand outside, the struggles he presents. But Golden retreats from this possibility by making struggle a "theme" Richardson intentionally presents, and then tames, in his fiction: "for Richardson .... life ... is at bottom of the psyche a wild conflict for dominance; and ... moral differences among people will depend on the degrees to which they can restrain the violence of their urges in the interest of social living" (p. 3). Golden sees Clarissa's moral "exaltation" in her virtue as an assertion of power over others (p. 108). But he differentiates between virtue and evil, a proper and improper assertion of self in such a way as to exempt Clarissa from participation in any of the compromising moments of struggle (pp. 119–20).

Margaret Doody and Morris Golden both recognize the importance of struggle in *Clarissa*—but both their treatments, however different from each other, differ from mine in the way they limit the scope and effects of this struggle. Both critics see struggle as imposed from without upon (the innocent) Clarissa; both see struggle as a transitory phase of Clarissa's experience which she decisively transcends; and both work with Clarissa to this end, in their own critical texts, by siding with the heroine in her struggles with Lovelace. It is my contention that the novel's struggles infect every reader and every interpretation of *Clarissa* (cf. chapter 6).

Once one accepts the centrality of struggle to this novel, then Clarissa's narrative no longer seems "impartial." Ian Watt's version of Richardson's contribution to the "rise of the novel"—"formal realism"—was most fully developed in connection with *Pamela*, but has been widely applied to *Clarissa* (See *The Rise of the Novel* [Berkeley: University of California Press, 1957], chap. 1: "Realism and the Novel Form"). By this account, Richardson's language provides a more just and effective mimesis of time, place, external circumstances, and individual psychology than any earlier narrative fiction. By contrast, I try to show how Clarissa's narrative, even at its most "objective" moments, is a powerful rhetorical system evolved to meet the exigencies of the struggle her life has become.

Chapter 2: Lovelace and the Stages of Art

If Robert Lovelace were to peruse the remarks made about him in contemporary criticism, he would take some pleasure in Martin Price's description of him as "one of the great characters of English fiction," and he would value Anthony Winner's analysis of him as a pre-Romantic example of a heroic revolt against "Christian and bourgeois realism." (In several ways Winner anticipates my treatment of Lovelace. See "Richardson's Lovelace: Character and Prediction," *TSLL* 14 [1972]: 53–75.) But perhaps most of all, Lovelace would feel entitled to sue modern critics for defamation of character. He would find himself described by Cynthia Woolf as "an embodiment of unrestrained will. He is the shrieking, completely selfish child grown older but not wiser" (*Samuel Richardson and the Eighteenth-Century Puritan Character* [Hamden, Conn.: Archon, 1972], p. 107). He would find Morris Golden insisting that Lovelace's aesthetic response to Clarissa's suffering proclaims his "central emptiness" (*Richardson's Characters*, p. 121). After this pronouncement, Lovelace might be confused to find Golden dipping into psychology to praise Richardson for describing Lovelace's "paranoid need to create artificial worlds in which he rules . . . a mad substitution of art for nature" (ibid., p. 141). But though it would be vexing to find Margaret Doody and Mark Kinkead-Weekes shaking their heads over Lovelace's evasions of the "real," and annoying to read Cynthia Woolf saying that he has "no identity . . . at all," I am sure he would be most incensed at Kinkead-Weekes's insistence that behind all of Lovelace's playful ways there is the "tragic" story of a man trapped by his own self-image (Doody, *A Natural Passion*, p. 114; Kinkead-Weekes, *Samuel Richardson*, p. 228; Woolf, p. 105; Kinkead-Weekes, pp. 153, 160).

How could such harsh critiques of Lovelace be made? We begin to understand when we note that all these critics belong to Clarissa's party. The varied terms of their critiques emerge from using Clarissa's categories of selfhood, and her values, to measure Lovelace: seriousness, consistency, sympathy, maturity, a full deep heart, and belief in the "real." In fact, many of these slanderous characterizations of Lovelace echo things said of him by Clarissa. But there is one important difference: while Clarissa often writes in the heat of battle, and mightily qualifies the force of her own criticism by spending hours considering whether to marry Lovelace, none of these critics will admit that possibility.

Chapter 3: The Battle for the Body

Critics have shown a good deal of ambivalence about the melodramatic scenes I treat in this chapter. Most find them powerful and memorable, but they are *embarrassed* by the way they become the models for a thousand stage melo-dramas in the nineteenth century. My treatment of these scenes works to make them "respectable"—first, by showing how they work semiologically; second, by linking them with Clarissa's more comprehensive acts of composition.

After completing this book, I found another work that marks out an ambiva-lent opposition similar to the one I have described through the relationship between Clarissa and Lovelace. In a fascinating study of Renaissance rhetoric, Richard Lanham traces the interplay of Platonic and Ovidian concepts of the self. "One—the central self, the soul—is complete, interior, stable . . . and uses a neutral, middle style and sincerity in discourse. In contrast is the classical rhetorical concept of man, the self 'presented' in discourse and daily life—exterior, role-playing, unstable." See *The Motives of Eloquence: Literary Rheto-ric in the Renaissance* (New Haven: Yale University Press, 1976).

Chapter 4: Building a Book into an Empire of Meaning

While I have linked Clarissa's death to the institution of a book that will represent the self and control adversaries, the "humanist" readers of the novel emphasize Clarissa's spiritual movement beyond vulgar earthly concerns; Margaret Doody, for example, has made herself an especially fervid advocate of Clarissa's apotheosis. I shall examine the "logic" of this position in chapter 7. For now, I shall content myself with pointing out what is *illogical* about applauding Clarissa for the refined cruelty with which she leaves this world.

Notice the way critics discuss Clarissa's "compassion" and "pity" for Lovelace while she is dying. Margaret Doody and Mark Kinkead-Weekes make much of Clarissa's spiritual progress toward the point where she can "forgive" Lovelace. And so wise a critic as Martin Price concludes his valuable discussion of the novel by saying, "the novel *Clarissa* succeeds in making charity its genuine concern" (*To the Palace of Wisdom* [Carbondale: Southern Illinois University Press, 1964], p. 285). But if this is so, why does Clarissa, in her final letters, always manage to say the virtuous thing that will be most galling to her friends and family? Lovelace insists that Clarissa dies so as to complete a *"Christian revenge"* (IV,86). He hypothesizes that, since Clarissa's "desire of revenge insensibly became stronger in her than the desire of life, [she became willing to die]. And still the *more* to be revenged, [she] puts on the Christian and forgives me" (IV,326).

Lovelace, as usual, overstates his case. Clarissa is not just putting on "the Christian," she clearly believes she *is* one. But the quality of Clarissa's charity should become suspect when one reads her harrowing final letter to Lovelace, with its stunning biblical curse on the "wicked . . . hypocrite," or when one notes that the word *curse* can often be substituted for Clarissa's use of the word *pity*, without any change in the meaning of the sentence (IV,437). It seems, however, that critics are determined to see Clarissa as the type of the forgiving Christian. So Cynthia Woolf, in her study of Puritan religious literature and *Clarissa*, explains Clarissa's virtue in terms of the Puritan tradition. Then she goes on to cite hilariously contradictory evidence to "support" her claim:

> Perhaps the most explicit lesson of social virtue taught by the example of
> Clarissa's suffering is the value of the capacity for pity. . . . The increase in
> this sympathy for others is evident in all of her relationships, but most evi-
> dent in her feelings about Lovelace. Against all of Miss Howe's insistence,
> for instance, Clarissa refuses to prosecute Lovelace for his villainy, for she
> has no need to revenge herself upon him . . . she feels compassion for him
> as another human being. "Let me then repeat, that I truly despise this man!
> If I know my own heart, indeed I do!—I pity him!—*Beneath* my very pity as
> he is, I nevertheless pity him!—But this I could not do, if I still loved him."
> [IV,410] —*Samuel Richardson and the Eighteenth-Century Puritan Charac-
> ter*, pp. 170–71.

Chapter 5: Richardson as Author: Gamester and Master

Richardson criticism has been haunted by one, often fruitlessly argued, issue
more than any other. It may be stated this way: to what extent are Richardson's
conscious intentions and aesthetic principles adequate to the work of art he produced? The "loyal" critics, like Eaves and Kimpel, do a scrupulous reading of
the correspondence, deduce an aesthetic program from Richardson's statements,
and then read the works in terms of that program. Two recent books work in
this manner: Donald Ball, *Samuel Richardson's Theory of Fiction* (The Hague:
Mouton, 1971); and Elizabeth Brophy, *The Triumph of Craft* (Knoxville:
University of Tennessee Press, 1974). The first half of Brophy's study describes
Richardson's aesthetic "precepts" (the moral purpose, engaging the reader,
epistolary form), and the second half describes Richardson's "practice." And
this dual focus is said to demonstrate that Richardson has full conscious control over the direction of his artworks. In chapter 7 we shall see why many
modern humanist readers wish to center their readings of *Clarissa* upon the
conscious intentions of the author.

At the opposite side of this critical issue are the "subversive" critics—like
Morris Golden, Leslie Fiedler, Ian Watt, and Dorothy Van Ghent—who are
interested in Richardson precisely to the extent that he *fails* to comprehend the
real (and purportedly "repressed") meaning of his works. These critics show
little interest in doing a careful reading of Richardson's letters (though Golden is
an exception). They assume that although Richardson voiced perfectly conventional aesthetic platitudes, his own practice carries on a powerful articulation of
cultural myths and psychological drives which he was unwilling and unable to
apprehend.

If the "subversive" critics find the position of the "loyal" critics naïve or uninteresting, the "loyal" critics develop a finely modulated contempt for the
license of the "subversive" critics, and a smug confidence that *their* prosaic way
of discussing the novels is the only really valid one. After their summary of Van
Ghent and Fiedler, Eaves and Kimpel parade their own humility in this way:

Readers who find abstract statements about social relationships or illustrations of the doctrines of psychoanalysis of primary interest *may* read *Clarissa* in the light of one of these myths or, *if they are clever enough*, make up their own. *We* will discuss the novel, as Richardson's *simple* contemporaries (including Diderot and Johnson) read it, in terms of the realistic surface, of its characters and of the emotions they feel and inspire and the attitudes they embody and convey. [*Samuel Richardson: A Biography*, p. 241; my emphasis]

Is there tenable ground between the daring flights of the subversive critics and the dour fidelity of the loyal critics? Mark Kinkead-Weekes avoids the fallacy of the "excluded middle" on this issue, by focusing on Richardson's activity in writing:

In projecting himself into his characters and allowing them to lead him, Richardson achieved real exploration, self-extension, self-transcendence. He threw differing facets of himself into dynamic conflict, by means of which he reached beyond his ordinary limits. . . . This process, moreover . . . can never be subject to full authorial control. [*Samuel Richardson: Dramatic Novelist*, p. 454]

This perspective allows us to deal with something that only the most "loyal" Richardson critic can avoid feeling: there are times when Richardson brings such a severe and impoverished moral perspective to bear on his own texts that he becomes the worst enemy of his own art. As Kinkead-Weekes suggests, "At the end of *Clarissa*, indeed, Richardson seems to realize that his deepest moral convictions run clean counter to the drama that gives his fiction its most vivid life" (p. 453).

The positions of the loyal and subversive critics are beset by the same fallacy —the idea that Richardson's awareness of his fiction is always at the same level, that what he says (whether it be right or wrong) must hold for the moments before, during, and after the work of art is produced. My notion of Richardson's aesthetic—as a calculated game with the reader—emerges from watching Richardson produce his art, placing each of his aesthetic statements and authorial decisions within the context provided by the gradual publication of *Clarissa*, and observing the responses this work provokes. This allows us to see Richardson as a plurality of authors: sometimes agile, flexible, insightful (i.e. sporting), and at other times rigid, dour, and authoritarian (i.e. a spoilsport).

Chapter 7: The Humanist Sublime

A reader of this chapter might receive the impression that all the prominent readings of *Clarissa* have been "humanist." This is not the case. There is a body of valuable criticism which has developed outside the orbit of "humanist" concerns. Leslie Fiedler's discussion of *Clarissa* in *Love and Death in the American Novel* is justly celebrated. It helped to loosen the "humanist" hold on the text. But however brilliant its insights, the close reader of *Clarissa* must end by feeling that the novel has been "used" to extract a myth against which Fiedler can carry out his reading of American culture and literature.

Valuable and original nonhumanist studies of *Clarissa* have been contributed by the following writers: William J. Farrell, "The Style and Action in *Clarissa*," *Studies in English Literature 1500–1900* 3 (1963): 365–75; Morris Golden, *Richardson's Characters* (discussed in the critical bibliography to chapter 1); Edward W. Copeland, "Allegory and Analogy in *Clarissa*: The 'Plan' and the 'No-Plan,'" *ELH* (1972), pp. 254–65, and his "*Clarissa* and *Fanny Hill*: Sisters in Distress," *Studies in the Novel* 4, no. 3 (Fall 1972): 343–52; and Anthony Winner, "Richardson's Lovelace: Character and Prediction," *Texas Studies in Language and Literature* 14 (1972): 53–75.

Late in my writing of this book I came upon one of the best single articles on *Clarissa*: Leo Braudy's "Penetration and Impenetrability in *Clarissa*," in *New Aspects of the Eighteenth Century*, ed. Phillip Harth (Essays from the English Institute, 1974), pp. 177–206. Braudy describes Richardson's "main theme" as the "efforts of individuals to discover and define themselves by their efforts to penetrate, control, and even destroy others, while they remain impenetrable themselves." Braudy relates this antisocial mode of self-definition to Swift's Gulliver and Samuel Johnson, and sees Richardson as one of the popularizers of a personal appeal to purity and principle which denies the value of the psychological and social "inconsistency and ambivalence" which Braudy finds affirmed in Pope.

My study overlaps with Braudy's essay at many points. But by examining the forms of language which Clarissa and Lovelace use to present themselves to their readers, I have come to see Lovelace very differently (Braudy analyzes him in terms of a Clarissean quest for identity); and because I insist on the discrepancy between the radical independence Clarissa desires and the entanglements she becomes involved in, I do not see Clarissa as rising above struggle and achieving the abstract and principled identity that Braudy seems to envision for her. Instead, she and the text she writes, Richardson protects, and critics tend, are forever engaged in social and political transactions which are nothing if not ambivalent and "inconsistent." The sources of this ambivalence are examined in the Tail-Piece.

Index

Aristotle, 215–16
Austen, Jane, 136–37
Authority, and compositional strategy, xii

Bachelard, Gaston, 67, 73
Barthes, Roland, xi, 25
Baudelaire, Charles: "L'Essence du Rire," 36
Belford: as gullible "reader," 42–45; as editor, 95; implicated in rape, 151; "true" critic, 261
Belfour-Richardson correspondence, 158–79, 260
Boswell, James: *Life of Johnson,* 221
Bradsheigh, Lady, ix, xiii; correspondence with Richardson, 131–32, 141, 145, 147

Chapone, Sara, 87
"Character," "Plot," and "Theme," xiii, 194–95, 213–18
Chicago school of critics, 216–17
Cibber, Colley, 166
Clarissa: and mimetic narrative, xi, 12–13, 41, 57; dream of, 15; creation of "self," 17, 21, 23, 87; as paragon, 21, 25, 89, 186–88; use of time, 23, 25; as ruling "subject," 88, 91; as trope, 237
Clarissa. See Richardson, Samuel
Coleridge, Samuel Taylor: letter to Joseph Cottle, 105
Comedy, 78–80, 82–86
Congreve, William: *The Way of the World,* 79
Crane, R. S., 216

Derrida, Jacques, xi; "La Double Seance," 54–55; *Of Grammatology,* 120
Diderot, Dennis: as humanist critic, 220; eulogy for Richardson, 222–32, 236, 242–44, 262
Donne, John: *Devotions,* 91

Echlin, Lady, 137, 166

"Familiar" letter-writing, 96–102
Fielding, Henry, 166, 220, 248, 249
Fielding, Sara, 220; *Remarks on Clarissa,* 232–33, 235, 247
Frye, Northrop, 78

Gopnik, Irving, 233–34, 238

Heidegger, Martin, 207
Hill, Aaron, xiii; suggested revisions to *Clarissa,* 144, 153–54, 156–57, 174, 181, 260

Johnson, Samuel: on Richardson, 133–34

Kinkead-Weekes, Mark, 181–82, 197, 219–20, 232, 239–41, 252–56, 262

Lovelace: dream of, 15–16; and rake's code, 29; and comedy, 30, 33, 36, 77; parodic displacements, 57; and fire symbolism, 66–67; and "otherness," 94–95; as storyteller, 96; Richardson's rival, 169; Richardson's parody of, 177

Melodrama: Richardson's use of, xi–xii; garden gate scene, 58, 60, 61, 67–68, 70; fire scene, 58, 61, 73; pen-knife scene, 58, 63–65, 73, 75, 93
Milton, John: and myth of fall, 71
Myth of Fall, 69–71; as Christian interpretive system, 71–72, 103

Nietzsche, Friedrich, xi, 25, 44, 68, 86

Ouroboros, 105, 263

Proposal scene, 83–85; restorations to, 201–03; as crisis in text, 202; counterfeit of, 207, 213, 264

Rape: as inaccessible center, 57–58, 105; as catastrophe, 72–73; as violation, 92–93
Richardson, Samuel: and Pygmalion tradition, 48, 168–71; as editor, 123, 126–31, 155; as author, 125–26, 131; co-founder of Magdalen House, 145–46
—*Clarissa:* abridgments of, x; revisions to, 181; index summary added, 182, 187–95, 208, 214; "restorations" to, 195–97, 201, 208, 214
—*Pamela,* 145, 153, 174
—*Sir Charles Grandison,* 87, 130, 141, 145